Kings and Pawns

ALSO BY HOWARD BRYANT

FOR ADULTS

Shut Out: A Story of Race and Baseball in Boston

Juicing the Game: Drugs, Power, and the Fight for the Soul of Major League Baseball

The Last Hero: A Life of Henry Aaron

The Heritage: Black Athletes, a Divided America, and the Politics of Patriotism

Full Dissidence: Notes from an Uneven Playing Field

Rickey: The Life and Legend of an American Original

FOR MIDDLE-GRADE READERS

Legends: The Best Players, Games, and Teams in Baseball

Legends: The Best Players, Games, and Teams in Football

Legends: The Best Players, Games, and Teams in Basketball

FOR CHILDREN

Sisters and Champions: The True Story of Venus and Serena Williams (Illustrated by Floyd Cooper)

Kings and Pawns

Jackie Robinson and Paul Robeson in America

Howard Bryant

MARINER BOOKS
New York Boston

Without limiting the exclusive rights of any author, contributor or the publisher of this publication, any unauthorized use of this publication to train generative artificial intelligence (AI) technologies is expressly prohibited. HarperCollins also exercise their rights under Article 4(3) of the Digital Single Market Directive 2019/790 and expressly reserve this publication from the text and data mining exception.

KINGS AND PAWNS. Copyright © 2026 by Howard Bryant. All rights reserved. No part of this book may be used or reproduced in any manner whatsoever without written permission except in the case of brief quotations embodied in critical articles and reviews. For information, address HarperCollins Publishers, 195 Broadway, New York, NY 10007. In Europe, HarperCollins Publishers, Macken House, 39/40 Mayor Street Upper, Dublin 1, D01 C9W8, Ireland.

HarperCollins books may be purchased for educational, business, or sales promotional use. For information, please email the Special Markets Department at SPsales@harpercollins.com.

The Mariner flag design is a registered trademark of HarperCollins Publishers LLC.

hc.com

FIRST EDITION

Designed by Chloe Foster

Library of Congress Cataloging-in-Publication Data has been applied for.

ISBN 978-0-06-330816-9

Printed in the United States of America

25 26 27 28 29 LBC 5 4 3 2 1

For Kevin Hogan, a great friend,
and Rakia Clark, a great editor

Contents

Part Four: Recognition

"There are men in high office in this community who would silence brave teachers, violate our free elections, write injustice into law—all in the name of patriotism."

—*Native Land*, 1942.

The film, with narration and songs by Paul Robeson, was deemed subversive by the U.S. Attorney General's office and has scarcely been shown since its debut.

Preface

Twoness

DECEMBER 1949, TEN DAYS BEFORE CHRISTMAS. Jackie Robinson, the most famous ballplayer in America, is home—the first Christmas on his new street in his new house in St. Albans, a quiet, integrated neighborhood in Queens boxed in by Jamaica to the east, Long Island to the west, and Idlewild Airport, New York's new, year-old airport to the south.* It is a festive time, houses adorned with Christmas lights, solo candles flickering from front windows. Ten days before Thanksgiving, Robinson's son, Jackie Jr., celebrated his third birthday. Over cake and ice cream, the family enjoyed another milestone: Robinson had just won the biggest accolade of his career: the National League Most Valuable Player award. His wife, Rachel, is pregnant with their second child. Robinson tells the newspapermen he hopes it will be a girl.

Three days a week, on Mondays, Wednesday, and Fridays, Robinson works the floor as a salesman at Sunset Appliance Store in Rego Park, not far from his house. At the time, ballplayers, even the best ones like Robinson, work second jobs during the offseason—but for Brooklyn fans, his celebrity is its own gift, a major coup for the store, and further

---

* Following the president's assassination, Idlewild Airport was renamed JFK International Airport in December 1963.

cements him as a Brooklyn hero, not some distant superstar who leaves town after the final out of the season, but one who stays, one of them. Customers who purchase an RCA Victor television from Robinson receive an autographed big-league issue bat or ball, and can arrange to have their photo taken with him on the days he is in the store. Even *The New Yorker*, the city's magazine for the wine and cheese crowd, ventures out to Brooklyn to pay a visit to New York's most recognizable salesman.

It is a precious snatch of time. In a little over a month, before his thirty-first birthday, Robinson will hand out cigars in Harlem, celebrating the birth of his daughter, Sharon. The home in St. Albans—a two-story, single-family Colonial with a spacious backyard on a quarter-acre lot at 112-40 177th Street—stands as a testament to the possibilities this country believes it offers all people, the possibilities for better, despite the unforgiving realities of Black life. Within this moment, coated in the sugary haze of professional success, a new home, a beautiful wife, and a growing young family warmed by the comforting glow of Christmastime, Jackie Robinson has never been more ascendant, more complete, more *American*.

Most veteran baseball men could not envision his success—or did not want to, anticipating it would eventually destroy segregation. Robinson's excellence justified the fear. During the 1949 pennant race, as the leaves began to change and the Dodgers charged toward the World Series, a Black newspaper columnist noted that in photographs, in print, and in interactions among the other Dodgers, America looked different than it had just two years ago. The presence of Robinson and his Black teammates no longer felt unique, as it once did, but ubiquitous. Perhaps even normal. Robinson was now not only voted the best player in the league but with him the franchise had never been better. The Robinson Dodgers had won the National League pennant twice in his first three years. Before him, Brooklyn finished first three times over the previous fifty.

The accolades and pennants proved he was a great player, but by lunchtime on the afternoon of July 18, 1949, after he had left Room 226 of the Old House building on Capitol Hill following his testimony before the House Un-American Activities Committee (HUAC), Jackie

Robinson had become more than a baseball player. He had testified to the committee against the political opinions of the great bass-baritone singer and actor Paul Robeson, who was more than twenty years Robinson's senior, himself once beloved by millions of Americans, himself like Robinson once a great football player, once, like Robinson, one of greatest athletes in the nation—and once, as Jackie Robinson was now, the most famous Black man in his country.

America in the summer of 1949 was consumed by fear, convinced it was culturally and politically being infiltrated by agents of the Soviet Union. The fears were stoked by the nation's highest political and thought leaders—Harry Truman, the Democratic president; Col. Robert McCormick and William Randolph Hearst, two leading newspaper titans; and a desperate Republican Party that had been out of the White House for nearly two decades. The GOP had been out of power for so long it believed its attack on universities, FDR and his New Deal of social initiatives—unemployment benefits, Social Security, and a host of programs future generations of Americans now take for granted as foundational—could no longer be fought along the dry, pasty lanes of policy, but through the mud of accusation: the New Deal was communist, its supporters anti-American, cooperation with the Soviets treasonous. Who was loyal? No area of American life went untouched by the specter of conflict with the Soviets. Reminiscent of the violence against labor unions, liberalism, and Black soldiers that followed World War I, Robinson testified against Robeson in a climate that was now being called the second Red Scare. Amid these silhouettes of fear, Jackie Robinson was seen as one of America's champions.

As Christmas neared, Robinson appeared at the Commodore Hotel in New York, accepting the George Washington Carver Institute's gold medal for improving race relations, a "glowing example of Americanism at its best." Frank Gannett, the founder of the Gannett newspaper chain, addressed the overflowing audience. "Isn't it a story to thrill every American?" he said. "Jackie Robinson stands out as proof that here in America there is opportunity for those Black or white, who have ability, determination, character and ambition . . . he is not only a great citizen, but a great American. Rather recently, he appeared before a Congressional committee and defended his race's loyalty and rejected for them any sympathy for Communism."

In the August 1897 issue of *The Atlantic Monthly*, the legendary scholar W.E.B. Du Bois wondered if it was possible for Black people to successfully balance the "double consciousness" of being subjected to a segregated society and still feel "American." In his essay "The Strivings of the Negro," Du Bois saw this inner conflict as the defining characteristic of the post-slavery Black experience.

As loyalty and conformity often disguised as anticommunism suppressed the fervency for civil rights that punctuated the war years, Du Bois's conflict increased in intensity for a Black America expecting an improved quality of life in peacetime. "This waste of double aims, this seeking to satisfy two unreconciled ideals," Du Bois wrote, "has wrought sad havoc."

The years 1945 to 1953, when America transitioned from the Great Depression and the politics of World War II into a cold war with the Soviet Union, shaped both domestic and foreign policy. But overshadowed by the explosive years that would follow, this critical period has largely been treated as dormant Black history. Historians have tended to view the 1954 *Brown v. Board of Education* Supreme Court decision, the 1955 murder of Emmett Till, and Rosa Parks's subsequent defiance of segregation as the springboards to the modern civil rights movement—yet these in-between years had a profound effect on Black America.

Jackie Robinson and Paul Robeson were central to this overlooked period. Both men served as a prologue of sorts. For the remainder of the 20th century and beginning of the 21st, they were the early prototypes of a new template—the prominent Black entertainer as national political spokesperson. In the 19th century, the voices of Black leadership were the abolitionists and educators, orators, and clergy. Today, the entertainers, actors, and professional athletes enter the political maelstrom and illustrate Du Bois's notion of double consciousness, performing for white mainstream audiences while being expected to both advocate for

Black issues politically *and* represent America at home and abroad, a conflict perfected during the Cold War. No race of people have been so politically overmatched. Malcolm X would refer to them as "puppets."

Through countless published biographies over several decades, Robinson's 1949 testimony against Robeson on Capitol Hill had long sat in plain sight, explored in only a page or two but usually by a single sentence—*Jackie Robinson testified against Paul Robeson*—an exposed root on the beaten path of the story of baseball integration.

The exposed root sat unbothered, to be stepped over and never tripped upon. As a professional who had traveled that road in short-, medium-, and long-form journalism for decades, how many times had I stepped over it, muscle memory reminding me to lift one foot over the other without questioning what it was, why it was there, and what it might lead to? And how many times had I read the Jackie Robinson story and realized the entire narrative was constructed through the perspective of one man: Branch Rickey?

Why was the exposed root so easily stepped over? Robinson and Robeson were, along with Joe Louis, Jack Johnson, and Jesse Owens, two of the five greatest Black athletes over the first half of the 20th century. Add to Robeson's resume a law degree from Columbia, an international concert singer, a groundbreaking stage and screen actor, and he was nothing less than a titan. The root needed pulling.

The answers to the questions were not profound. The lens of the hearing never focused on Robeson, who was seen as only a prop for Robinson's patriotism, unworthy of rediscovery, especially as the Robinson/Rickey integration story—sports as the pathway to equality—became virtually unchallengeable. The excavation of Paul Robeson complicates Robinson and Rickey and destroys, almost completely, the easy, uncomplicated tale of interracial heroism Americans have long preferred.

It was about a decade or so ago when researching another book about the history of the political voice of the Black athlete when I finally stopped, looked down, and inspected the root. By the time I reached my own adolescence in the 1980s, the domestic elements of the Cold War focused on nuclear annihilation, the USA versus the USSR in the Olympics, "Fallout Shelter" signs in government buildings, *The Day After.*

The years when the federal government turned on its own citizens, corporations fired employees accused of subversion, and neighbors spied on neighbors had long since ended. For my generation, that type of hysteria where no one could be quite trusted to be what they seemed could only be found in *The Twilight Zone* reruns—until the 9/11 terrorist attacks reignited suspicions.*

In our house, Paul Robeson was a disembodied figure, a name without a story, appropriate for the market-driven 1980s in many ways. With the disappearing of Robeson also came the disappearance of questioning the effect of free-market capitalism on Black communities, a once vibrant question replaced by the celebration of individual wealth. When I attended college in Philadelphia in the mid-1980s, Robeson grew more present, especially on the Temple University campus. He had lived in West Philadelphia and had died there only a decade earlier, and though his name still resonated throughout the Black communities, it did so in regal, broken fragments.

The late Harry Belafonte once referred to Robeson as "one of our kings." How, then, could a king become so obscure, especially to his own people? His disappearance could not merely be a function of time because he had not been gone that long. Sand does not replace sand so quickly. The rise of hip-hop and the films of Spike Lee in the late 1980s and early 1990s forced a revival of Malcolm X, a reclaiming of him by Black America, wrested from his historical framing by the white mainstream, which during his time did not love him. To a new generation, Malcolm X became timeless, as Ossie Davis eulogized him following his 1965 assassination: "Our shining Black prince." Paul Robeson has yet to receive such a reappraisal.

---

* The "If you see something, say something" campaigns offered a McCarthy-era reminder of the disturbing ease in which Americans allowed the government to surveil its public spaces and private thoughts, once in the name of anticommunism, now as a means of anti-terrorism.

Prior to the fateful day Jackie Robinson appeared in Room 226 of the old House building, the continuum of Du Bois's double consciousness wrestled with itself, during World War I when Black leadership made the strategic choice to temper its domestic militance only to have Black soldiers targeted at war's end; in employing the opposite strategy during World War II, aggressively campaigning for civil rights during the war years only for Black soldiers to be targeted again physically by white vigilantism and economically by their government, which excluded them from the G.I. Bill and the opportunity to join in the postwar prosperity that created the American middle class; to fight segregation and be called communists for it.

Today, the nation is experiencing a similar period of retrenchment. Loyalty oaths have resurfaced. In 1949, across the flag of the *San Francisco Examiner* read the words "America First" in block letters and the slogan, "An American paper for American people." Today, "America First" has been revived with the familiar hostility of its antecedent. In April 2024, the state of Florida announced it would make courses teaching the "evils of communism" a requirement for grades as low as kindergarten. The University of Nebraska relented to the right-wing assault on Black history, forcing its instructors to rename its "Race and Sports" sociology class "Sports and Culture." In May 2025, the White House stated that "children will be taught to love America" and will be taught to "be patriots." With modern terminology, the antiliberal playbook of the 1950s has returned, once more, by conflating progressive politics with communism. The election of a Black president and a subsequent political movement against police brutality—amplified by the visibility of Black professional athletes—was met with a similar questioning of the loyalty of Black citizens and a merciless legislative assault on their gains, aggressively reestablishing a regressive white nationalist, Christian hierarchy that hasn't been part of a presidential mandate since the days of Woodrow Wilson, more than a century ago.

Within these pages is the story of a moment in the continuum, when Jackie Robinson and Paul Robeson, seven years apart, embodied Du Bois's dilemma in Congress, one man appearing in conflicted service to and the other hunted for ferocious critique of a country that would ultimately and decisively wound both. Through their actions and strategies, both men—along with the NAACP, the Black press, and the Black veterans who believed serving their country would finally make them American—would embody the 19th-century words of Du Bois that have encapsulated the expanse of the Black American journey: "One feels his two-ness,—an American, a Negro; two souls, two thoughts, two unreconciled strivings; two warring ideals in one dark body, whose dogged strength alone keeps it from being torn asunder."

The word *American* reverberated throughout that evening at the Commodore, and continued at banquets as Robinson crisscrossed the country, the word *hero* rarely far from his name. The Oregon Daily Journal referred to him as a "clean-cut American Negro athlete" and lauded Robinson for protecting American values, ostensibly in direct opposition to Robeson. Countless newspapers followed.

JACKIE ROBINSON GIVES CRITICAL PAUL ROBESON JOLT ON WHISKERS

Paul Robeson and Jackie Robinson were both Negroes. In their respective lines of endeavor—singing and baseball playing—each was an artist; however, any similarity between the two comes to a sudden conclusion there.

In 1949, at the apex of the American ideal, Jackie Robinson had been placed in opposition to a man he would never meet, whose hand he would never shake. No quarrel had preexisted between the two. He had been lauded as an American hero for all that he had done, but what exactly in the moment had he done? As the calendar moved into a new decade, soon to become one of America's darkest, that question lay before Jackie Robinson and the disparate forces and organizations—Black and white—who believed as a condition of Black America fulfilling the patriotic half of Du Bois's twoness, his presence before HUAC was essential.

Book One

America's No. 1 Negro

Part One

Hope

(1942–1945)

Chapter One

I

THE NEW HAVEN LURCHED NORTHEASTWARD, leaving New York City farther in the distance, leaving behind the end of something. The train hugged the southern Connecticut shoreline, passengers eager to secure a seat on the right of the car for better access to the absorbing summer views of Long Island Sound. Alongside the Yankee Clipper and The Comet, the New Haven was once a prestigious member of stylish service cars from the golden age of train travel, but the New Haven would soon be one of the few survivors of the industrialist J.P. Morgan's voracious capitalism—his dream of monopolizing the eastern seaboard rail devoured by greed, the Depression, and very soon, automobiles. Ironically, Morgan's most important rail line would be kept alive by the federal assistance American businessmen said they loathed, by a government needing transportation lines for a world at war.

The train eased north, inland through Rhode Island, winding upward into Massachusetts, heading toward a new and uncertain world. Among the passengers were servicemen and women staring out at scenic New England, staring into their thoughts, thinking about the inevitable fighting that awaited, fighting for a world many of the uniformed passengers aboard knew they'd never live to see.

The train arrived at South Station. The enlisted headed for the Boston Navy Yard, the cluster of outposts occupying Boston's inner harbor that now comprised the epicenter of the city's muscular shipbuilding war complex, consisting of the Chelsea Naval Hospital, the Chelsea Annex, the Charlestown Navy Yard, and the South Boston Annex. One newspaper described Boston as "dim against the submarines offshore."

Days earlier, the *Boston Herald* reported that 8,600 miles west, U.S. Marines landed at Guadalcanal. *The Boston Globe* brought news of Europe, of a German Nazi leader named Schmidt, "who warned that future intervention on behalf of the Jews in Holland would be punished by forcing those involved to share the fate of the Jews." It was August 1942.

Among the passengers on the New Haven, leaving a version of the world behind, was Paul Robeson, who had come to Boston to star in Margaret Webster's version of *Othello* for a weeklong engagement at Brattle Hall in Cambridge. Robeson stood at a certain remove from the rest of the cast the way stars did, having already been famous for the previous quarter century. The show highlighted the Cambridge Summer Theatre schedule, and eager scouts eyed the week as a test run to a potential Broadway opening.

Robeson had been a stage star since 1925, when playwright Eugene O'Neill cast him, untested, as the title character in *The Emperor Jones*. Robeson's signature bass baritone, the voice seemingly born from the richest soil of the earth, had been discovered by accident—he couldn't whistle on cue, so he broke out in song. Nearly 20 years later, two weeks before arriving in Boston, Robeson shattered attendance records at consecutive concerts in New York and Fairmont Park in Philadelphia.

He had been famous for so long. Robeson made his film debut with Oscar Micheaux's 1925 silent picture *Body and Soul*. In 1929, he played Carnegie Hall for the first time, and even then, he was already famous—for sports. During World War I as a teenager at Rutgers, Robeson had been one of the greatest college football players. In 1917, as a junior, he received college football's highest honor, selection to the prestigious All-America team compiled by the godfather of American football, legendary Yale coach Walter Camp. Camp's fingerprints could be found all over the modern game—yard markers, the two-point safety, the quarterback, line of scrimmage, the reduction of players per side from 15 to 11. Camp had wrested football from its foundations in English rugby to create something uniquely American—and now he was telling the nation that Paul Robeson was one of the greatest he'd ever seen play the sport.

In 1921, Robeson played defensive end for Akron in a nascent pro football startup, the American Professional Football Association. The next year, when Robeson moved to the Milwaukee Badgers, the two-year-old venture changed its name to the National Football League. While playing in the NFL, Robeson earned a law degree at Columbia. It appeared he could succeed at anything. A century later, Shana L. Redmond would author a biography about Robeson titled *Everything Man*.

Robeson was a giant to a Black community inspired by his soaring achievements, especially in interracial settings. Robeson was raised during a period of hardening segregation, enormous racial unrest, segregation justified by a belief—held by white (and routinely Black) Americans—that Black people were not sufficiently socialized to live on equal terms with whites. The term of the day used for African Americans and predominately Black countries was "backward." Leaders of both races were often in agreement: Black people must earn their way out of second-class citizenship, an attitude that led to the great scholar W.E.B. Du Bois's belief in a "talented tenth." The best of the race would provide the example.

In 1939 and 1940, at the peak of his fame, Robeson galvanized a nation ambivalent about the prospect of entering the war when his rendition of "Ballad for Americans" was carried across the airwaves nationwide. By the time he arrived in Boston, it was no exaggeration to say that Paul Robeson was the most famous Black American in the world.

II

FOR A COUNTRY AT WAR, something as ephemeral as a stage play did not appear to be major news by comparison, but Robeson's presence in Cambridge was not trivial: no Black man had ever played Othello—Shakespeare's tragedy of the jealous Moor who marries and murders his white wife—in an interracial cast on American soil. Shattering a centuries-old, ironclad racial barrier was national news. Southern politicians preemptively mobilized against the production.

In 1930, Robeson and his wife, Eslanda, had relocated to London, where they had lived for nearly a decade and where Robeson had been playing Othello in the British theater opposite Peggy Ashcroft as Desdemona. But he would not be the first Black Othello in America. In 1916, when Robeson was a college freshman, the all-Black Edward Sterling Wright Players performed the play at the Lafayette Theatre in Harlem, the Walnut Street Theatre in Philadelphia, and the Grand Opera House in Boston, with Wright playing the lead. Robeson's tremendous reception as Othello in London led to him being approached for a Broadway run, with Lillian Gish set to play Desdemona. The project dissolved as the nation, or so went the thinking, was not "ready" for the play's interracial lovemaking and violence, which would be amplified by Robeson's physical enormity—he was 6 ft., 3 in., 250 pounds. Robeson himself could be counted among that number reluctant to perform a role in America where, in addition to marriage and murder, Othello, self-destructing in jealousy, slaps Desdemona—"a good stage slap," according to the *New York Daily News*. "I feel that in London, trouble couldn't possibly arise on racial grounds . . . but they certainly wouldn't stand in America for the kissing and the scene in which I use Miss Ashcroft roughly," Robeson said in 1930. "I wouldn't care to play those scenes in some parts of the United States."

Energized by the war's mission of freedom, Robeson arrived at Brattle Hall, the cramped and creaky Dutch Colonial Harvard Square theater house built, nine years before he was born, in 1889. The world was engaged in a fundamental conflict, the idea of democracy against fascism, the unifying rhetoric of a country mobilizing as one was thrilling to Robeson, and he was additionally buoyed by the action: the raw steel and sweat of the American war machine, the grim-faced soldiers on the New Haven about to man warships built a mile or so from where Robeson would perform.

Being in Boston heightened his sense of purpose. Robeson and the city mirrored one another, two symbols coalescing in the shadow of wartime—Robeson of Black aspiration and achievement, Boston of the American ideal. When he wasn't performing, Robeson aided the local war effort, making several appearances across the area to raise money: to Gloucester, to aid the Russian War relief, and to Central Square, where he set up a table on a sidewalk and raised $2,000 in war bonds for the Cambridge Women's War Savings Committee.

Webster, the respected Shakespearean actor-director intentionally chose to open *Othello* in Cambridge for its reputation of tolerance, of being cool amid overheated racial matters. The announcement of the play brought fears of violence or preemptive edicts to cancel the show, but when tickets went on sale in early July, the entire week sold out in hours.

Othello had traditionally been played by white men in blackface. On Broadway in 1935, the British actor Philip Merivale played the lead. *Time* magazine reported that Merivale possessed a "grave, bony face" and "beetling mobile brows and eyes whose whites can gleam with tragic fury in a sepia-colored face." A "sun-tanned" Walter Huston played the role a year later on Broadway.

The punditry long debated Shakespeare's vision of Othello's racial identity, but both Robeson and Margaret Webster agreed the Bard's intention was for his Moor to be of sub-Saharan origin. The Black man who once played Othello, the legendary stage actor Ira Aldridge, was New York–born but never played Othello in the United States. Aldridge's Othello debuted in London in 1826, but it would take 116 years for America to be "ready" for a Black Othello.

Six days before opening, Webster told *The Boston Globe* she believed Cambridge was where a "Negro star can be tried out with fairness and tolerance," because Boston audiences were known to be "intellectual and sympathetic." Financiers were reluctant to back the production, convinced American audiences would recoil. Several news stories reverted into debate—if Othello even needed to be performed by a Black actor. "Miss Webster," *The Globe* wrote, "says she thinks Shakespeare himself wouldn't have cared for a coffee-colored Othello, who looks as if he merely has a Palm Beach tan."

That Robeson would be the vehicle for the first rendition of *Othello* in the United States and perform in Boston carried a certain preordainment. Boston, with all of its 17th-century mercantile contradictions—building enormous wealth from the slave trade while proud of its acceptance of its small Black population—was one of the early epicenters of the American antislavery movement. If Boston would not later be known for its racial activism, much of the city's history of abolition has been preserved. A statue of the great antislavery activist Wendell Phillips, its base carrying the inscription, "Prophet of Liberty. Champion of the Slave," stood on the corner of Charles and Boylston Streets, in the Public Garden across the street from the Boston Common.

Enslavement was not a theoretical subject for Robeson. His father, William, had been born enslaved in Marion County, North Carolina, in 1844, before escaping north to Philadelphia when he was 15 years old. The statue of Phillips was dedicated May 4, 1915, a month after Robeson's seventeenth birthday. Around the same time, Robeson, a high-school senior, entered a state oration contest, selecting Phillips's 1861 lecture on the Haitian revolutionary Toussaint L'Ouverture. Twenty-seven years later, here Robeson was, now a 44-year-old man and internationally known, walking the same crooked and cobblestoned streets of Phillips, Tubman, Sojourner Truth, Garrison, and Douglass, walking for the same purpose.

Boston was a thrilling success. The Harvard Society named Robeson an honorary member. *The Globe* expressed surprise by the "manly softness" of his voice and, even what it considered his inelegant patches, saw Robeson's power as an actor. *Boston Herald* theater critic Elinor Hughes raved. The Associated Press asserted Robeson's performance answered the "long-debated question of whether Shakespeare intended a Negro or a white man for the role of the jealous Moor of Venice." Ralph Warner of the communist *Daily Worker* saw Robeson on stage in both artistic and political terms. "In these war days, when Negro youths are taking up arms in defense of their America, and Southern bourbons are seeking to revive the spirit of the KKK," the newspaper wrote, "Robeson's Othello is a valiant plea for human rights."

For years, Robeson had grown more pointed in his criticisms of racism and fascism, and the week as Othello confirmed his addition to a historical continuum, connecting backward to the heritage of protest and political oration that defined abolitionism and forward in Cambridge, successfully contributing to a piece of theater that would crush a long-held prohibition—Shakespeare's Moor would no longer be in blackface, or anything other than unambiguously Black, and no longer banned from America. As he had followed Ira Aldridge on the stage, so too would others follow him. Within a decade of Robeson's Cambridge debut, Othello would be almost exclusively cast to Black actors for the next 80 years. It had been true: Robeson's trip from New York to Boston signified the end of something.

At Fort Riley, Kansas, unaware of his destiny, of Robeson in Cambridge, and of *Daily Worker* reporter Nat Low and *The Boston Record* columnist Dave Egan, was 23-year-old Army draftee Jackie Robinson. Egan suggested baseball's war shortage provided a perfect opportunity to admit Black players.

Low, the sports editor of the communist newspaper, wrote on July 30 that Pittsburgh Pirates President Bill Benswanger would hold tryouts for three Black players within the month. One was 20-year-old Negro League catcher Roy Campanella. "Negroes are American citizens with American rights," Benswanger told Low. "I know there are many problems connected with the question, but, after all, somebody has to make the first move."

The production left Cambridge for Princeton, New Jersey. The *Boston Herald* saw the disparate wartime threads attacking the contradiction of segregation. Under an editorial titled "Hope for the Negro," the newspaper saw new possibilities:

> Has the war, with its strong emphasis on democracy and the rights of individuals who risk all for their country, somehow softened our attitudes toward the Negro? A lively discussion is taking place here regarding the unwritten rule which bars Negro baseball players from the American and National Leagues . . . Miss Hughes reminded readers that Paul Robeson's appearance in Brattle Hall, Cambridge, was, "the first occasion upon which an artist of his race has played the part in this country with a cast of white actors." It is both comforting and discomforting to read her characterization of him as, "this remarkable actor, honored more in Europe than in his own country . . ." Unjustified economic barriers cannot persist once the people realize how devoted the Negro is to his country and how little he asks.

III

THE PRODUCTION'S ARRIVAL IN PRINCETON assumed a more personal tone. Robeson was born in Princeton on April 9, 1898—33 years to the day of Robert E. Lee's surrender at Appomattox, officially ending the Civil War—an irony considering Princeton was often considered the northernmost outpost of the Confederacy. Robeson's father, Reverend William Drew Robeson, once led a respected congregation, Witherspoon Street Presbyterian Church, out of Princeton. Cyrus Bustill, his great-great-grandfather on his mother's side, baked bread for the Continental Army and, according to family history, was thanked personally by General George Washington for fortifying his exhausted troops during the Revolutionary War. Robeson returned to Princeton the prodigal son.

He had played Princeton two years earlier, in 1940, in O'Neill's *The*

Emperor Jones (Robeson had also starred in the film version), and his return, enhanced by the energy from Cambridge turned Princeton into a major event. The week of shows at the McCarter Theatre sold out so quickly, two more were added. Prior to Princeton, Webster announced *Othello* had been chosen to come to Broadway, but Robeson's crowded concert schedule meant the debut would have to wait a year.

Princeton reinforced Cambridge. Robeson was the star. Special praise went to José Ferrer, who was part of the Princeton Class of 1933, and Uta Hagen (Ferrer's real-life wife) for her portrayal of Desdemona. The more intrepid reviewers confronted the play's historic significance. "In a nation increasingly aware of racial problems," *The Baltimore Sun* critic Allen W. Harris wrote, "the story of the star-crossed love of a Negro and a young and beautiful Venetian aristocrat is innately dramatic."

Beneath the pageantry of Robeson's homecoming lay an unspoken tension: Princeton was not a joyful place for Paul Robeson. With its racial hierarchies and pre–Civil War practice of students and faculty bringing their slaves to the College of New Jersey campus (as the school was known until 1896), Princeton—the town and college—represented an American caste system. "Rich Princeton was white," Robeson once recalled. "The Negroes were there to do the work."

Princeton was the site of family hardship. A personal dispute with Woodrow Wilson, then the president of Princeton, led to the removal of William Robeson as pastor of Witherspoon Street Presbyterian Church and drove the family from Princeton to Westfield and then to Somerville, where Robeson eventually attended high school. Robeson leaned heavily on his father, as his mother, Maria, had died when Paul was in the first grade. William's resoluteness in the face of discrimination made the father even more heroic to the son. "I marvel that there was no hint of servility in my father," Robeson would write. "Just as in youth he had refused to remain a slave, so in all the years of his manhood he disdained to be an Uncle Tom." When Wilson was elected president, he brought Princeton to Washington, authorizing the segregation of federal facilities and agencies, including the mail service, which resulted in Black federal employees regulated to lower-paid jobs, and separate restrooms, drinking, and eating facilities. Robeson recalled being Black in Princeton as being part of a permanent underclass tolerated only in positions of subservience, never to be seen as equals.

IV

ROBESON'S *OTHELLO* MADE ITS BROADWAY debut Tuesday, October 19, 1943, at the Shubert Theatre. For a quarter century, Robeson had been a star, and now he was a megastar, fully amplified by the power of Broadway. As an actor, he had received appreciation for his stage presence ("Paul Robeson has majesty.") and criticism for his perceived deficiencies ("At least once, his physical movements are grotesque . . ."), but his insistence on emphasizing Othello's Blackness crossed what had been an impenetrable bar, modernizing the work with a contemporary urgency a white man in blackface could not duplicate. Where past critique and scholarship focused on the dilution of Othello's sub-Saharan ethnicity, Robeson emphasized it, giving his Othello an enduring unambiguous self.

The rise of *Othello* and Robeson's personal voice were concurrent. His success challenged the generations of pseudoscience thought to confirm Black inferiority both in the scientific community and in the world's imagination. Three months before *Othello* opened on Broadway, Robeson was honored at a dinner in Berkeley, California, and he used his stage success to challenge the notion. "There can be no question anywhere," he said, "of a 'backward' people if they are given the opportunity of complete equality." A year earlier, in the fall of 1942, Robeson addressed an integrated auditorium in New Orleans with a stirring message: "I have seen whole people ground down, depleted, crushed. But not so these great black people," he said. "Nothing the future brings can defeat a people who have come through three hundred years of slavery and humiliation and privation with heads high and eyes clear and straight."

Robeson's sharpening voice resonated with fellow Black artists. Lena

Horne, a rising young singing and acting talent, met Robeson three years earlier, in 1940, when she was a 23-year-old rising talent. Horne struggled with discrimination, both in its practice and its emotional effect on Black people. At Café Society, the club in New York's West Village that was secretly a mecca for Black progressive thought, Horne told Robeson how much she "hated her own people for being pushed around, and hating white people for doing the pushing." Robeson became a mentor to Horne as she found her political voice. As Robeson redefined Othello, the obviousness of the American contradiction of how it treated its Black citizens had elevated Robeson's importance to the country's racial discourse:

> **PAUL ROBESON PLAYS OTHELLO TO THE LOUDEST CHEERS IN YEARS**
>
> The cheers were long and loud and earnest last night when the curtain went down on 'Othello' at the Shubert Theatre, such cheers as have not been heard in the theater in years . . . Othello, the Moor, trusts, is tricked and deceived into hating Desdemona and is hurt. When Robeson plays him he ceases to be just a Moor of a dead past and becomes the Negro of today, still tricked, deceived, hurt. Shakespeare, a broad-minded man, understood these things long ago.

In his *New York Daily News* theater column "Little Old New York," Ed Sullivan told his readers Robeson could not be measured by his singing, acting, or touchdowns, but as a potential world figure. Sullivan understood the total significance of Robeson, the segregated orders his excellence threatened, and the responsibility to Black people Sullivan saw belonging to him—but curiously not to his white fellow countrymen or elected officials. Eleven days after *Othello* debuted, Sullivan published a column titled "Saga for a Nonpareil":

> What other worlds left are there for Rutgers' Robeson to conquer? . . . The only big role left for him to play now, is as spokesman for his race,

> and this is a drama in which he must play a leading part. But in this, Paul Robeson must be aware of the Iagos who murmur innuendoes that inflame the Negro and arouse the whites . . . The issue must be resolved in the realm of reason . . . Such a man as Robeson, revered by his own race, and admired by the white race, can here, achieve the most important triumph that has ever distinguished him. If he can do this, what has gone before in his career will seem in miniature . . . Robeson has figured in many kickoffs, and he has won. He must win this one, for his country.

V

AS *OTHELLO* EXPLODED AT THE box office, Robeson found himself in a position familiar to the famous Black performers that would follow him in future decades, and that was to follow Ed Sullivan's template and be a "spokesman for his race." But what exactly did that mean? In Sullivan's eyes, it meant accepting his success as proof that America's racial prohibitions were more annoyance than systemic, that the fruits of his talents offered a pathway forward for all Black Americans, even though virtually none of them possessed his otherworldly gifts. The translation of Sullivan's challenge was not for Robeson to be a spokesman for Black Americans, but for him to defend the environments that allowed him to receive the standing ovations showered upon him nightly at the Shubert—and to use his influence to convince Black citizens that wide opportunity was possible without drastic societal change.

It would be a nearly impossible ask. A year earlier, in 1942, a white supremacist group in California threatened a senatorial campaign designed to attack the "arrogant minorities who refuse to accept their rightful place in American life and who use the war emergency to further their own selfish ends," and singled out Robeson—whose growing profile was both inspiration and threat—to be hanged, tarred, and feathered.

Anger toward Black prosperity was not a fringe attitude. With no intention of competing for jobs or accepting racial equality postwar, white violence against Black citizens was a daily, normal occurrence.

Attacks on Black workers in Mobile, Detroit, Harlem, Beaumont, and Los Angeles contradicted the war-effort solidarity Robeson once found so encouraging. The Black press and Communist Party—which concurrently advocated for desegregation but were never allies—responded by pressuring high-profile institutions to live up to the wartime ideal.

The optimism that baseball would be a leader in that aspiration was premature. The Pirates had no intention of integrating. Team President Bill Benswanger was incensed by Nat Low's tryout report and forcefully disavowed it—with the self-satisfied help of the *Pittsburgh Courier*, whose antipathy toward the *Daily Worker* illustrated the rift between the Black and communist newspapers. "The sports editor of the *Daily Worker* put words in my mouth," Benswanger told the *Courier*'s Wendell Smith. In positioning the *Courier* as the more reputable source, Smith wrote with an unsubstantiated confidence that Benswanger supported integration, and, when the time came for Pittsburgh to audition Black players, it would be the *Courier*, and not the *Worker*, that Benswanger would trust to choose the players. Smith quoted Benswanger as being "all for it" on integration.

A month before Robeson's *Othello* debut, the United Furniture Workers of America sent letters to Baseball Commissioner Kenesaw Mountain Landis and the 16 major-league teams, urging the signing of Black players. Bills were posted around New York highlighting the contradiction of liberty and segregation. One Communist Party poster depicted a split image: a Black soldier lying dead in a foxhole on one side and a Black pitcher warming up on the other, with the caption, "Good enough to DIE . . . but not good enough to PITCH!"

The Black press instituted the "Double V" campaign, its own pressure initiative led by the *Pittsburgh Courier*, which meant victory over the Axis abroad and victory over segregationists domestically. The Double V had not been initially directed at baseball during the summer of 1943, but sports could not be divorced from the burgeoning push for civil rights. FDR had been under pressure from Black leaders—the legendary labor leader A. Philip Randolph, especially—to desegregate the military; the W.E.B. Du Bois–led *Crisis* at the NAACP debated the wisdom of Black soldiers risking their lives for a country that intended to relegate them back to segregation upon their return.

Landis had been tipped off that baseball would be the Double V's next target. In mid-October, the *Pittsburgh Courier* and *The Los Angeles Tribune* informed Pacific Coast League President W.C. Tuttle they would picket the league offices. Tuttle alerted William Bramham, the jowly, segregationist head of minor league baseball, that protests were planned for the first week of December in New York. In his letter dated October 15, 1943, Tuttle wrote to Bramham that, "I have no doubt that in the near future we are facing a race situation" and referenced a protest that had occurred at a PCL game a year earlier.

Tuttle was something of a character. He was not a lifelong baseball man, but of Hollywood. A screenwriter and novelist, having written dozens of silent films, mostly westerns, Tuttle had been tapped to head the PCL because he had enjoyed the game, not lived it. That meant he was not part of the longtime clique of east coast and southern baseball executives who controlled the nervous system of the national game. Tuttle told the two Black newspapers they had "placed the cart before the horse," and that "until the Major Leagues recognize and use colored players, the Minors cannot do so."

Bramham immediately understood Tuttle's error: he had acknowledged baseball's unacknowledged conspiracy to bar Black players—and had put it in writing, to two newspapermen, no less. Bramham measuredly wrote back to Tuttle a week later: "I think the third paragraph of your letter is very unfortunate in that it places the Major Leagues in a situation we should have no part in." Bramham then followed the stock baseball line: baseball had no rule prohibiting Black players, but added, reminding Tuttle of his letter's confidentiality, "As the negro race has a professional baseball league of its own, I cannot understand the incentive behind their trying to inject themselves into our organization which can but augment the fury of a growing and very dangerous and difficult race question which certainly will not be conducive to better relationship between the races."

Privately, Bramham was furious. Tuttle had essentially admitted baseball was segregated by directive from the top—which meant Landis. A Landis loyalist, Bramham wrote to Landis the same day, enclosing Tuttle's letter to him with the following paragraph:

> *Dear Judge Landis,*
> *Of all the damn fool things that have come to my desk, the attached copy of [a] letter from President Tuttle, of the Pacific Coast League, takes the cake.*

Facing the embarrassment of a public demonstration, Landis strategized, opting to open the door instead of having protesters outside of it. He would invite the Black press to the meeting—with a star attraction, Paul Robeson.

The invitation was stunning. In 42 years, neither the American nor National Leagues had ever acknowledged the existence of a color line, even though no Black player had appeared in Organized Baseball, or O.B., as Major League Baseball then called itself.

But why Robeson? Late in his long life, longtime Black sportswriter Sam Lacy would say it was *Defender* publisher John Sengstacke who extended the invitation to guarantee headlines. Landis would say it was his idea. Both make sense. In October 1943, no one in America was hotter than Paul Robeson, who also happened to have been teammates two decades earlier in the NFL with Jimmy Conzelman, who was the player coach of the 1922 Milwaukee Badgers for the final three games of the season and was now an executive with the American League's St. Louis Browns.

Having Robeson in any room at that time would be seen as a coup—and he was playing just down the street. At that time, a reporter, Jerome Beatty, had been tailing him for a story that would appear in the May 1944 issue of *The American Magazine*, with the headline "America's No. 1 Negro."

• • •

Robeson accepted the last-minute invitation. The meeting would take place Friday, December 3, 1943, in New York City, in Room O on the second floor of the Roosevelt Hotel, during the annual owner meetings. There was no prior notice that Robeson, who lived just a few blocks away at 38th and Park, would be in attendance, or that a delegation of Black journalists would be on the agenda. Baseball's segregation had been so complete that the invite itself remained wholly suspicious—but something felt new. Romantically, Robeson attributed the opportunity to the war. In the face of Nazism, perhaps attitudes were changing. His *Othello*, the banned play for which America hadn't been ready for more than a century, was sold out every night. Eventually, it would run for 296 performances—a Broadway record for a Shakespeare play. He had already changed history, opening a door that had been closed to Black actors, and now Paul Robeson headed to the Roosevelt to confront the national pastime, with the intention of opening another.

Chapter Two

I

PAUL ROBESON AND BASEBALL CIRCLED each other largely along the periphery of his enormous fame. Despite his Renaissance mastery, baseball was the rare stage where Robeson was not the star. As a law student at Columbia, Robeson took a moonlighting job on the baseball coaching staff. The Lions' best player on that squad was Columbia Lou, the Iron Horse himself, Lou Gehrig.

Robeson was not a standout baseball player. Even if he did excel at the sport, there would have been no place for him to play. When he graduated from Rutgers in 1918, organized baseball was segregated. The Negro National League was two years from existence, and neither the National Basketball Association nor the NFL yet existed. Given his pride, talent, and pedigree, Robeson most certainly would not have joined a league that reinforced his perceived inferiority. Existing photos of Robeson, the baseball player, mimic similar images of him on the Rutgers campus and the football field, the dynamic figure separated from his classmates because of his race and size. He was a rugged catcher, but he hit just .176.

That did not mean Robeson was oblivious to the power of the sport. Baseball soared in popularity during the 1920s as Babe Ruth transformed the insular dead-ball game Robeson once played into a game of awesome power and influence. Once Landis was brought in as commissioner to restore credibility after the members of the Chicago White Sox consorted with gamblers to fix the 1919 World Series, baseball was the model for all professional sports, and part of that model was total segregation.

Neither the Black nor the mainstream newspapers wrote of the delegation in advance, a silence that could have been interpreted as an expression of the low expectations on the part of the white papers and caution by the Black papers to do nothing to jeopardize such an unprecedented opportunity. The week before Thanksgiving, word of Robeson's acceptance began to circulate, and hundreds of letters piled into the mailrooms of the Roosevelt, on 45th Street between Madison and Vanderbilt Avenues, and the Hotel Commodore, Landis's New York residence, at 42nd Street and Lexington, next door to Grand Central Station. The labor movement, especially the heavily leftist CIO locals concentrated in New York, organized a letter-writing campaign to Landis. Black leadership followed suit. On November 24, Roy Wilkins, the number two man at the NAACP, wrote to Landis that baseball integration would "do much to strengthen the American democratic way of life." The Friday after Thanksgiving, Claude Barnett, the director of the Associated Negro Press, praised the commissioner, treating him with deference, as though segregation was a universally offensive social blight. Barnett remarked that Landis's "attitude of total fairness, known the nation over" would contribute to eliminating "whatever barriers have existed in the past." On congressional stationery, William Dawson, the Black U.S. representative of Illinois's First District, wrote to Landis sympathizing with the "difficulties" that would come with integration and the "courage" its eradication would require, but wrote he was confident because of Landis's "fairness and fearlessness in all matters" under his jurisdiction.

The setting was rife with symbolism: The owners would be facing the great Robeson, in a hotel named after Teddy Roosevelt, whose surname had been given to Jack Roosevelt Robinson—the man who would change the American century—as a middle name.

Or had it? A 1957 *Ebony* magazine article bylined by Robinson's older brother Mack, the 1936 Olympic silver medalist in the 200 meters, as told to *Chicago Defender* columnist A.S. "Doc" Young, quietly put into question Robinson's most fundamental element: his name.

> Incidentally, throughout this article, I've called my brother "Jackie Robinson." You call him Jackie, too. Everybody does. But I really don't know where that "Jack" business started. It was always my understanding that my mother named him "Roosevelt Robinson." As far as I know, the "Jack" or "Jackie" part is only a nickname.

The 1920 and 1930 Census entries corroborate Mack Robinson—and revealed his own accepted name to also be a nickname. Recorded two and a half weeks before Jackie's first birthday, the census reports the family living in the Cairo area of the Ragans Militia District in Grady County, Georgia, along the same strip of road as a "convict camp," roughly 30 miles north of the Florida border. The census misidentifies the family name as "Robertson," but the youngest child's name is listed not as "Jack," but "Roosevelt." The 1930 entry, from Pasadena, California, correctly identifies the family surname as "Robinson," but still lists the youngest child's name as "Roosevelt." Both Census entries refer to Mack as "Matthew Robinson." Somewhere between elementary school and his graduation from John Muir High School, Roosevelt Robinson gave way to a new creation, Jack Roosevelt Robinson.

II

FOR 73 YEARS, THE OFFICIAL minutes of the meeting between Paul Robeson and the owners of the 16 major league teams sat in the possession of the Commissioner's Office, leaving historians at the mercy of incomplete newspaper accounts, offering second- and third-hand speculation of what was actually said within the secret halls of power. In 2017, Major League Baseball donated the ledgers to the National Baseball Hall of Fame and Museum. For the first time, the transcripts of the historic meeting were made public, and the actual words of Robeson, Landis, and the owners would finally be known.

The Joint Meeting of the National League of Professional Baseball Clubs and the American League of Professional Baseball Clubs was scheduled for 10:30 a.m. Dick Young, the legendary baseball writer for the *Daily News* and later the *New York Post*, famously nicknamed the owners the "Lords of Baseball," because of their imperiousness and immunity to outside forces—nobody told them what to do. They controlled the country's most popular sport, and, in 1922, they had even convinced federal legislators to exempt the game from existing antitrust laws, allowing it to operate as a total monopoly. The Lords were untouchable—and here they were, assembled at the Roosevelt, the venerable names responsible for the creation of the modern game, its very foundations, stadiums, teams, and history.

The 77-year-old Landis presided. Forty-four representatives from the 16 teams attended. Secretary Leslie O'Connor recorded the minutes and took the roll: the American League President William Harridge, who was flanked by three deputies; Harry Grabiner of the White Sox, sitting in for team owner Grace Comiskey; Alva Bradley and Roger Peckinpaugh of Cleveland; Jack Zeller of the Tigers; Tom Yawkey and his president and GM, the Hall of Fame second baseman Eddie Collins, representing the Red Sox; George Weiss of the Yankees; Connie Mack and his son, Roy, for the Philadelphia A's; Clark Griffith, owner of the Washington Senators; and Bill DeWitt and Don Barnes, two of three owners in for the St. Louis Browns, along with Barnes's assistant Jimmy Conzelman.

Across the table was National League President Ford Frick, and owners and representatives for the National League: Bob and John Quinn of Boston; Branch Rickey and three deputies for Brooklyn; Philip Wrigley of the Cubs; Warren Giles of Cincinnati; Leo Bondy of the Giants; Robert Carpenter, his son Robert Jr., and Herb Pennock of the Phillies; William Benswanger of the Pirates; and Sam Breadon of the Cardinals.

John H. Sengstacke, publisher of the weekly *Chicago Defender*, addressed the owners first. Sengstacke was the nephew of Robert

Sengstacke Abbott, the *Defender*'s founder who had been grooming Sengstacke to succeed Abbot and take over the paper since Sengstacke was a teenager. Sengstacke was just 31 years old, but he oversaw the dominant Black newspaper in the nation. Despite his relative youth, Sengstacke was also the president and founder of the Negro Newspaper Publishers Association. Following Sengstacke's address would be Ira F. Lewis, the publisher of the *Pittsburgh Courier*, and then Howard Murphy, secretary of the Negro Newspaper Publishers Association.

In addition to Sengstacke, Lewis, and Murphy, the Negro Newspaper Publishers Association delegation was comprised of *Michigan Chronicle* publisher Louis B. Martin, *New York Amsterdam News* publisher Dr. C.B. Powell, Cleveland's *Call and Post* publisher William Welker, and two advisory members, the *Courier*'s Wendell Smith and Dan Burley, the managing editor of the *Amsterdam News*.

At approximately 10:45 a.m., as John Sengstacke prepared to speak, Landis called the meeting to order and addressed the delegation.

> COMMISSIONER LANDIS: Mr. Sengstacke, I am interfering with your plans just a little. I have brought Paul Robeson here. I don't need to introduce this man to you, gentlemen. When he comes to a meeting, there is no thing that I recognize that has any relation to intolerance or lack of forbearance, or to racial controversy. I brought him here on my own invitation—now, you understand that, don't you, Sengstacke? I told you I was doing that because this man has sense, and this man has not been fooled by the propaganda that there is an agreement in this crowd of men to bar Negroes from Baseball.
>
> I don't know what, beyond that, he understands, but I am informing him and these other men that are here with you, Mr. Sengstacke, of this: I have been here only twenty-three years, and maybe I don't know what is going on—I don't know; I won't testify to that; but so far as I know, and from all that I have learned in twenty-three years, there is no such agreement.

God knows these men are not cowardly enough to be afraid to put it on paper, and to have it as a haymow agreement; and I am not crook enough to stand up and enforce such a haymow agreement. Now, do you understand that?

MR. SENGSTACKE: Yes, sir.

COMM. LANDIS: With respect to that question, these clubs are on their own. Have that in mind in presenting this question.

You go ahead and talk now, Robeson.

Wearing a dark, double-breasted suit and the goatee of his title character Othello, Robeson faced the sea of white men at the rectangular-shaped table, having been introduced by Landis as a man willing to testify that baseball—a game that had not employed a Black player since 1887—did not discriminate against Black players as a matter of official policy. Plumes of cigarette, cigar, and pipe smoke wafted in the air. Robeson stood at the podium in front of a ruling class of men, most of whom had been born, as he had, in the 19th century. One man, Philadelphia's Cornelius McGillicuddy, better known as Connie Mack, was born during the Civil War, one year after William Robeson escaped north from bondage and ten days before the Emancipation Proclamation.

MR. PAUL ROBESON: I want to thank Judge Landis for permitting me to say a word to you gentlemen. I would say before I begin that I come as one who is an athlete himself, and as an American. And I can in no way disassociate myself from my friends around here. I came up with them. They represent the Negro Publishers Association, and have, perhaps, more definite knowledge of the problem about which you would want specific questions—for example, as regards negro ball players—than I would have. There are many distinguished negroes in the room.

I come only because I played a lot myself, and because I feel very deeply about this problem of getting negro ball players into the leagues. I played against Frankie Frisch when he was at

Fordham, and I was a catcher at Rutgers. I was just telling the Judge that, when I was a catcher, we had a pitcher who wound up pretty slowly, and by the time I drew back, Frisch was practically around second.

I later coached at Columbia, when Gehrig was playing. I, as you know, was an All-American football player, and played pro football. Problems have come up that face you owners and managers, Judge Landis has said—you have heard him say—that there is no agreement against negro ball players. However, we know the problem that must confront you when the question comes up: Shall we hire negro ball players?

First, there is the question: Shall other players play with them? I know about that from my own experience. I have played with Southern boys in football. At first, they wouldn't play, but at the end of the game, every man shook my hand.

When I went to play pro out in Akron, years later, the first fellows that greeted me were players from the South. As far as the public is concerned, certainly we have seen in various sports—in boxing, in football, again, and in track—that the American public is ready to accept negro athletes.

I have had great experience showing what can happen in America today. I am playing Othello—and there were bets that that could not be done in America. I have done it in Boston; I have done it in Philadelphia; are now a smash hit on Broadway. And I can think of no greater acclaim that I have ever received than I do every night in this theatre—a real demonstration to me of what the American democratic spirit can mean.

You face, I know, serious problems. There is no question about the quality of the ball players; there are plenty of them around. You need ball players, and it has gone beyond, I think, the question of letting it slide. Some say it is going to be a difficult problem. Well, we live in difficult times; we have to take up difficult things, and show that we stand foursquare on what our country can mean.

> I never presumed that there was any agreement among you gentlemen to bar negro players, but merely that you hate to initiate a policy that has not been initiated before. We live in times when the world is changing very fast, and when you might be able to make a great contribution to not only the advance of our own country, but of the whole world, because a thing like this—negro ball players becoming a part of the great national pastime of America—could make a great difference in what peoples all over the world would feel toward us as a country, in a time when we need their help.
>
> As I say, I speak purely as an individual, and as a former athlete . . . I played football myself. I don't know why colored fellows aren't in the pro football leagues. I would probably feel, if I were playing today, that I would go to Halas, Conzelman, and other fellows that I played with and say, "Give me a chance to play some football." So, I think I could ask for a chance to play baseball.
>
> I have played in most of the parks, either in football or something else, all over the country, and I have a sense of a different spirit today. I hope that something can be done.
>
> I sincerely hope the Judge will permit the other negro representatives, who really know much more about this than I do, to say a few words.
>
> Thank you, Judge.

As Robeson departed, Landis looked at him and said, "We are much obliged to you sir." The room broke out into sustained applause.

III

WHEN ROBESON JOINED THE THEATER, the popularity of baseball—and its unspoken segregation—directly affected his old sport, professional football. Landis was the entrusted moral spine of the national game, and now free of scandal, baseball was the sport to emulate. The NFL had been integrated at its inception in 1920 as the APFA. Fritz Pollard, Robeson, and the great Native American Jim Thorpe all overlapped in the new league—Thorpe was even the NFL's first president. By the mid-1920s, just as baseball had in the 1880s, the NFL gradually winnowed its number of Black players to zero. The national pastime embraced segregation, and the NFL dutifully followed its lead.

Robeson's old friend Pollard—the two had known each other since college and worked summers together in Newport, Rhode Island—last played in the league with Akron, the old Pros now renamed the Indians, for four games in 1926. His last full-time NFL head-coaching job was back in 1921, his first and last year of coaching. Though the game fielded Black players, the legendary founders of the sport, Green Bay's Curly Lambeau and Chicago's George Halas, for example, did not sign Black players.

Robeson accepted the Lords as people of honor and good will and invoked the name of Halas as a man of reason, when he was, in fact, one of the key architects of ridding football of Black players. Halas had played against Robeson as a player-coach. He founded the Bears in 1920 and, as owner, would not field a Black player for 32 years.

Two years earlier, Halas had personally witnessed Jackie Robinson in action against his Bears at the College All-Star Game at Soldier Field in Chicago. The 22-year-old Robinson was sensational, and if not for the NFL's ban against Black players, Robinson would have joined the NFL, as would his two Black UCLA teammates, Kenny Washington and Woody Strode. Instead, Robinson played semi-pro football with the Honolulu Polar Bears, leaving the territory just before the attack on Pearl Harbor.

Yet, in front of the Lords, Robeson leaned into Du Bois's twoness, just as Ed Sullivan had implored him to do weeks earlier, believing in a shared struggle and describing Halas as a reasonable man willing to integrate the game with a simple phone call. Pollard would go to his grave loathing Halas for being one of the game's great racists. Washington owner George Preston Marshall would endure as the league's most racist owner, the NFL equivalent to Boston's Tom Yawkey, but Halas more than did his part to keep Black players out of the NFL.

A different Kenesaw Mountain Landis appeared once Robeson left. The Landis who now turned toward John Sengstacke was not the man deferential to Robeson, but the Judge Landis of fearsome reputation: hard, bullying, and menacing.

> COMM. LANDIS: You go ahead now, Mr. Sengstacke. You want to talk, don't you?
>
> MR. SENGSTACKE: Yes, I do.
>
> COMM. LANDIS: Go ahead.

Sengstacke, like Robeson, appealed to the Lords' sense of wartime patriotism, repeatedly referring to the "national unity" required to beat the Axis. "We do not, and you do not, either, agree with those who argue that there is no longer room in the world for the ideas of fair play," Sengstacke told the room. "We believe that the most powerful will is inspired not by the concentration camp or the purge, but by the processes of liberty. Unity is the demand of the hour."

Sengstacke leaned into the American ideal: domestic solidarity against a foreign enemy. "Organized baseball's unwritten, but effective practice, of exclusion against some players because of their color helps to spread the 'master race' theory among Americans on a mass basis," Sengstacke told the owners.

Ira Lewis of the *Courier* appealed to the collective pocketbooks of the owners. "I am sure it would make such a difference in your turnstiles as to make you wonder why you hadn't done it years before," he said.

He too spoke of "national unity," but broke from the deferential tone of Robeson and Sengstacke, preferring baseball's record to its words. Lewis told the owners he had been a fan of baseball since 1894 and, like "all Negroes in the United States of America, I have felt the bitter pangs of sorrow and disappointment over unfair and unjust attitudes of organized baseball towards Americans of color." Landis took immediate offense. Lewis listed the potential obstacles to integration—interracial living quarters and travel—and offered solutions. "On the question of travel . . . we wish to point out to you gentlemen the fact that Negro stage performers, like Mr. Robeson, for instance, with white casts manage to handle this perplexing problem themselves." Lewis then noted the box-office successes of integrated college football and boxing. "I think," Lewis said, "the public is ready for the change."

Landis's exasperation toward Lewis simmered. "Your Honorable Commissioner has stated that there is no written law barring Negro players participating in organized baseball," Lewis said. "We thank Judge Landis for his statement. But we believe—"

"Just a moment," Landis interrupted. "I went beyond that. Please don't say that is what I said."

"I think Mr. Sengstacke said—"

"I know," Landis interrupted a second time. "But you were here when I made the statement. You must pardon me for this."

"Certainly."

"You were here when I made the statement, and now you are saying what I said. You say that I said there is no written rule."

"That is right."

"I say," Landis said, "there is no written rule; there never has been. There is no verbal rule; there never has been. There is no haymow rule or subterranean rule or understanding, expressed or implied, between leagues or between any two clubs of any league."

"Thank you, Judge," Lewis said to Landis.

"Now that," Landis said, "is my statement. Did you get that, Mr. Sengstacke?"

"Yes, sir."

Landis then looked at the Black delegation.

"Did you other members of the committee get that? If you put that statement out, I want you to add what I have said."

"Exactly. Thank you, sir," Lewis said firmly to Landis. "But we believe there is a tacit understanding—there is a gentlemen's agreement—that no Negro players be hired."

Howard Murphy closed the presentation, offering a four-point plan to integrate the sport. According to the official minutes of the meeting, Sengstacke said to the owners, "This completes our statements. If there are any questions that you would like to ask any members of our committee, we would be happy to answer them at this time."

Landis looked at the owners.

"Has anybody any questions?" he asked.

Silence.

"Apparently," Landis said, "there are no questions."

The delegation began to depart, but Landis remained infuriated by Lewis, who did not appeal to the owners' sense of fairness but indicted their half-century blockade of it. Landis could no longer hide his condescension, which was, by the laughter of fellow owners at Landis's pique, seemed appreciated by the Lords of Baseball, unused to being told how to run their business—especially by a room of Black men.

MR. SENGSTACKE: Thank you very much, Judge Landis.

COMM. LANDIS: It has been a very complete presentation of the question.

MR. SENGSTACKE: We appreciate your having given us the opportunity.

COMM. LANDIS: Although your colleague, this Pittsburgh "Courier" fellow, can't get it out of his hide.

(Laughter)

MR. SENGSTACKE: We will correct that. He understands.

COMM. LANDIS: And he looked me right in the eye when he said it.

(Laughter)

COMM. LANDIS (CONT.): We are much obliged to you, gentlemen, for coming here.

IV

THE JOINT MEETING NEARED ITS close. The last presenter of the day, Homer Chaillaux, national director of the Americanism Commission of the American Legion, implored the owners to support the exporting of baseball around the world as a method to spread American values and confront subversion, to keep the youth of the world from being "ensnared" by communism. Even as wartime allies, Chaillaux was deeply mistrusting of the Soviets. This was the same Chaillaux, who in 1935 had accused his denomination, the Methodist Church, of having been infiltrated by communists.

With German Jews desperate for asylum, this was also the same Chaillaux who spoke in Franklin, Indiana, in May 1939, three months before Hitler's invasion of Poland, and proposed a ten-year ban on immigration into the United States, a position effectively guaranteeing the closure of American borders to Jews.

After Chaillaux completed his remarks, the Lords discussed the tedious business of the game, Landis agreeing to grant the Cardinals and Browns additional night games during wartime to help with struggling attendance, the owners mulling proposed amendments of existing major- and minor-league rules and tweaks to the season schedule. Then, Branch Rickey, part owner and president of the Brooklyn Dodgers, interrupted the monotony.

"Mr. Commissioner, are we to understand that the report from this meeting, in response to the delegation that came in here today, is to be simply that the matter was not considered?"

Landis responded to Rickey's question as would the head of a cartel: he told the room what the official position of the sport would be. He told them what to think and how to present their thoughts. He spoke with a lawyer's precision, repeating the denial of a prohibition against Black players, practically verbatim to the denial he issued to the delegation, each word closing a potential loophole.

> COMM. LANDIS: No, no. The announcement will have to be that it was considered—and my recollection now is that it was considered, and you gentlemen all remember that it was considered; you each participated in the consideration of it—and that no action was taken on it; that the matter is a matter for each club to determine in getting together its baseball team; that no other solution than that, in view of the nature of our operations, is possible.

The matter, in fact, was not considered. Robeson was given an ovation but was not asked a question. Nor were the publishers—because, days earlier, Landis told the Lords no questions would be asked. When the delegation departed, Landis conducted the remainder of the meeting with no discussion period. The meeting had been moments from adjournment—until Branch Rickey spoke.

> COMM. LANDIS (CONT.): Do I state what you have in mind?

Sam Breadon was a powerhouse figure in the room. A middle-school dropout from Greenwich Village, he had owned the Cardinals outright since 1920, the same year Landis was named commissioner. Breadon was part of the consortium that hired Branch Rickey in 1917, and it was under his ownership and Rickey's leadership that the Cardinals had both created the modern-day farm system and, in the process, overtook the New York Giants as the National League's premiere franchise. The Yankees were the running dynasty in baseball, but after they had won their first title in 1923, only Breadon's Cardinals had ever beaten them in the World Series, in 1926 and 1942.

Nineteen forty-two would also be Rickey's last year with the Cardinals. His relationship with Breadon had deteriorated, and after winning the World Series, Breadon fired him. Rickey moved on to Brooklyn after 25 years with the Cardinals, and now the two men sat across the table, existing as rivals and co-conspirators.

With St. Louis being one of the most hostile and segregated cities in baseball, integration was not a subject on which Breadon wanted a prolonged discussion. He would never own an integrated team; he would sell his share of the Cardinals in 1947, the year of Jackie Robinson's arrival, and be dead of cancer two years later. As a franchise, the Cardinals would not integrate until 1953, nearly a decade after Robeson's address. Eager to close the meeting, Breadon answered Landis before Rickey could respond.

> MR. BREADON: Yes, sir.
>
> MR. RICKEY: I thought that we should all have in mind the same thing.
>
> COMM. LANDIS: Yes. Is there anything more, Mr. O'Connor?
>
> MR. O'CONNOR: No.

For the second time, the meeting nearly ended, but Branch Rickey was not finished. With nearly three-quarters of a century of hindsight, the following exchange between Rickey and Landis provided the first tangible evidence of Rickey's intention to integrate the sport: he was the only person in the meeting seeking clarity, even if only to ensure the Lords had their story straight.

The silence also exposed the owners, who from media and history, would receive the dispensation of being good men whose greatest crime was lacking vision. The official minutes of the 1943 meeting tell an indisputably different story: Their commitment to keep Black players out of baseball was total, an active silence.

Branch Rickey clearly wanted to engage with Landis, but he also was one of them, part of the club, and his comments reflected this duality: aware of the future but offering language that would maintain the conspiracy—and buy him time.

> MR. RICKEY: Mr. Commissioner, there is one further step for our consideration on that matter. Some of our clubs are beset with a great many petitions and a great many visitations, such as you saw here today. That they become embarrassing is

not the point; they become time-taking, and, from a publicity standpoint, they become important.

Is it in order for a club to say that this is a matter requiring not only our League consideration, but joint consideration, and that the club itself is not able to give further statement than it has now given, whatever that is?

Is that the position? Is that a good position to take? Is it permissible or advisable for us to make that statement?

COMM. LANDIS: I don't think it is, for this reason: that three Major League managers were quoted in Negro newspapers as saying that, but for the bar, there would be a footrace run by sixteen Major League managers to sign Negro ball players. I called in those three managers, and, while there was no admission that they had made those statements, I think it is a fair approach to the truth to say that such was the unconvincing quality of their evasiveness in reply to my questions, they all did make the statement.

Whereupon, I gave out an announcement a year ago last summer that any club was perfectly at liberty to hire one or twenty or twenty-five Negro players. I gave out that statement: that there never had been an agreement, written or unwritten, vocal or otherwise, and that each club was absolutely and completely at liberty in that respect, as they were in respect of any other players coming from any other race or belonging to any particular church or anything else.

I think your suggestion would carry with it an implication that they were not at liberty; that it would require League action—and I don't think that would be good. I think that would be indefensible.

MR. RICKEY: It was hardly a suggestion, Judge. It was an inquiry.

COMM. LANDIS: Well, it was an inquiry, but suspicious men might think that—

MR. RICKEY: Yes, that is right.

COMM. LANDIS: I don't think that anybody ought to say that. We can't say that. In the first place, it isn't true, and, if any of you gentlemen want to hire a Negro player, you are as much at liberty to do that as you are to sign up any other player, be he in human form. That is our whole theory, and we must keep away from the other idea.

Again, I say to you, as I have said to these delegations: I have been there twenty-three years. Not only has there never been any agreement, written or haymow, or any other kind of an agreement, but I never have heard it discussed among you gentlemen on the basis that there was an agreement or understanding. Never have I heard it discussed.

MR. J.A.R. QUINN: I have been going to these meetings for more than forty years, and this is the first time I heard as much as I heard in here today.

MR. GRIFFITH: I make a motion we adjourn.

It was fitting Griffith ended the meeting, for few team owners would be more associated with the history of racism in the game than the Senators' Clark Griffith. His Senators and George Preston Marshall's Redskins were located in the nation's capital—and both teams were two of the most racist in professional sports. When most teams had integrated seating, Griffith Stadium only sold seats to Black fans in the right field corner. When Griffith moved his team from Washington to Minnesota in 1961 and renamed his club the Twins, he was proud of his reasoning: Minnesota was full of good, clean, white people.

Boston's Bob Quinn had never heard as much about adding Black players as he heard that day. The reason was obvious: the thought of integration was so preposterous, it never received their consideration. Quinn had answered his own question.

COMM. LANDIS: Is there anything further, Mr. O'Connor?

MR. O'CONNOR: No, sir.

COMM. LANDIS: Has anybody anything further?

(No response.)

COMM. LANDIS: The meeting is adjourned, gentlemen.

(Whereupon, at 12:40 P.M., the meeting adjourned.)

Chapter Three

I

THE MAN WHO EMERGED MOST victorious from the joint meeting was the least deserving: Kenesaw Mountain Landis. In the next day's morning editions, most major papers did not even mention the presentation, and none prominently. It was, to the mainstream population, not news. The influential *Brooklyn Eagle* was dismissive. "Paul Robeson, the great star of stage, screen and airways, gave an eloquent speech pleading for the inclusion of colored players in organized baseball. It was said that Robeson's speech was well-received, but no action was taken," the paper reported. ". . . it is a good guess that the Negro problem will remain unsolved as far as baseball is concerned." The *San Francisco Examiner* concluded that Landis "added to his many distinctions the other day by saying exactly nothing in several hundred well-chosen words." Robeson's name produced a headline in the major dailies—he was always big news—but as an example of how inconsequential the meeting had been treated at the time, the top story nationwide did not concern Robeson or integration, but rather focused on William D. Cox, disgraced owner of the Philadelphia Phillies.

Nine months earlier, in March 1943, Cox was part of a consortium that purchased the team and ran the club for just four months before his own manager, Bucky Harris, accused him of betting on games. Ten days before Robeson's address, Landis barred Cox from baseball for life. First jury, then judge, Landis listened to Cox over a six-hour appeal hearing. As executioner, Landis reached the same verdict.*

Whether out of sheer naivete or a painfully misguided attempt to apply public pressure on the Lords, Black newspapers wildly overplayed the afternoon. Robeson spoke in high terms ("Because baseball is the American game, it is up to baseball to see that discrimination does not become the American pattern."), but several executives offered polite, noncommittal assessments. AL President Harridge said the presentation was the highlight of the three-day event, hearing such "clean-cut, tactical, straight-to-the-point colored gentlemen who evidently knew what they were after and had taken the proper steps to get it," but no member of the baseball leadership, in private session or in print, offered an actual pathway toward integration.

The Black press, meanwhile, positioned Landis as audacious. *The St. Paul Recorder* reported the meeting was conducted in good faith ("The consensus was Judge Landis wouldn't have invited the publishers committee in to talk if the league owners hadn't had something good one way or the other in mind.") and predicted, "There is sure to be some action on the question of Negroes in the big leagues this winter. Watch for it." Nat Low of the communist *Daily Worker* was enthusiastic ("Major Leagues Pave Way for Negroes"), but the most extreme response was reserved for the front page of the *Pittsburgh Courier*, courtesy of its sports editor, Wendell Smith.

PUBLISHERS PLACE CASE OF NEGRO PLAYERS BEFORE BIG-LEAGUE OWNERS

JUDGE LANDIS SAYS NO OFFICIAL RACE BAN EXISTS IN MAJORS

NEW YORK–"I want it clearly understood," thundered gray-thatched Kenesaw Mountain Landis to 44 owners and officials of major league teams

---

* In denying his appeal, Landis made William D. Cox the first and to date the only owner in Major League Baseball history to be stripped of his franchise. In the wake of the ruling, Bob Carpenter and sons, part of the powerful DuPont family, would take over the Phillies and own the team from 1943 until 1981.

> at the Roosevelt Hotel here in New York last Friday morning, "that there is no rule, nor to my knowledge has there ever been, formal or informal, or any understanding, written or unwritten, subterranean or sub-anything against the hiring of Negroes in the major leagues!" That was the unqualified, official bombshell that Landis hurled at representatives of major league clubs at a joint session of the American and National Leagues.

In addition to calling them a "bombshell," Smith described Landis's words as his "admirable, honest position," that his voice "pierced the smoke-filled room," and that as the "walls of the packed conference room bulged with tension," Landis's voice "roared defiantly" at the Lords. Smith's story added, "This was an historic meeting." In a companion column appearing the same day on the *Courier*'s sports front, Landis's own words should have diluted the enthusiasm ("I can't speak for the owners at all," he said. "Really, there is absolutely nothing I can tell you."), but Smith continued undeterred.

Smith not only vastly mischaracterized Landis, but his hyperbole also revealed the powerlessness of the Black press. Integration rested not on leverage or commitment, but on flattery, appealing to Landis's ego and his ostensibly peerless jurisprudence. His overreaching sentences of pro-labor and anti-war activists during World War I contributed to the destruction of the left-wing political movements of the late 1910s and early 1920s.

Why did the *Courier* so badly overplay the story? Part of the reason may have been competition with the *Daily Worker*, which a year earlier appeared more aggressive on the integration question. In the spring and summer of 1942, the communist paper was fierce, running a Lester Rodney story with a 60-point headline that read, "CAN YOU READ, JUDGE LANDIS?" In response, the *Courier* appeared to be marking its territory.

II

THE BLACK PUBLISHERS VIEWED THEMSELVES as soldiers in a world battle, but Kenesaw Mountain Landis did not see Black people as comrades, nor did he see the war as a welcome opportunity for Black Americans to prove their patriotism. In the war, Landis saw a dangerous moment that threatened the white hierarchy and in FDR a president promising enough hope to make Black citizens believe he was their champion. While the Black press enthused, the segregationist Mississippi Democrat (and Paul Robeson archenemy) John Rankin attacked FDR's newly formed Fair Employment Practices Commission from the House floor as a threat to all white men. "When they go to the railroad brotherhoods and tell the white men working on our railroads, who have been good to the Negroes of this country, that they have to make engineers and conductors out of them, and that they have to accept them on terms of social equality, I say they are insulting the white railroad men of this country, and doing the Negroes an irreparable injury."

Two headlines in the *Washington Afro-American* underscored the attitudes of the owners. The first, "Clark Griffith Won't Budge on Use of Colored Players," quoted Griffith's long-held refusal to integrate ("It is my belief we should have white baseball leagues and colored baseball leagues."). The second quoted the legendary Yankee executive Ed Barrow, bedridden at the time but quoted as appearing supportive of integration ("I have no objection to employing colored ball players . . . If we find it necessary to hire colored, we will do it."). The *Afro-American* optimistically headlined the story, "Yankee boss Oks Colored Players."

Another item, unrelated to baseball, also caught Griffith's suspicious eye: an unsigned editorial titled "Can We Beat the Japs?" that illustrated the wide and, to Griffith, nefarious ambitions of the Double V campaign. In it, the editorial stated,

> The South today spends more time in perpetuating segregation than in making munitions. The Navy boasts that its fighting ships will never be taken by the Japanese or served by colored officers. Any railroad car or bus, no matter what its military urgency, will not move until all colored passengers are in a jim-crow car.

Griffith was furious. On December 10, on Senators letterhead ("Washington American League Base Ball Club"), Griffith included a clipping of the editorial in a letter to Landis, explaining that his statement was a reprint of an old quote and alerted Landis that the Black press interpreting the commissioner's comments in New York as well as Barrow's quote as proof that the league was now "favorable to the negros entering professional ball." In his letter, Griffith circled one paragraph *("Not a word has been said at home about a new emancipation for the colored people, who are deprived of a vote and who are fettered with segregation.")* of the *Afro-American* editorial in red marker.

Griffith sent the letter to Landis, and the two engaged in an exchange rife with the racial paternalism and the suspicions of a coming threat: communist elements were influencing Black people to insist on civil rights:

> *I want you to pay particular attention to the editorial which is captioned "Can We Beat the Japs?" This article will give you a good idea what is really in the minds of the negro. The insinuations in this article that the negro isn't ever free and that he is expecting a "new birth" pretty nearly verifies the fact that he is listening to a lot of outside paid-for propaganda.*

On December 14, Landis replied, "Dear Mr. Griffith: I have your letter of the 10th. The trouble with the whole thing is the misuse of the black man. Politicians, black and white, are exploiting him and have been doing that thing since the first slave ship touched the west coast of Africa and sailed away with the first Negro bound and gagged—headed for slave labor in the western hemisphere. A good Christmas to you, and give my love to your lady. Truly yours, KML."

Landis viewed the racial tensions that marred 1943 as proof that integration was a great mistake—especially in the military and labor forces. The races required separation. He seemed alarmed by the idea of entrusting Black people with defending the country—and the baseball men around the league privately provided Landis with ample grist for his beliefs.

Red Sox GM Eddie Collins had already placed *Boston Record* columnist Dave Egan on Landis's radar when Egan advocated for integration to solve wartime player shortages. "The solution, logically, is to hire colored ballplayers." The Harvard-educated Egan would be one of the few white mainstream columnists in the country who routinely supported integration. Collins, like Robeson, was Columbia-educated. He was also one of the few prominent members of the Chicago White Sox curiously spared by Landis during the infamous 1919 "Black Sox" betting scandal that created the commissionership. Collins was one of Landis's most trusted lieutenants in thwarting the use of Black players. The same day of Egan's piece, January 26, 1943, Collins sent a letter, written on Boston American League Baseball Company letterhead, to Harridge:

Dear Mr. Harridge:
Here is another from our friend again.

The Judge called me about this writer the other day, so I take it you must have shown him one of the clippings I sent you. Maybe he will "enjoy" reading this one.

A week later, an incident occurred between Black soldiers and local police in Dallas, a repeat of similar encounters between enlisted men and the white communities nationwide who did not appreciate the presence of Black soldiers. On February 2, *The Dallas Morning News* reported the arrest of five Black soldiers after a "near riot, the second in a month between Negro soldiers and civilians." J. Alvin Gardner, president of the Double-A level Texas League dutifully sent Landis a copy of the article. ("Dear Judge, Thought you would be interested in reading about the above incident that took place here yesterday.") After another Texas skirmish nearly pitted armed Black soldiers in conflict with local residents, Landis received a clipping of the news story from another intimate with an ominous note, "Dear Judge: It almost happened!"

• • •

The Black publishers would never again meet with Landis. He had outmaneuvered the Black press, using Robeson to do so, and, in return, was heralded in its pages. They believed the presentation would result in further dialogue. It did not. Landis had beaten the newspapermen with language. Baseball may not have ever adopted an official edict to bar Black players, but each individual owner had no intentions of signing one. Despite Wendell Smith's description of the 1943 meeting as "epochal" and Smith personally telling Landis that day the commissioner had made "millions of Black and white friends due to his courageous stand on Negro ball players," nothing concrete followed—except Landis's uncompromising insistence on segregation and privately mocking integrationists. Black leaders presented themselves as loyal Americans, and the owners just wanted them to go away.

The 1943 meetings would be untethered to history, added occasionally to the list of thwarted attempts at integration, but Robeson's address and Rickey's exchange with Landis provided important foreshadowing. Meanwhile, integration disappeared as an issue. The next year, it received no mention during the 1944 league meetings or very much during the year in the press. During the season, no team made a serious attempt to sign a Black player. In contrast to Wendell Smith's euphoria, Landis would threaten any player, manager, or executive discussing integration favorably in the press—Chicago's Jimmy Dykes and the Dodgers' Leo Durocher, most prominently—with suspension. Decades later, Roger Kahn would write it was an open secret that Landis privately threatened any executive attempting integration with a lifetime ban. The next milestone would occur November 25, 1944, when Kenesaw Mountain Landis, rigid overseer of the game for a quarter century, suddenly died of a heart attack.

III

WITH LANDIS DEAD, BRANCH RICKEY began rewriting baseball history. His origin story was a moral tale, featuring Charles Thomas, the catcher who played for Rickey when he coached Ohio Wesleyan in 1903. Prohibited from lodging with the rest of the club on a road trip to South Bend, Indiana, Thomas was allowed by the hotel to sleep on a cot in Rickey's room. To his horror, Rickey discovered his Black catcher sobbing, jabbing fiercely at his dark skin, attempting to scratch his permanent, disqualifying impediment free from his body. Rickey, the Bible by his bedside, would say Thomas provided the foundation for him to one day undo the injustice.

There was a more practical reason for Rickey's mobilization that Rickey omitted from the tale: no team in baseball was under more pressure to integrate than the Brooklyn Dodgers, and no executive in the sport was in more contact with an agitated local public than Branch Rickey.

Under Republican Governor Thomas Dewey—and much to the anger of the national GOP trying to win back the White House and Congress—New York enacted the Ives-Quinn Act, outlawing job discrimination in the workforce. While pro-integration forces explored how to apply the new law to baseball, in the city, Mayor Fiorello La Guardia was also under pressure from a coalition of several religious and social justice groups. One 1945 combined effort, the Campaign to End Jim Crow in Baseball, was sponsored by such names as artists Stella Adler, Langston Hughes, Canada Lee, and Paul Robeson.

Pressure on La Guardia translated into pressure on Rickey. La Guardia immediately asked Rickey and Yankee President Larry MacPhail to join the advisory board. In the summer of 1945, MacPhail met with two members of the La Guardia Committee. One was Dan W. Dodson, the son of a sharecropper and raised in the Texas cotton fields who would earn a doctorate degree and join the faculty at New York University before being tapped for the committee by the mayor in 1944. One of Dodson's great victories would occur in 1946, when he discovered New York colleges were limiting the number of Black, Catholic, and Jewish students through a heinous system of secret quotas. According to *The New York Times*, Dodson's research was essential to ending the practice.

Dodson and a second committeeman, Schuyler N. Warren, met with MacPhail for two hours at Yankee Stadium. Appearing amenable on racial issues, MacPhail told the two men integration would be an asset to the Yankees because "good Negro players would draw more at Yankee Stadium than he would lose."

The pressure mounted. Black and communist newspapers constantly targeted the New York teams to integrate, and now the city was involved. The Dodgers were the most targeted of pro-integration demonstrations. In the rare times when the newspapers would speculate which team would be the first to add Black players, invariably the answer was Brooklyn—and it wasn't because of the Mahatma's inscrutable moral code. It was because of pressure.

Unlike St. Louis, Brooklyn was home to many Eastern European immigrants. Labor influences were strong, including the communist paper *Daily Worker*. Brooklyn was a powerful demographic mix for social justice. The conservative wings of the mainstream press did not hide its anti-Semitism in describing New York or its conviction that the New Deal led to strong labor and strong labor led to socialism. The right-wing syndicated columnist Westbrook Pegler referred to "the foreigners of New York" and "parasites from the European compounds of the city of New York," when describing its liberal, immigrant, and often Jewish electorate. An aggressive critique of the political and economic system was occurring in a country by Americans whose politics skewed to the left of mainstream liberalism, and much of that left-wing political activity was taking place in Brooklyn.

New York City had elected three prominent leftists to government—all of whom were close personal friends of Paul Robeson. In 1943, Harvard- and Amherst-educated Benjamin Davis Jr. was elected to the city council representing Harlem. Davis was Black, a communist, and a member of the NAACP. Vito Marcantonio was elected to Congress, representing East Harlem as a New Deal Republican and member of the American Labor Party. Brooklyn elected a communist, Peter Cacchione, to city council in 1941. Each of the politicians had wired Landis before Robeson's 1943 appearance. As the view of communists grew less popular, future accounts, especially from the Black press, would diminish their influence, but the leftist voice was loud and sustained. When it focused on baseball, it focused first on Landis, and then, uncomfortably, on Branch Rickey.

In June 1945, Cacchione brought a delegation of pro-integration activists to visit Rickey, and the Young Communist League presented him with a petition of 10,000 Brooklynites supporting integration. Cacchione threatened protests in front of the Dodgers' Montague Street business offices. The Giants and Yankees received similar challenges.

The Lords still resisted. Two months earlier, on April 24, 1945, the owners met at the Hotel Cleveland. A successor to Landis had yet to be finalized, so his trusted longtime secretary, Leslie O'Connor, presided as acting commissioner, and for the first time, the Lords began facing the inevitability of integration—and did so with dread. Earlier that month, in Boston, the Jewish city councilor Isadore Muchnick threatened to revoke the Red Sox permit for Sunday baseball, and, in response, the Red Sox agreed to conduct what would be an infamous tryout of Negro League players Jackie Robinson, Marvin Williams, and Sam Jethroe. Robinson and the two other players donned Red Sox uniforms, took batting and fielding practice, and never heard from the Red Sox again.

Seventeen months earlier, Rickey's exchange with Landis extended the 1943 meeting. Now, in Cleveland, O'Connor addressed the owners directly, according to the official minutes of the meeting.

> MR. O'CONNOR: Now, gentlemen, a problem that is becoming more acute all the time is this question of Negro admission to the Major and Minor Leagues. New York has adopted a very rigid statute. Illinois is in the process of doing so. I think the Federal Congress has one before it, and it is good politics, so we must assume it is very apt to go through.

O'Connor read a proposal from the newspaperman Sam Lacy, now of *The Washington Afro-American*. Lacy proposed to be a de facto scout between the Negro Leagues and Organized Baseball. Lacy suggested the Lords appoint a "colored man" to make a survey of "Negro baseball" whose responsibility would be to "ferret out those men whose ability, personality, character, habits, etc. fit them for the job. I ask for your consideration. . . . This is sort of [a] compromise for me as a colored man, in that it embraces the element of 'appeasement,' but if it accomplishes anything I shall feel compensated in some measure for suggesting it."

Rickey was the first to speak when the owners began discussing Lacy's proposal, moving to approve the meeting. According to the official minutes of the meeting, Horace Stoneham of the Giants seconded the motion. Sensing positive momentum, Clark Griffith immediately shut down discussion, just as he attempted to do in 1943.

> MR. GRIFFITH: And nothing else from this meeting.

The Lords unanimously agreed. O'Connor would meet with Lacy, reiterating that the meeting would not be public. O'Connor stressed secrecy because "any publicity would only hamper their efforts."

Jack Zeller, the general manager of the Detroit Tigers, sided with Griffith, opposed to any proposal that suggested a pathway toward baseball including Black players. He would vote no. "Unless," he said, "we are talking about helping the Negro baseball leagues."

For the first time in the history of the game's recorded transcripts, the baseball leadership other than Branch Rickey seemed to acknowledge that segregation could not exist in perpetuity. Griffith made clear he expected Lacy's survey to be a bureaucratic exercise designed to buy time, but Leslie O'Connor, who had served Landis for the judge's entire quarter-century tenure, turned harshly to Griffith.

> GRIFFITH: That is all you are going to talk about. You are not going to talk about using them with us.
>
> O'CONNOR: And you are not going to meet the New York situation unless you meet it square on. You are not going to meet it by refusing to talk about it.

IV

ALBERT B. CHANDLER, FORMER GOVERNOR of Kentucky, officially succeeded Landis. He went by his nickname, "Happy." Five months after the owners meeting in Cleveland, on October 23, 1945, Branch Rickey signed Jackie Robinson to a minor-league contract. He was to report to Montreal for the 1946 season. Given his appearance before the Lords two years earlier, the signing indirectly represented something of a personal triumph for Paul Robeson. Even if Landis had attempted to manipulate him, the pressure the unions and communists had placed on the game was not insignificant. Once, the 1943 meeting stood orphaned from history, now Robinson and Robeson were linked in a historic journey. When the signing was announced, Robeson happened to be in Montreal, Robinson's future home, performing a two-night engagement at Plateau Hall.

SINGER PAUL ROBESON LAUDS ROBINSON DEAL

"This is the greatest step ever taken by organized baseball on behalf of the American Negro. Its effect upon the game, indeed upon the entire racial problem, should be far-reaching," said Paul Robeson, colored international concert singer in Montreal last night when informed of the signing of Jack Robinson, 26-year-old Negro second basemen to a Montreal Royals contract. "Great pressure will naturally be brought to bear upon the Montreal Club and also upon Commissioner Chandler in this matter. It is to be hoped that the club will stand its ground now that this important decision has been made. There will be strong dissent from certain quarters naturally, but the Montreal Baseball Club can rest assured that it will be supported in this move by all liberal minded Canadians and Americans," he concluded.

Privately, the Lords felt betrayed. Only Horace Stoneham of the Giants applauded the news. The rest were enraged. Eddie Collins showed his contempt for the Negro Leagues by expressing the difficulty of reaching the majors from "college or sandlot ball." Collins dismissed Robinson backhandedly. "More power to Robinson if he can make the grade."

Larry MacPhail had been outmaneuvered from a direction he did not see coming: Branch Rickey. MacPhail was likely even more stung to discover his old mentor Rickey had secretly signed Robinson even earlier than October, in a deal over the summer—just as he and Clark Griffith felt they had devised a plan to better fund the Negro Leagues to maintain a patina of separate and equal. In his public statements, MacPhail contended separate leagues respected Negro League sovereignty and published an extensive report arguing that integration would be a terrible mistake, but he was too late. Rickey had won the day.

MacPhail's fellow owners attempted to soothe his defeat—and their own. The Pittsburgh Pirates were managed by Robeson's old college rival Frankie Frisch, the old Fordham Flash himself. The Pirates hadn't won a pennant in eighteen years, but the Lords were not focused on improving their teams. On October 26, Pirates owner Bill Benswanger, who wound up never holding a tryout for Campanella, reacted to baseball's newly available talent source by writing a forlorn letter to MacPhail.

> *Dear Larry,*
> *Thanks for your dope on the negro baseball player.*
> *The least I can say is that such a delicate and controversial matter your opinions ride side by side with my own. The recent occurrence, in my opinion, did not help either Organized baseball or the negro.*

From the White Sox, owner Harry Grabiner, whose White Sox hadn't reached the World Series since fixing it in 1919 and finished fifth or worse 18 times in the ensuing 25 years, wrote to MacPhail that he believed MacPhail's defense of segregation "outlined the picture perfectly, fairly, and adequately."

The most telling consolation letter MacPhail received arrived from the Athletics Base Ball Club of Philadelphia. From Connie Mack, age 81, born December 22, 1862, sixteen months into the Civil War. As the owner-manager of the Philadelphia A's, Mack would both win and lose more games than any man in baseball history. He was the patriarch of the sport, older than both leagues, and his letter to MacPhail, dated October 29, 1945, best illustrated the institutional attitudes that awaited Jackie Robinson.

Dear Mr. MacPhail,
Many thanks for sending me the statement in regards to the negroes in baseball.

It was a great disappointment to me to see that Branch Rickey had signed a negro for his Montreal Baseball Club. If all Major League Club owners would just let Branch have all the negroes, feel that we would all be better off in the long run. Hope you feel as I do in regards to this.
With kind regards,
CONNIE MACK
President

Five and a half months later, Mack would hold court with another important group of co-conspirators, the baseball writers. In the event the Dodgers were scheduled against the A's and Robinson was in uniform, the octogenarian said he would not field his team and urged reporters to quote him. The Philadelphia writers, including Red Smith of *The New York Times*, chose not to publish the story, fearing the old man's words might hurt his reputation. Mack echoed the same sentiment publicly that he wrote to MacPhail privately. "I used to have respect for Rickey," Mack told the writers. "I don't anymore."

Part Two

Transition

(1946–1949)

Chapter Four

I

IT WAS A NEW TIME. The war was over, and the global death tolls—of soldiers who were paid to fight, of children, parents, and grandparents who were not—were staggering, incomprehensible even to the coldest eye: 2.5 million dead in India, 1 million each in Yugoslavia and the Philippines, 8 million-plus dead in Germany, 3 million in Japan, 5.6 million in Poland, 20 million dead in China, and 24 million more in the Soviet Union. The United States suffered 418,000 casualties, a grim luxury for the country protected by oceans, spared from fighting wars on its own soil—but America's war dead still equaled the entire population of Oakland, California.

The nation emerged victorious and heroic, something to behold in a devastated world. The industrial city of Eindhoven in The Netherlands, bombed mercilessly by the Germans and now grateful to its Allied liberators, named two main thoroughfares after Churchill and Montgomery, and four after Americans Eisenhower, Patton, Marshall, and FDR. America, as Robeson had preached throughout the war and appealed similarly to Landis and the Lords, could be a worldwide model of freedom. Victory allowed America to see itself as an ideal of enormous possibility that would translate postwar, and much of the world believed so, too.

Emerging from the Great Struggle, Americans clung evermore tightly to its credos, its belief in merit, that the only barrier to one's prospects in the United States was the limit of their imagination. Manifesting freedom was how to attain it, and it was this seductive idea that would become a leading cultural export. In triumph, the philosophy surged with greater intensity, even as the United States in the fall of 1945 remained unequivocally segregated. America's relationship with merit formed an enduring contradiction that coursed through the national bloodstream. No amount of evidence to the contrary could shake that conviction—not that the entire nation by law or custom insisted on second-class Black citizenship; not that white Americans had never hesitated to reinforce that insistence with violence; not that a standing U.S. senator, Mississippi's Theodore Bilbo, told the country following the war it must choose between "separation or mongrelization"; and not that instead of reacting to his signing of Robinson as an impressive scouting coup, Branch Rickey's fellow owners saw it as the deepest, personal betrayal.

Dan M. Daniel assured his readers in *The Sporting News* that Jackie Robinson posed no threat to segregation. The impetus to integrate the majors, Daniel suggested, came not from "Negro baseball circles" but from "high-pressure groups"—shorthand for the Communist Party—his way of telling baseball fans that the Black baseball establishment was comfortable with segregation.

Daniel sought to assuage white anxieties that baseball was yet another frontier where whites would have to compete with Blacks for their jobs. Daniel told his readers Black players simply weren't good enough to take big-league jobs from white players. "It is quite conceivable that the story has received far more attention than it is worth," Daniel wrote. "Robinson has not been signed by the Dodgers and insofar as can be discerned, never will play for the Brooklyn club in the National League." Daniel reinforced his assessment with inside information directly from Dodgers team President Branch Rickey. "'He is not now major league stuff and there is not a single Negro player in this country who could qualify for the National or the American leagues,' Rickey admitted to this writer." Daniel's voice was not anomalous. *The Sporting News* wrote condescendingly that Robinson's value was not as a potential star but as "a symbol of emancipation." The Cleveland fireballer Bob Feller said at the time there wasn't a Black player in America talented enough to compete with the white players currently in the game. As the man of the moment and not a hypothetical, Feller was referring specifically to Robinson.

Over the following weeks, Rickey addressed skeptics who doubted the legitimacy of the signing. He told the *Pittsburgh Courier* that Robinson could one day join the Dodgers, but only "if capable." Three weeks before Christmas, an editorial in the *St. Louis Post-Dispatch* titled "Democracy on the Diamond" declared, "Whether Jackie Robinson is or is not a good ballplayer is the only thing that matters."

Whether or not Jackie Robinson was or was not a good ballplayer was, in fact, the *least* important thing that mattered, for he had obliterated the International League for Montreal in 1946, but his promotion to the Dodgers was uncertain. He was 28 years old and, as a collegiate, was once the greatest athlete in the nation. As the only Black player in the minors, he had been subject to hostilities and remained sensational. He had come from the Negro League's Kansas City Monarchs, where Branch Rickey said no worthy players existed, and won the 1946 batting title with a .349 average. He scored 112 runs in 124 games, tying for the league lead. He stole 40 bases and led all second basemen in fielding percentage. He was pure athlete, 5 ft., 11 in., 195 pounds, with an electric playing style that made him a must-watch–the-football power with a sprinter's burst and box-office appeal. People paid to read about him in the papers, and they paid to watch him play live.

Robinson excelled in any environment. When Montreal visited Louisville, a segregated city whose fans (and players) were known to be especially venomous, the Colonels adopted a game plan: put Jackie

Robinson on his ass as many times as possible. See if he was a man. See if he could take it. Robinson had encountered the tactic before: October 14, 1939, at Stanford Stadium in Palo Alto, California, against the Stanford Indians.* On one play, a 20-year-old Robinson was brought to the turf by a Stanford defender, who then punched him in the face. The UCLA Southern Campus yearbook the next year would caption a photograph of the play: "Stanford men are amazed as a teammate plays a dirty choke on Robinson."

Pitchers routinely threw at hitters to test their courage, to create that split-second of fear that might break their concentration, that might turn a hit into an out. The Louisville pitchers threw at Robinson for a different reason: to confirm their beliefs that Black people, as a race, lacked fortitude. White Southerners believed Black people were incapable of handling pressure, couldn't stand tall during the fight, and they accepted this bit of paternalism to reinforce the Southern caste system. Black people were childlike, unready for the adult responsibilities of democracy. Challenge their comfort, and they would break.

Louisville threw relentlessly at Jackie Robinson. They made him "skip rope" (intentionally throwing fastballs at his feet to make him scamper around the batter's box, the baseball equivalent of the old Western trope of shooting at a cowboy's feet to make him "dance."). They gave him a "shave," throwing directly under his chin. They threw beanballs: fastballs aimed directly at his head, an especially deadly threat in those days before batting helmets. They would prove he would wilt. He did not. "When we saw that he didn't scare," Louisville pitcher Otey Clark said of Robinson after the season, "we let him alone."

Rickey said merit would determine Robinson's promotion to the Dodgers, but as spring camp broke, he turned vague. During the final month of the 1946 season, each of the top ten hitters in the International

* Stanford changed its school teams' name from the "Indians" to the "Cardinal" in 1981.

League had been called up to their respective teams, except Robinson, the best hitter in the game.

The Sporting News said word out of Brooklyn was that Rickey had changed his mind. "Rickey has turned cold on the idea of bringing up the colored boy to the National League this campaign." Rickey was too busy pumping up a kid pitcher named Johnny Van Cuyk, whose big-league career would consist of appearing in only seven games over three years.

On some occasions, Rickey confounded his coaches, considering leaving Robinson in the minors for a second full season—a thought that would have never applied to a white player who had been as dominant as Robinson. On others, Rickey would be uncharacteristically rigid: either Robinson would make the Dodgers directly out of spring training or he wouldn't be brought up at all in 1947, an oddly unequivocal position for a business as volatile as baseball, where injury or performance, trade or circumstance, could alter personnel decisions in an instant.

Even that great elixir—winning—did not sway Branch Rickey. While Robinson destroyed the International League, the Dodgers and Cardinals were deadlocked for the 1946 National League pennant. During the final month, the teams would never be separated by more than two and a half games. Tied on the season's final day, a best-of-three playoff decided the pennant. The Cardinals swept Brooklyn, then beat the Red Sox in the World Series. Late in the race, one New York paper suggested Brooklyn might call on Robinson to put the Dodgers over the top, a suggestion Rickey quickly dismissed. Two evenly matched teams were separated by an indiscernible margin with the season on the line, and Branch Rickey left Jackie Robinson, the most explosive of pennant-winning secret weapons, sitting in the minor leagues.

Speculation opened the new year. The January 8, 1947, *The Sporting News* dedicated a full page to debate Robinson's professional prospects. Lloyd McGowan of the *Montreal Star* covered Robinson in 1946 and concluded he would be a pedestrian but serviceable major-league player. "There isn't much Robby can't do with the bat," McGowan wrote. "On merit alone, Robinson should rate a place on the Dodgers."

Cy Kritzer of the *Buffalo News* disagreed. Robinson's terrific 1946 was to Kritzer merely the result of adrenaline. "There are many around the International League who still believe, after watching the Negro star do everything expected of a future major-leaguer, that he was playing over his head in 1946," Kritzer wrote, "that his crusading zeal to pave the way for other members of his race actually increased his ability. In time, like an old-fashioned alarm clock, such things as inspiration, zeal, ardor, all run down." Kritzer consulted respectable voices in the game to reaffirm his lack of faith. "Robinson won't make the major leagues this coming season," Kritzer quoted Yankee manager and future Hall of Famer Bucky Harris.

The article was titled "The $64 Question Mark." Robinson integrating the game was the obvious issue, but the coverage of him revolved around merit, insisting Jackie Robinson was just another ballplayer. Only a few stories directly mentioned integration. McGowan addressed it on the periphery. Kritzer never mentioned it at all.

When Rickey signed Robinson in 1945, *The Durham Morning Herald* reporter Jack Horner predicted "the Negro player will be so uncomfortable, embarrassed, and out of place in O.B. that he will soon get out of his own accord." Feeling betrayed by Rickey, no entity was more hopeful for this outcome than the Lords. In the summer of 1946, a six-member steering committee led by Larry MacPhail issued a devastating private report to Happy Chandler, revealing the game's true fears: integration represented an existential threat to the future of baseball.

Under the section titled "Race Question," the committee concluded integration was fueled by political opportunists (i.e., communists) only seeking publicity. "Certain groups in this country, including political and social-minded drum-beaters, are conducting pressure campaigns in an attempt to force major league teams to sign Negro players," the report read. "Members of these groups are not primarily interested in Professional Baseball. . . . They single out Professional Baseball for attack because it offers a good publicity medium. These people who charge that baseball is flying a Jim Crow flag at its masthead—or that racial discrimination is the basic reason for failure of the major leagues to give employment to Negros—are simply talking through their collective or individual hats."

When the La Guardia Committee met with Larry MacPhail a year earlier, MacPhail told the two investigators that he did not fear integration because good Black players would result in greater ticket sales for the Yankees. The private report to Chandler told a different story: the owners were convinced more Black players would attract more Black fans, and sitting next to the Black fans would repel white ones, who would stop paying to watch the game. Robinson's excellence, the report concluded, threatened every team's financial health:

> The employment of a Negro on one AAA League Club in 1946 resulted in a tremendous increase in Negro attendance at all games in which the player appeared. The percentage of Negro attendance at some games at Newark and Baltimore was in excess of 50%. A situation might be presented, if Negroes participate in Major League games, in which the preponderance of Negro attendance in parks such as the Yankee Stadium, the Polo Grounds and Comiskey Park could conceivably threaten the value of the Major League Franchises owned by those Clubs.

The report destroyed the theory that money, as well as any appreciation of merit in the American tradition of fairness, would incentivize integration (the owners believed Robinson portended *less* money). The authors of the report were National League President Ford Frick, Cardinals owner Sam Breadon, Cubs owner Phillip K. Wrigley, American League President William Harridge, MacPhail, and Boston owner Tom Yawkey—all of whom were present three years earlier when Paul Robeson addressed the owners, and no one could blame Landis, who had been dead 18 months.

The report's conclusion was unmistakable: the teams must act in concert, but Branch Rickey had gone rogue and threatened the entire operation. The report did not hide its disdain for what they believed Rickey and the Dodgers had done to their sport. "The individual action of any one Club may exert tremendous pressure upon the whole structure of Professional Baseball," the document read, "and could conceivably result in lessening the value of several Major League franchises."

II

RICKEY SPENT SPRING TRAINING PREPARING for acts of insurrection. To his enemies, he had betrayed the white race. The newspapers derisively called him "the great emancipator," and it was standard for stories about Rickey to contain some reference to Abraham Lincoln—especially as a framed rendering of Lincoln hung above his desk at Ebbets Field. W.G. Bramham, the segregationist president of the minor leagues, said, "Father Divine will have to look to his laurels, for we can expect Rickey Temple to be in the course of construction in Harlem soon." Several news stories referred to him as "Massa Rickey."

Rickey was considered a shrewd judge of character, but when it came to integration, he was blinded by his own naivete. Rickey possessed many of the same racial prejudices of his contemporaries, but he believed in America's exceptionalism. Robinson's gifts, Rickey believed, would dilute the prejudices of white players, as would their self-interest when they received the playoff money Robinson would help them earn by winning. Rickey was so convinced of this outcome that he publicly announced he would seek player input regarding Robinson's promotion—an extraordinary step in those rigid years before free agency, when the team enjoyed complete control over players. The only plausible explanation for Rickey's actions was his certainty that his players would accept Robinson, perhaps even more enthusiastically than he had.

Rickey was so convinced of Robinson's ability that he secretly decided to make Robinson a Dodger. In the March 29 *Pittsburgh Courier*, Wendell Smith attributed a front-page blockbuster to an "unimpeachable" source: the Dodgers would purchase Robinson's Montreal contract on April 10, and he would be Brooklyn's Opening Day first baseman.

Smith's scoop contained two additional important pieces of information: Robinson himself had already been informed by Rickey he would be a Dodger as early as March 5, which meant Robinson knew from virtually the first day of camp that he had made the club. The vague newspaper stories regarding Robinson's status were merely Rickey's attempts at misdirection. The secret promotion also explained why Robinson had been playing first base from the very start of camp. While the white dailies insisted Robinson was only being judged by his play, it was Smith who confronted the element directly. "Robinson's sensational playing in spring training exhibitions has assured him of the job. The only obstacle in his way currently is the possibility of wholesale rebellion on the part of the present members of the Brooklyn club."

Members of the white mainstream press would claim in later years awareness of Rickey's intentions, but they honored his confidence by remaining quiet. Rickey's leak to the Black press may have been strategic, for certainly Smith's "unimpeachable source" was an authorized member of the Dodgers, if not Rickey himself. Had it not been, it is unlikely the highly suspicious and careful Rickey would have allowed such explosive speculation to go unaddressed. Most likely Rickey would have ordered Smith's reporting debunked by a press ally. It is also likely that the daily reporters covering the team did not routinely read the Black papers, even the well-known *Courier*. In any case, no newspaper followed up on Smith's exclusive, which was only the biggest, most important sports story in America.

The Dodgers trained in Havana because of Cuba's more tolerant racial climate, but whenever Rickey anticipated resistance, it was Jackie Robinson who was made to suffer. Rickey set the Dodgers up at the lavish Hotel Nacional. Robinson, Roy Campanella, and two other Negro Leaguers, the older lefthander Roy Partlow and Don Newcombe, a young Negro League righthander, arrived at the hotel. The quartet received a warm welcome by hotel staff before being summarily transferred to dilapidated segregated housing in a remote part of Havana. Robinson was furious at the Cubans but then discovered it was Rickey who ordered the relocation, fearing backlash from the hotel's white American guests.

A year earlier, during Robinson's first spring camp in Sanford, Florida, a mob formed over his presence, and he; his wife, Rachel; and their infant son, Jackie Jr., were forced to flee town. It was a harrowing, defining experience, and, contrary to the mythology that he was awoken from a deep sleep and sprang into action to protect his player, Rickey was not in town that night. He wasn't in the state or even the time zone. Rickey was in Fulton, Missouri, at Westminster College, where he was a trustee, as the school honored President Harry Truman and former British Prime Minister Winston Churchill with honorary degrees for helming the Allied victory. It was where Churchill's remarks, titled "Sinews of Peace," contained the foreboding sentence, "From Stettin in the Baltic, to Trieste in the Adriatic, an iron curtain has descended across the continent." Churchill's famous words, forever known after as the "Iron Curtain speech," served as the de facto start of the Cold War.

Just as owners would rather lose than improve their teams with Black players, Dodger outfielder Dixie Walker refused to play with Robinson. "As long as he's not with the Dodgers," Walker said two years earlier, "I'm not worried." His stance had not changed. As Rickey sensed the unwelcoming mood of his players, he opted against testing democracy after all, rescinding his decision to canvass player opinion on Robinson and leave his promotion solely in the hands of himself and the rough-hewn Dodger manager, Leo Durocher.

On the third day of camp, *The New York Sun* reporter Herbert Goren filed a dispatch from Havana:

DODGERS SPLIT ON HOW THEY FEEL ABOUT

JACKIE ROBINSON AS POTENTIAL TEAMMATE

HAVANA—Jackie Robinson, calling Branch Rickey a sincere man, said today he believes his chances of making the grade with the Dodgers this

> season depends largely on how well he performs in spring training with Montreal, specifically, in the 11 exhibition games with Brooklyn.
>
> But a canvass of the Dodgers heightens the task confronting Robinson. It is mainly antagonistic. Robinson will have to undo an undercurrent of resistance. Not all the Dodgers feel that way, but a great many do.

Anonymous Dodgers told Goren of their secret hope Arky Vaughan would make the team. Vaughan, a future Hall of Famer who was attempting a comeback at age 35, was a career shortstop who had never played a single inning at first base, but the players hoped Vaughn's presence would squeeze Robinson from the roster. "It was not so much that Vaughan can be more helpful than a Robinson at his best as the thought that Arky can keep Robinson from establishing a precedent, which, in one man's mind, is regarded with distaste."

Robinson hit .355 in nine games for Montreal against the Dodger regulars, more proof he could compete against major-league competition. When the Dodgers arrived in Panama for a stretch of games, Black Panamanians rushed to Olympia Stadium in Panama City in anticipation of seeing Robinson in person. A week before opening day, on April 9, 1947, team press secretary Arthur Mann personally delivered to reporters in the Ebbets Field press box a handwritten release, penned by Mann, punctuated by Rickey, confirming Wendell Smith's scoop of two weeks earlier. The Associated Press wire story appearing in hundreds of newspapers the following day described Mann's historic bulletin as *terse*. "The Brooklyn Dodgers today purchased the contract of Jackie Roosevelt Robinson from the Montreal Royals," the statement read. "He will report immediately."

The day Mann circulated the press release of Jackie Robinson's callup, Paul Robeson was celebrating his 49th birthday. The paths of the two men born 21 years apart were so similar, they literally trod the same ground. On November 24, 1917, fourteen months before Robinson was born, Rutgers football played the heavily favored Newport Naval Reserves (who were "invincible," according to *The New York Times*) at

Brooklyn's Ebbets Field, the ballpark Robinson was about to make famous. Rutgers won the game, 14–0, but it was the 19-year-old Robeson who would not be forgotten.

ROBESON A MARVEL

> Robeson, the colored lad, who held down the left wing of the New Brunswick line, was a marvel in his position. Nothing seemed to escape him. He was chiefly responsible for the big gains around the ends, and it was he who intercepted the forward passes that the Newport men tried to gain by. He furnished excellent interference or was through the line to nail the runner if his opponents had the ball. Robeson seemed to be everywhere at once.

On the same field, Jackie Robinson integrated Major League Baseball for the first time since the late 1800s. As Robinson stood with his teammates, the lone Black face in the Dodgers' lineup, he was reminiscent of Robeson two decades earlier at Rutgers: the dynamic Black talent surrounded by unwelcoming white classmates. In the press, mention of Robeson's race would always serve as a warning, alerting readers to integrated competition, and so, too, would the practice remain with Robinson. Robinson and Robeson would routinely be described as "dusky," "husky," and "colored." Robeson arrived at Rutgers as a sports and arts prodigy, but like the Dodgers treated Robinson, the white members of the Rutgers football and glee clubs organized a boycott to keep Robeson from playing. Just as opponents had employed dirty tactics against Jackie Robinson, Robeson's white teammates maimed him on the football field. In separate incidents, his own teammates broke Robeson's nose, separated his shoulder, and, in one practice, stepped on his right hand so severely the cleat ripped his right index fingernail off. None of Robeson's towering academic or athletic ability immediately translated to acceptance; two decades later, part of a continuum, Robinson entered the same crucible, his arrival framed through the lens of merit, when race, just as it had been with Robeson, stood at issue.

III

DAN DANIEL TOLD HIS READERS Robinson would never wear a Dodger uniform, and now Jackie Robinson was the Dodgers' starting first baseman. One of the first calls Rickey received was from Philadelphia general manager Herb Pennock. According to Roger Kahn's 1993 book, *The Era*, Pennock apparently told Rickey, "You just can't bring the nigger here with the rest of your team, Branch. We're not ready for that sort of thing in Philadelphia. We won't be able to take the field against your team if that boy is in uniform." Kahn was long an intimate of Robinson. He covered the Dodgers in 1952 and 1953 for the New York *Herald-Tribune* and personally knew all of the principals. Until his death in 2020, Kahn's primary sourcing gave him a fierce proprietorship of the Robinson story, and he could be vicious in his rebuke of a competing narrative. As he advanced in years, the foundation of Kahn's reportage was his memory, and memory, fickle at best, was the only surviving source for a private telephone conversation between Branch Rickey and Herb Pennock, a well-known opponent of integration who would be dead of a heart attack nine months after Robinson's debut.

What cannot be denied is the sentiment of the exchange. Rickey told Pennock the Phillies would forfeit if they did not play. A week after Robinson's debut, the Phillies arrived in Ebbets Field for a three-game series, memorable only for the racist verbal attacks on Robinson by the Phillies and their manager, Ben Chapman. Ford Frick responded, not by sanctioning Chapman or his players, but by forcing an enraged Robinson to endure the humiliation of staging a photo with Chapman.

When the two teams ultimately met in Philadelphia, the games were played, and the Phillies won three of four, but not before Pennock harassed the Dodgers. Their usual hotel, the Benjamin Franklin, refused the Dodgers if they included Robinson. After being turned away by several Center City hotels, the Dodgers wound up in Rittenhouse Square, at the one place that would accept a Black guest, the Warwick hotel, on 17th and Locust Streets.

Robinson showed signs of emotional fraying before the season had even begun. With two weeks remaining in spring training, he told *The New York Sun* he did not want to join the Dodgers if "resentment persisted." In a rare departure of America's insistence on merit, Herbert Goren wrote directly, "The only thing keeping Robinson off the Dodgers, plainly, is the attitude of the players." Dixie Walker immediately requested a trade. Four other Dodgers (Carl Furillo, Hugh Casey, Kirby Higbe, and Bobby Bragan) agreed to boycott the team. The St. Louis Cardinals initially voted not to play against the Dodgers. As in Philadelphia, the Chase Hotel in St. Louis refused Robinson accommodations. For decades, *The Sporting News* was one of the loudest and most influential voices against integration.

When white hostility escalated, Rickey insulted Black people. One night before the Dodgers left for Cuba, Rickey met with a few dozen Black professionals in Brooklyn and stunned the room by telling them the greatest obstacle to Robinson's success would not be death threats, opponents refusing to face him, or teammates boycotting playing with him, but, in his words, "the Negro people themselves!"

"You'll strut. You'll wear badges. You'll hold Jackie Robinson Days . . . and Jackie Robinson Nights. You'll get drunk. You'll fight. You'll be arrested. You'll wine and dine the player until he is fat and futile. You'll symbolize his importance into a national comedy—and an ultimate tragedy." Rickey ended his broadside by demanding that Black people not use Robinson's arrival as "a triumph of race over race." More succinctly, Branch Rickey believed instead of feeling happiness and hope that greater opportunities were possible in the wake of Robinson's arrival, Black people would see a single Black player, alone in a league of 400 players, 16 white managers, dozens of white coaches, medical and front office staff, and an overwhelmingly white fan base as an example of Black superiority.

Without leverage, the outraged group responded to Rickey's insults by pledging cooperation: the opportunity was too important to risk, but the price was an even deeper isolation of Jackie Robinson. Per Rickey's order, proud Black people could cheer—as the Panamanians exulted whenever Robinson came to bat during the spring—but not *too* much, lest the white public be offended. Supportive Black people must not be too effusive in Rickey's eyes, or else they, and not the Pennocks and Chapmans, the Furillos and Bragans of the world, would jeopardize his "noble experiment." Too much happiness from Black fans would only infuriate whites, and that would only intensify the resistance. *The Sporting News* followed Rickey's lead, advising Black fans to exercise "understanding" and "patience," which were "qualities his race has long utilized in its amalgamation into American life—especially in the South." Conditioned that Black people could not be trusted with equality, the Black press echoed Rickey's warnings with class condescension—the public behavior of the "lower members" of the race could ruin everything.

Just as the Lords believed white ticket buyers would refuse to sit next to Black fans, Rickey was convinced the exuberance of Black fans seeing Robinson's success would alienate whites from the sport, yet there is no record in the American, National, or joint league meetings' minutes of Branch Rickey directing his considerable oratory to appeal to whites of any social status to also meet the moment and adjust their own prejudices. There are no surviving materials of the great man challenging his fellow owners and executives who believed he betrayed them to exercise tolerance or adhere to the wartime commitment to freedom or fairness. No record exists of Rickey announcing to the press a new day of integration and imploring the league for support and leadership the way he had, by his own admission, cruelly admonished a group of Black professionals. Despite Bobby Bragan being one of the first players who threatened a boycott and undermine Rickey's entire plan, Rickey would one day reward him with his first coaching and managerial opportunities. Integration was not a mutual responsibility for Black and white America, but rather a burden for Jackie Robinson and his people to endure whatever was next to come as a price of admission. As deeply as Americans claimed fairness as an embedded credo, Robinson's inaugural journey embodied the very opposite of merit.

IV

THE DODGERS BEAT THE SECOND-PLACE Cardinals by five games in the pennant race before losing to the Yankees in a classic seven-game World Series. Despite being wounded during the season (by Ben Chapman, the hotel refusals, the unpredictable reactions), Robinson concluded gingerly that the imperfect systems had nevertheless worked. Rickey, Frick, and Chandler had not been intimidated into expelling him from the game, as the Black players of the 19th century had been. That gave Robinson hope: he would be alone for now, but others would follow.

Robinson was a celebrity, winning the NL's inaugural Rookie of the Year award, and receiving offers to join organizations, to speak, to lend his name to issues, causes, products. A quickie autobiography with Wendell Smith was already in the works. A week before the regular season ended, Robinson appeared on the cover of *Time*, America's most famous news magazine.

In the popular retelling, Robinson was content with America as a flawed country of good intentions whose racial shortcomings were borne of ignorance but not malice, and thus the violence it had inflicted on him during 1947 did not obscure the country's potential. Such accommodation offered the impression that Robinson possessed boundless patience. He did not. For Rickey and for America, hope was an enduring, endless commodity that would shape his first season and all of its subsequent retellings as a universal triumph, but for Robinson, hope was a perishable item to be consumed within a certain due date or lost. His restraint in the face of hostility resonated with the mythmakers, for America loved the Black people who did not fight back, whose suffering came without responding with force—the true language in which America was fluent. That defined the nation's moral conscience, but Robinson's first year began the slow disintegration of his faith in his country. What was not immediately clear at the time, as America transitioned from hot war to cold, was that Branch Rickey had a private, additional vision for Jackie Robinson that would complicate the plans he had for himself.

Chapter Five

"Criticism, like charity, should begin at home."

—*Mansfield (Ohio) News Journal*, January 25, 1941

I

APRIL 1947 BEGAN A PIVOTAL period in the lives of Jackie Robinson and Paul Robeson. On April 11 at Ebbets Field, Robinson jogged out to first base for the first time wearing the crisp, white flannels of the Brooklyn Dodgers in a 14–6 exhibition game thrashing of the Yankees before 24,237 witnesses to the end of segregated baseball. Earlier that morning, equipment man Dan Comerford, who joined the Dodgers in 1905, handed Robinson his new uniform, number 42—which coincidentally matched the number of years Comerford had been with the team. Robinson had been the Dodgers' best first baseman that spring, but in an insult to his ability that would resonate into the next century with Black professionals of all industries, Rickey was still being accused of selecting Robinson not for his .355 spring training average but to make an unearned social statement—Jackie Robinson, handout recipient. "Not charity, but a chance," one Black newspaper defensively countered. Like Paul Robeson on the train heading to Boston for his *Othello* debut five years earlier,

Robinson stood on a major-league diamond, standing at the end of something.

A week before, U.S. Attorney General Tom Clark began compiling a dossier that would soon be known by the menacing acronym AGLOSO: the Attorney General's List of Subversive Organizations, groups the government claimed were sympathetic to communism. On April 15, as Robinson made his historic regular-season debut against the Boston Braves, the House Committee on Un-American Activities reported subversion had infiltrated the nation's college campuses, singling out, among a handful of others, Paul Robeson as a "sponsor of communism."

Robinson indirectly became HUAC's next target. On April 21, 1947, six days after Robinson's big-league debut, Alvin Stokes, an opportunistic Black staffer at the Bergen County Sheriff's Office, convinced his congressman, the anticommunist New Jersey Republican J. Parnell Thomas, who was reshaping HUAC into a fearsome vehicle to expose communism, to allow him to covertly investigate Black organizations for communist infiltration. There was no better issue than communism for an ambitious Black outsider to ingratiate himself to Republican politics and prove his loyalty—and at the time, no bigger name to put in front of the committee, as friend or foe, than Jackie Robinson.

Stokes grew up in Westwood, New Jersey, about 35 miles from Westfield, where Paul Robeson spent much of his early adolescence. He was six years younger than Robeson and significantly less talented, but the two shared certain similarities in regard to being afforded opportunities that barely existed in America previously. In 1922, Stokes was the first Black graduate from Westwood High. He then enrolled in Columbia, overlapping briefly on campus with Robeson. In the 1930s, he became involved in New Jersey Republican politics, his break coming when J. Parnell Thomas was appointed HUAC chair for the 80th Congress. Stokes would lead many an investigation, and yet because he was Black his name did not appear on the masthead as a formal committee staffer.

• • •

Branch Rickey had already been annoyed that communist news outlets—Lester Rodney and Nat Low of the *Daily Worker*—were trumpeting Robinson's signing as an example that the years of letter-writing and public pressure contributed to Rickey's actions. During the 1943 owners meeting when Robeson addressed the Lords, Rickey, at the time new to Brooklyn, admitted as much to Landis that the Dodgers were constantly under pressure from local pro-integration advocacy groups—but there was no way Rickey would admit he had given in to public pressure, not from the press, the Black press, and especially not from the communist press.

The Dodgers were already sensitive to the idea that the CPUSA was taking credit for forcing integration, and were thus amenable to working with Stokes. Arthur Mann, Rickey's trusted assistant, referred to May 26, 1947, as the date the Dodgers agreed to cooperate with the committee. Robinson appearing in front of the committee provided enormous career value to Stokes and to Rickey, whose bold integration of the national pastime could not afford to be threatened by the taint of communism—especially when four years earlier, the now-embattled Robeson had addressed the sport.

II

THE COUNTRY WAS CHANGING. Earlier in the year, Truman signed Executive Order 9835, forcing all federal employees to sign oaths pledging their loyalty to the United States—or be fired. As anti-communism rose in volume, Paul Robeson was prominently in the headlines, eroding the public esteem he enjoyed just a few years earlier when he stood at the apex of his popularity.

While he electrified audiences, the government had been surveilling Robeson. J. Edgar Hoover long considered Robeson to be suspect for his involvement in the two issues Hoover found most threatening: liberal politics and civil rights. He also knew the extent to Robeson socialized with left-wing organizations because the FBI had been tailing him since 1941. The country loved Robeson for his rendition of "Ballad for Americans," but the GOP did not, replacing him with Bing Crosby at the 1940 Republican convention. MI5, the British intelligence counterpart to the FBI, had been tracking Robeson (file no. KV/2/1829) since 1930. Within the FBI's voluminous stacks of surveillance of American citizens, Robeson was file number 100–12304.

By the time of Robinson's callup to the majors, Robeson had already played the role Robinson now entered as a chrysalis: the famous Black man Americans cited as proof that segregation could coexist within a democracy. While his country now looked to Jackie Robinson as its new symbol of its benevolence toward Black people, Robeson believed America was embracing the darker, authoritarian impulses that can accompany power. During the war, *The Kingsport Times*, the local newspaper of Kingsport, Tennessee, printed a simple motto to the right of the American flag that appeared in the top right corner of the paper's front page: "War Vets, Wear it. Citizens, Respect it." Yet Tennessee was notorious for its violence against returning Black soldiers. Seventy-five years later, the rise of post-9/11 patriotism in American life would attempt to reinforce the image of Black soldiers as respected national heroes, but at the time, no Black man in America was in more danger from his fellow white citizens than one wearing a military uniform in public.

Three weeks into the new year, the American Theater in St. Louis reneged on an agreement with Robeson and issued segregated seating for his concert. Robeson joined the picket line in dissent. The next morning, he vowed to "talk up and down the nation to talk about race hatred and prejudice," announcing he would be quitting concert performing for the next two years to focus on civil rights. "It seems that I must raise my voice, but not by singing pretty songs," he said. "The next two years will be critical and important ones for our country. Some of us have to speak up and appeal to the people to respect the common rights of others." The next day, while returning to St. Louis after a recital at

Lincoln University, the wheel of Robeson's Buick dislodged from its axis, nearly killing him, his longtime accompanist Lawrence Brown, his driver, and the driver's son. Investigators concluded someone had tampered with the wheel. On January 31, Jackie Robinson's 28th birthday, the headline in the Black press *St. Louis Argus* led with a 60-point headline that read "ATTEMPT ON LIFE OF PAUL ROBESON AFTER CRUSADE."

In April, Robeson was scheduled to perform before an audience of 6,500 at the University of Illinois, but, for the first time in his 22-year career, he said he misremembered the date and failed to appear. Two days later, when he arrived at the Shrine Mosque in Peoria, Illinois, the city canceled his appearance. The tightening dragnet around him created by Hoover and HUAC finally encircled him.

It had been a long time in the making. More than a year earlier, in September 1946, Robeson led a seven-member delegation of Black leaders to the White House to meet with President Truman, one that included the legendary educator and Pan-Africanist Mary McLeod Bethune, with the hopes of securing a federal anti-lynching bill, legislation the notorious Democratic representative John Rankin of Mississippi said would give a free pass for Black men to rape white women. The meeting was inspired by an assault and false arrest months earlier in Batesburg, South Carolina, on Isaac Woodard, a Black Army veteran. In uniform, Woodard was beaten so severely he was left permanently blind. Newspapers reported Woodard's eyes had been gouged out. The NAACP launched a national investigation. The case spurred national outrage, forcing Truman to reluctantly use government resources to bring federal charges against Linwood L. Shull, the Batesburg police chief. Heavyweight boxing champion Joe Louis raised thousands of dollars for Woodard, and the famed director Orson Welles dedicated several of his national radio broadcasts to the beating. Robeson's organization, the National Negro Congress, launched a "100-day campaign" to end lynching. For all of the national attention, furor, and evidence against him—during the trial Shull admitted under oath he struck Woodard repeatedly across the eyes—an all-white jury acquitted Shull in less than 30 minutes.

The meeting with Truman went poorly. Truman told the group he was troubled by lynching, but the political timing was not good to take action. A month before the meeting, the NAACP was investigating another set of murders: two Black couples were ambushed by a white mob and shot to death on the banks of the Apalachee River near Monroe, Georgia. During the investigation, the NAACP uncovered another lynching in Gordon, Georgia, that newspapers referred to as "forgotten": a miner named John J. Gilbert was found shot to death 500 yards from his home. "It seems evident that he was waylaid, as Gordon citizens state, by some unknown party who planned the killing," according to one newspaper account. "Rumor has it, in whispers, that possibly and even probably," Gilbert was murdered by local whites upset by his "participation in a recent unionizing movement in the chalk mines."

At the White House, Robeson asked Truman how the United States could support justice for Holocaust victims during the ongoing Nuremburg trials while allowing atrocities to persist against Black Americans at home. In a response that would shape the State Department's attitude toward him for the rest of Robeson's life, Truman told Robeson it was unwise to compare domestic and international situations. Truman responded to Robeson's concerns about white vigilantism by rebuffing him with the claim that the United States and Great Britain represented the last refuge of freedom in the world, to which Robeson exploded, "The British Empire is one of the greatest enslavers of human beings" and added if the American government would not protect them, Black people "would have to protect themselves." Taking Robeson's words as a threat, Truman brusquely adjourned the meeting.

In a speech September 23, 1946, that was broadcast over the Mutual Broadcast System, an embittered Robeson began, "I stand here ashamed. Ashamed that here in the Capital of the world's first genuine democratic government, it is necessary to seek redress of a wrong that defies the most fundamental concept of that precious thing we call democracy . . . I speak of the wave of lynch terror and mob assault against Negro Americans. Since V-J Day, scores have been victims, most of whom were veterans, and even women and children . . . but I am not ashamed to stand here as a servant of my people, as a citizen of America, to defend and fight for the dignity and democratic rights of Negro Americans—to fight for their right to live." Five days later, Robeson held a rally at the National Mall, where he read what was termed in the press a "new Emancipation Proclamation" at the foot of the Lincoln Memorial.

Following the disastrous White House meeting and the subsequent rally, Robeson flew to California to appear before the Joint Fact-Finding Committee on Un-American Activities in Los Angeles. Now known as the Tenney Committee, the group—chaired by California State Assemblyman Jack Tenney and originally infamous for its role in removing Japanese American citizens to internment camps—was rebranding itself by targeting "subversives." Tenney asked Robeson several times if he were a member of the Communist Party. "I consider myself anti-fascist and independent," Robeson replied under oath. When Robeson urged collaboration between the United States and the USSR, a point he made with Truman—his life was at greater risk in America. "Millions of Negro people are no longer willing to be shot at," he told the committee. "They understand that anti-lynching legislation must be passed. I could go to Georgia and be dead tomorrow." The next day's Stockton *Record* headline read, "Communism Praised by Robeson at Probe."

Now, months later, Robeson's performance was cancelled in Peoria. The day before he was to take the stage, the Tenney Committee announced it concluded Robeson was a supporter of communist-front organizations. The Peoria city council immediately declared Robeson was "a speaker or artist who is an avowed or active propagandist for un-American ideology."

III

HOW HAD ROBESON GONE FROM the bass-baritone voice Americans embraced and loved to one of the prime targets of the government? The country's mood had shifted against the Soviet Union, and cooperating with government agencies against the Communist Party now seemed to be an acceptable action, but his had not.

He had never hidden his politics, which were decidedly anti-capitalist. Robeson believed socialism remedied wealth inequality. It was common to see him performing around the world for labor—for the Scottish miners, the dockworkers in Oakland—or umpiring a softball game at Camp Wo-Chi-Ca, the communist-affiliated summer camp for kids in Hackettstown, New Jersey, singing campfire songs at Camp Kinderlaand, in Tolland, Massachusetts, or siding with striking electrical workers in Buffalo. Government, he reasoned, had a responsibility to educate its citizens, to keep them out of poverty. He held to his "deep conviction that for all mankind a socialist society represents an advance to a higher stage of life—that it is a form of society which is economically, socially, culturally, and ethically superior to a system based upon production for private profit."

Capitalism had failed the nation through the Great Depression, Robeson felt, and a world in economic despair signaled devastation for Black people. "To be a poor man is hard," Du Bois wrote in 1897, "but to be a poor race in a land of dollars is the very bottom of hardships." Capitalism also required a permanent underclass. "Under the caste system in Princeton," he wrote, "the Negro, restricted to menial jobs at low pay and lacking any semblance of political rights or bargaining power, could not hope for justice but for charity."

In *Spain in Our Hearts*, his landmark book on the Spanish Civil War, historian Adam Hochschild would reflect on this period between the world wars almost quaintly, when Americans were amenable to the different economic choices of socialism and communism: "Vanished also is the widespread conviction that the capitalist system was in crisis and could endure no longer and that a blueprint for the future existed, even if there were quarrels over whose blueprint was right." Yet the issue was not that future generations of Americans would conclude capitalism was no longer worthy of critique as much as they had succumbed to the devastating and unrelenting punishments—legal, extralegal, societal, and violent—America would inflict on its citizens who dared ask the question.

In the early part of the 20th century, the socialist platform was a nascent, but increasingly attractive, alternative to capitalism. In the 1912 presidential election, Eugene Debs won 6 percent of the popular vote, more than 900,000 votes overall. The great labor leader A. Philip Randolph joined the Socialist Party in 1917 and, with his business partner Chandler Owen, founded the radical newspaper *The Messenger*. President Woodrow Wilson would call Randolph the "most dangerous Negro in America." The first issue of *The Messenger* appeared in November 1917. In his inaugural editorial, Randolph explained the necessity of dissidence and addressed the American contradiction of democracy beginning at home. "Negroes are lynched—one every four days . . . Negroes are disenfranchised . . . Twelve million Negroes are discriminated against in places of public accommodation—Jim Crowed on railroads and street cars—set apart in the government service as if they were lepers . . . How can I hear what you say when what you are is continually thundering in my ears?"

The magazine would routinely be confiscated as subversive by the U.S. mail service, and the publication's promotion of Black political advocacy and consideration of socialism in the face of deepening economic inequality saw the government accuse Randolph more than once of sedition. In one early issue, the magazine made a direct appeal to Black people to relinquish capitalism with an article titled "Some Reasons Why Negroes Should Vote the Socialist Ticket" and proceeded with a 25-point list. ("7. Because Negroes are the first and hardest hit victims of the high cost of living on account of the starvation wages they receive.")

Robeson's domestic hopes rested on the Roosevelt New Deal policies and the expectation that the destruction brought on by the Great Depression would leave Americans more receptive to alternative economic systems, but the public attributed Robeson's successes to the very systems he opposed. Free markets made it possible for the son of an ex-enslaved man to become a world figure. Robeson did not completely disagree, but where the public deemed the American model a success because of the individual who made good, Robeson focused on the collateral damage the system caused: capitalism was also responsible for the poverty that was an inevitable consequence of a few, far above the rest, and worse, for corporations to dominate everyday workers. Robeson resented being seen as illustrative of segregation being merely unfortunate, but not debilitating. "It means little when a man like me wins some success. Where is the benefit when a small class of Negroes makes money and can live well? It may be encouraging, but it has no deeper significance," Robeson said in 1941. "I feel this way, you will understand, because I have cousins who can neither read nor write. I have had a chance. They have not. That is the difference, and I believe that no political philosophy that does not include a chance for all of them can possibly endure."

He did not believe what he symbolized to some elements of white society to be particularly honorable: whites did not celebrate Black success stories, but rather, they weaponized one individual's success to indict millions of Black people who struggled—he saw his fame constantly leveraged in opposition to his own people. White Americans' appreciation of hard work only applied in relation to one another. They had not, Robeson argued, ever intended to compete against Black people—in the classroom, for jobs, for housing, for social status, on-screen, or on the ballfield. He recalled white animosity to be at its highest whenever Black people succeeded in fields deigned to belong to whites, remembering the white high school administrators angered by his success, even as he brought prominence to the school, an animosity intensified by his confidence, size, and self-assuredness. His excellence was not treated as earned against whites but allowed by them, a tribute to his talent, certainly, but also—should he forget his place—their benevolence.

Robeson did not see socialism as the great scourge the country was being told it was, even as the national tone grew more harshly against world communism. While both mainstream whites and the Black press were convinced the Communist Party's interest in race relations was opportunistic—an effective tool attacking an American vulnerability—a vast majority of the CPUSA members were political liberals and progressives whose politics extended beyond party affiliation. The Party did what neither Democrats nor Republicans would: commit to eradicate racism and improve the Black standard of living. When Robeson began honing his liberal political voice while living in 1930s London, he did so not as a rogue, but as part of the preexisting tradition of Black intellectuals amplifying the Soviet commitment to American racial equality. He was part of the small, but committed, wave of Black Americans who would either relocate to Russia or promote anti-capitalism as the preferable route toward freedom for Black people. Robeson's art had been predated by Ira Aldridge, his politics by the writer Claude McKay, who was one of the first Black intellectuals to explore the Soviet experiment. W.E.B. Du Bois visited the USSR extensively in 1926. Writers Dorothy West and Langston Hughes spent time in Russia during 1932 and 1933. Three of Robeson's in-laws—his mother-in-law and two brothers-in-law—would live in Russia, and he and Eslanda sent their son, Paul Jr., to school in Russia until the outbreak of the war in Europe.

"Robeson has been criticized for favoring the Soviet Union—before the war and before Russia became one of our most valuable allies," an Oregon newspaper wrote in a 1943 editorial. "However, Robeson's actions did not necessarily indicate acceptance of Russia's economic system, rather they told more plainly than words that a black-skinned man had found a home."

Between dispatches from writers such as Hughes, West, and Du Bois, the Soviet Union, in the years before the war, grew in attractiveness as a destination. The story of the thousand or so Black American migrants who expatriated to the USSR would be decoupled by American historians, Black and white, from the larger story of the Great Migration, but their main reason to leave America was largely similar: escaping from the American South. "The blacks who chose to go to the Soviet Union followed the same impulses that inspired the Pilgrims, as well as the generations of immigrants who followed in their wake, to cross the Atlantic for a new life," the writer Joy Gleason Carew wrote of the expatriating Black citizens as a common historical phenomenon. "It was simply a search for a country without discrimination or racial prejudice."

The appeal of the Soviet Union to Black Americans could be best seen not through the convoluted rubric of U.S.-Soviet foreign relations, but rather through the political disenfranchisement, daily hardships, and violence of Black life in the United States. Any alternative that provided relief from lynchings, poll-taxes, segregation, and broken promises was worth listening to—American propaganda was as dangerous as Soviet. The Communist Party viewed Black Americans as an oppressed working class in their own country. "It is a sad indictment of American politics that the only political platform that seemed to recognize the reality of my life belonged to the Communist Party," James Yates wrote in his 1987 memoir, *Mississippi to Madrid*. Yates, a Black Mississippian, served as one of the roughly one hundred Black Americans who volunteered to fight with the communists during the Spanish Civil War from 1936 to 1939.

In October 1939, Robeson sailed on the SS *Washington* back to New York, holding out fleeting hope that America would respond to the global threats of Nazism and fascism after choosing to allow the Spanish government to fall at the hands of Franco, Mussolini, and Hitler. The Spanish Civil War was a complicated triangle of interests, but in its time, thousands of idealistic Americans enthusiastically volunteered to fight, many joining the International Brigades—one such brigade, the XV, was nicknamed the Abraham Lincoln Brigade. Robeson, the anti-fascist, would join the Spanish loyalist cause, which would immediately place him, and almost any other citizen who openly defied the State Department's mandate to not cross into Spain and join the conflict, in the government's crosshairs.

That Americans would voluntarily defy their government to fight the very forces that would comprise the European Axis powers only a few years later further illustrated the idealism and commitment of the period—and underscored the lengths to which Western governments actively preferred a fascist takeover to an elected left-wing government. Following Italian dictator Benito Mussolini's 1935 invasion of Ethiopia,

20,000 New Yorkers marched in Harlem in protest. Communist groups marched from 120th Street between 2nd and 3rd Avenues to Bradhurst and Edgecombe Avenues in solidarity with Black Americans. The rally caught the attention of Mussolini, who was quoted in an Italian newspaper editorial: "Harlem Negroes have enough concern with their brethren Christianity being lynched daily in the United States without worrying about the blacks in Ethiopia."

While Black leadership distrusted the communist interest in Black people, the CPUSA made a serious impression on James Yates. In defiance of the U.S. government, Yates scaled the jagged Pyrenees into Spain and fought on the side of the communists against Franco. Robeson's outspokenness made him a hero to the Spanish and to the American volunteers who risked their lives for their values, especially the largely forgotten Black volunteers like Yates. In 1937, Robeson had announced he had established a veteran's fund for the Black soldiers upon their return. When word reached the frontlines that Robeson had defied the U.S. government and entered Spain, many of the Black soldiers did not believe it—Robeson had loomed so large in the Black imagination. It had to be a myth that the Great Robeson was standing with them in-country. The rumor ultimately became fact: Robeson was indeed singing for the troops in Spain. A superior showed one of his Black soldiers a photo of Robeson surrounded by Spanish Loyalist fighters. "A warmth stirred within me when I saw that picture," recalled James Yates, who served in the German International Brigade. "I tried to explain in Spanish to the lieutenant how I thought there was no other man or woman who represented freedom for mankind more than did Paul Robeson, and about his endless struggle for the rights of Black people. Occasionally, I would say '*Comprende?*' and he would reply, '*Si, Si.*'"

Yates served in Spain with Milton Braxton, whose younger brother Angelo Herndon in 1932 was sentenced 18 to 20 years in prison for union organizing white and Black laborers in Georgia and possessing "communist literature." Herndon served three years before his conviction was overturned. Herndon was represented by Benjamin J. Davis Jr., an Atlanta-born Black Amherst- and Harvard Law–educated attorney whose experience with the Communist Party platform and principles on the case resonated so deeply he would join the Party in 1935. The literature had a similar effect on James Yates. "Their platform stated, 'The Negro people suffer doubly. Most exploited of the working people, they are also victims of Jim Crowism and lynchings. They are denied the right to live as human beings." In addition, the platform endorsed the "abolition of poll taxes and other limitations on the right to vote . . .' To a man like me those words were heady stuff. Those who have difficulty understanding this have never walked in my shoes."

IV

ROBESON'S FAME DID NOT PROTECT him from the indignities reminiscent of Hollywood.. The British began its surveillance of him when the Savoy Hotel in London denied him entry, an insult MI5 decided turned Robeson "antiwhite, and slightly anti-British." His ventures into Hollywood were not based in the vanities of being a movie star as the end to the means, but to bring dignity to the Black experience. Just as with his singing concerts, where he strove to legitimize the Negro spiritual as an enduring and important world music, Robeson wanted his film roles to elevate Black actors.

Instead, Robeson found Hollywood degrading. The roles reinforced servitude the kind of greed and moral depravity that was used a justification to institute Jim Crow segregation, as in the case of one of his most famous roles, the 1933 film version of *The Emperor Jones*. He was most appalled by the movie he had once most anticipated: the 1935 film *Sanders of the River*, which Robeson believed was going to be a groundbreaking film. Filmed in various regions of east Africa, distributed by United Artists, the British production of an Edgar Wallace story featured Robeson as Bosambo, a native chief Robeson believed would give dignity to the African cultures and traditions, but for Robeson, the film ended up an abomination, depicting Bosambo as a supporter of European colonialism. Robeson would later say the filmmakers recut scenes after filming that reinterpreted his Bosambo character as a savage, preferring to be controlled by Sanders, the British regional commissioner. Robeson actively denounced the film and distanced himself from it upon its release. Even the Robeson-friendly *Sunday Worker* criticized Robeson as playing a leading role in a "slanderous attack on African natives who were pictured as being well-satisfied with the 'benevolent' oppression of English imperialism," and in an interview with Robeson told him, "You became the tool of British imperialism and must be attacked and exposed whenever you act in such pictures or plays." The deepest insult that Robeson had been misled by the production came from a Canadian newspaper, which described the film as a story of "a few white men who rule over the millions of natives in Central Africa by their wisdom and daring."

It was *Sanders of the River* that cemented Robeson's belief that the film industry was not only comfortable in its stereotypical depictions of Black characters but preferred them. Soon after, Robeson announced he would no longer act in Hollywood films. "What I won't do anymore is work for the big companies, which are headed by individuals who would make me a slave, like my father, if they could."

Robeson would then lean even more deeply into his political voice. He would only associate himself with projects that were political in nature, with progressive themes that forecast the disparate authoritarian crackdowns that were coalescing into the creation of an antidemocracy in America. One such project was *Native Land*, a 1942 film directed by Leo Hurwitz and Paul Strand, where Robeson narrates a series of vignettes focused on threats to civil liberties, the violent anti-labor tactics of strikebreakers, and the elements of right-wing extremism in the 1930s established during the first Red Scare, which served as a warning for authoritarianism in the coming years.

V

THREE WEEKS BEFORE CHRISTMAS, after Jackie Robinson had made the cover of *Time* magazine, the Justice Department made the

AGLOSO list public. The December 5 edition of *The New York Times* reported the names of 51 organizations the government had deemed subversive. Fifteen percent were directly committed to supporting Black civil rights domestically and African independence internationally. The Veterans of the Abraham Lincoln Brigade was also listed.

Clark listed the Council on African Affairs—chairman, Paul Robeson. Another organization Clark believed to be a threat to national security was the National Negro Congress, the same organization Robeson brought to the White House in 1946.

Hoover had long seen enough. A year earlier, in a confidential memo dated November 25, 1946, he asked the FBI's New York office to begin building a case against Robeson that could result in a successful prosecution. "The Bureau desires that your office prepare a report in summary form in this case setting forth by witnesses only such information of a legally admissible character and will tend to prove, directly or circumstantially, membership in or affiliation with the Communist Party, and knowledge of the revolutionary aims and purposes of that organization," the memo read. The same day, Truman ordered his Justice Department to investigate the backgrounds of federal workers to guarantee their allegiances—including those who had already signed loyalty oaths.

On New Year's Eve, Alvin Stokes of HUAC called Branch Rickey to discuss Jackie Robinson, his politics, and the possibilities of Robinson standing up publicly against communism. Arthur Mann and Stokes agreed to meet January 2, 1948. Robeson held the conviction the nation was descending into authoritarianism, uncommitted to protecting Black citizens and reviving the anticommunist hysteria of the first World War period. Simultaneously, J. Edgar Hoover and the FBI had reached a conviction of its own: to arrest Paul Robeson.

Chapter Six

I

THE UNITED STATES HAD NOT held a formal inauguration since January 20, 1941, eleven months before Pearl Harbor. With The Netherlands, Belgium, and France under Nazi occupation, Mussolini predicting Great Britain would fall within 70 days, and America still uncommitted to joining the war, Franklin Roosevelt stood on the East Portico of the Capitol and accepted the presidency for a ninth year. With Vice President Henry Wallace by his side, FDR stirred the 75,000 freezing spectators with the defiant declaration that "democracy is not dying." Four years later, in 1945, after a terminally ill FDR defeated Thomas Dewey but peace not yet attained, FDR's fourth-term inauguration was a modest one, held at the White House, not at the Capitol, for only the second time in the nation's history.

Now in 1949, the war was three and a half years won, and FDR had been dead nearly four years. The United States held a tenuous monopoly on the atomic bomb. Ready to fulfill Henry Luce's expectation of an "American Century," Washington returned to its grand tradition and reopened the city to inaugurate Harry Truman.

The 1949 inauguration would be the biggest presidential spectacle the nation had ever witnessed. Newspapers described the atmosphere as "circus-like." The taxpayer price tag was a record $650,000 (the equivalent of nearly $8.5 million today). Public officials estimated the crowd to be a record 1.3 million spectators. The presidential parade ran seven miles long, including a stretch of Constitution Avenue that included the Capitol standing majestically in the background. Seated in a black convertible beside his top-hatted Vice President Alben W. Barkley, Truman waved to the throngs of well-wishers that lined both sides of the street. A line of floats carrying the governors of the fifty states traveled the parade route. A phalanx of Naval Academy Midshipmen marched in honor of the President. Soldiers represented the three established military branches and the brand-new one, the Air Force, just sixteen months old. Black and white soldiers marched together for the first time in an inauguration, a byproduct of Executive Order 9981, Truman's pen stroke a year earlier, at long last, desegregating the military.

January 20, 1949, was no ordinary inauguration. It was the announcement of a superpower—the kind of ostentatious public military display Americans of later generations would associate unfavorably with totalitarian regimes. The show of muscle was Truman's response to communism. First, the loyalty oath, then the investigating of citizens, and now the military parade. Forty thousand troops marched beneath an air armada of 650 warplanes. Cutting above the Capitol was a fleet of Northrop P-61 Black Widows, the first American fighter planes designed for night combat. Accompanying the Black Widows were several newly modified Corvair B-36 bombers. A year earlier, the B-36 had been reconfigured to travel from North America to Europe for a single purpose: the ability to drop America's heaviest nuclear weapons directly onto Soviet soil without needing to refuel. The B-36 was nicknamed "The Peacemaker."

Truman's inauguration confirmed Robeson's suspicions that winning the war would turn the United States even more aggressively against the Soviets—and America had the bomb. Truman used the remainder of FDR's term to establish communism as an enemy and his election as a mandate. Less than thirty minutes into his new term, Truman told his nation the USSR could exist only as a mortal enemy.

Truman's speech lasted twenty-one minutes. It was interrupted by applause twelve times.

The speech only increased the temperature, reigniting talk of a preemptive American attack against Russia. America was the only country in the world that possessed nuclear weapons, and Russia, mourning tens of millions of dead, was never more vulnerable.

American newspapers hailed Truman as marvelously uncompromising. Henry Wallace saw Truman as misleading, comparing communism to democracy instead of America's economic system, capitalism. To Wallace, Truman was coarse and unstatesmanlike, and his combative rhetoric was far from defensive. "No statement by an American leader has ever so clearly spelled bankruptcy for our nation," he said afterward. "[Truman's statement that] Capitalism and communism cannot live together in one world makes war the only alternative . . . we cannot fight ideas with guns."

The Times of London was one of the few mainstream outlets to consider Truman as the aggressor. With a prescience that would soon be sharply felt by the coming American generation, *The Times* wrote, "A sequel may well be to extend the conflict between Russia and the United States to other parts of the globe; during the next decade the Cold War may be fought in the Middle East and Southeast Asia as much as in Europe."

The 1949 inauguration was the first to be televised nationally. More Americans would hear Truman's speech than all of the previous presidential inaugural addresses combined. The Voice of America radio broadcast sent Truman's words overseas. At home, ten million television viewers watched. Truman had set the American attitude heading into the 1950s. With the president explicitly announcing the Cold War, the journalist I.F. Stone said Truman's inaugural speech left him "sick at heart." It was, in Stone's words, "shallow, naive, childishly arrogant, and self-righteous, a call for war thinly masked as a pledge of peace."

II

IN THE NEARLY TWO AND a half years since his White House clash with Truman, Paul Robeson's movements, associations, and public statements were ceaselessly monitored by the FBI. The walls were closing in on progressive, left-wing politics. The country pursued Cold War victory by threatening political beliefs at home.

Roughly a decade earlier, a 1938 Gallup poll posed a question to America: "Do you believe in freedom of speech?" Ninety-six percent of respondents answered yes. The pollsters offered two follow-up questions: 1) "Do you believe radicals and communists should be able to hold meetings and express their views?" and 2) "Do you believe communists should be able to hold meetings and express their views?" Only 40 percent of Americans affirmed the former, 36 percent the latter. When U.S. Attorney General Tom Clark announced the AGLOSO list in December 1947, he released an accompanying statement, saying, "'Guilt by association' has never been one of the principles of our American jurisprudence." Yet, guilt by association would precisely be the nation's guiding principle. Two-thirds of Americans approved of nationwide "loyalty boards," which surveilled government workers in search of any past or present communist affiliation.

Fear was the nation's greatest weapon. While many of his contemporaries scrambled to survive by renouncing their radical pasts as naive indiscretions, naming names of friends, colleagues, and even family, Robeson kept his word to leave the stage and screen to raise his voice in political support of Black people. In response, the government squeezed him more tightly. In one California newspaper, a reader reprinted part of the state's American Legion response to her inquiry on Robeson, claiming HUAC told her Robeson belonged to 62 communist-front organizations, "a number of which [had] been declared subversive by the attorney general of the United States." Another FBI report on Robeson suggested the number was greater than 70. By refusing to adjust to the mood of the country, Robeson had been transformed from celebrity to adversary.

• • •

During Wallace's 1948 presidential campaign, Robeson crisscrossed the country for Henry Wallace and, in doing so, highlighted a central political dilemma for Black voters. To Robeson's mind, there was no question the Progressive Party best served African Americans. He was appalled by Truman, and the Republican party, once the Party of Lincoln, operated with various ranges of hostility toward civil rights and the New Deal. Black people gravitated toward the Democrats because of FDR, but its Southern bloc was so committed to segregation, it chose to challenge its own incumbent president and ran South Carolina Governor Strom Thurmond against Truman. That left Truman for Black voters, a man whose grandparents were Missouri slaveholders and was raised to sympathize with the Confederate cause. As a young man, Truman was a segregationist, once writing to his wife, "I think one man is just as good as another so long as he's honest and decent and not a nigger or a Chinaman . . . I am strongly of the opinion that negros [*sic*] ought to be in Africa, yellow men in Asia and white men in Europe and America." Truman saw race as bad politics and was more hesitant on civil rights than FDR, succumbing only to pressure and the reality that his political survival—and that of the Democratic Party—increasingly relied on the Black vote.

After the White House summit in 1946, Robeson distrusted Truman. In his whistle-stop train campaign during the 1948 election, Truman did not use the term "civil rights" when addressing white audiences, while Henry Wallace unashamedly incorporated civil rights as a core principle of his breakaway Progressives. Wallace pledged to eliminate segregation socially and in education. He spoke openly of universal health care and racial equality as a national necessity, not a dream. Black voters responded favorably to Wallace's third-party upstart charge early in the campaign. To Robeson and Du Bois, and, to a lesser extent, men like A. Philip Randolph (who, unlike Robeson, began disavowing his former enthusiastic support of socialism as the country shifted), the needs of Black Americans so often differed from mainstream thought that, as a constituency, Black people could not be satisfied by either party.

In return for his commitment to racial justice, the national media ridiculed Henry Wallace. Nearly five years earlier, convinced his politics were too radical and dreading the prospect of FDR dying in office and Wallace replacing him, Democrats removed Wallace from the 1944 ticket in favor of Truman. Wallace was seen by the Washington press as an out-of-touch dreamer incapable, and unwilling, to engage in the tough, bare-knuckle sparring required to stand up to the Soviets and win at global politics. His desire for cooperation with world governments would spawn a pejorative that would terrify American politicians (especially Democrats) for the next 40 years: *soft on communism*. The hardline Democratic machine believed Wallace was a communist or, at the very least, a fellow traveler.

Mainstream columnists attacked Wallace by demonizing his base, conjuring fears that a Wallace presidency would leave average white Americans behind; Wallace was more concerned about "the Negro and the Jew" than with "hard-working Americans." At the Progressive Party convention in Philadelphia, writers depicted the large swaths of Black Wallace supporters as "jolly, drawling Negroes having a grand old time," the image of the unserious, uneducated Black voter, at the expense of white industry conjuring the racist images of Reconstruction that spawned the revival of the Ku Klux Klan.

Politically, Truman was not incorrect—the public did not support civil rights legislation. A Gallup poll on civil rights published the week of the convention reported 54 percent of Americans outside of the South rejected segregated seating on buses and trains when crossing state lines compared to 84 percent of Southerners who supported the practice. Robeson protested in support of fair employment, but only a third of Americans supported federal employers hire "without regard to race, religion, color or nationality." The Black press had been urging federal anti-lynching statutes for decades, but less than half of Americans believed the federal government should intervene in the event of a lynching.

Wallace campaigned on a racial justice platform, but Black leadership was unmoved, instead joining the mainstream voices convinced Wallace represented the communist agenda. The NAACP and the Urban League opposed Wallace, even if his campaign and his white supporters vocally supported integration.

Randolph, in retreat, chose pragmatism, using the threat of Wallace to force Truman to act. Randolph even publicly advocated Black recruits refuse induction into a segregated military and never threw his full support behind Wallace. On July 26, the day following Wallace's acceptance of the Progressive nomination, Truman relented to Randolph's backroom pressures. Defying the national poll numbers, Truman signed Executive Order 9980, which ordered fair employment practices throughout the federal government, repudiating three decades of Woodrow Wilson's segregation. On the same day, Truman also signed Executive Order 9981, which desegregated the military. It was a truly historic moment, even though Truman did not exactly throw his heart into the issue. Robeson was one of the voices urging Black voters not to fall for Truman, warning he would accept Black votes while ignoring Black voters.

Truman finished the Wallace campaign and backed up his historic pen stroke on October 29, the final week before Election Day, by appearing in Harlem, his one and only campaign stop in a Black community. As Robeson and left-leaning advocates saw Truman's gestures as political expedience, Democrats would receive lasting dispensation from a grateful Black electorate, even as the Democratic Party's entire Southern bloc remained committed to segregation.

III

THE BLACK VOTE WON TRUMAN the election. Defeat that had once appeared a certainty made victory even sweeter, but he'd won through superior politics. By desegregating the military and guaranteeing fair opportunity, at least on paper, Truman neutralized Wallace's advantage with Black voters and isolated the Robeson-backed Wallace threat as leftists that real Americans could not trust. This resonated with Black Americans hungry to be seen by whites as loyal Americans. The legacy of the 1948 presidential election was the faith Black voters would place in the Democratic Party while often reaping the barest of minimums for their crucial support. Black leadership had rejected Wallace and the scores of white Americans who were willing to provide their support to racial justice with their vote and believed Democrats would reward that loyalty. Randolph's backroom realpolitik defeated Wallace as much as Truman.

The election was a disaster for Wallace and Robeson. Wallace did not carry a single state, while Strom Thurmond's segregationist States Rights Party won South Carolina, Alabama, Mississippi, and Louisiana. In addition to his executive orders, Truman became the first American president to campaign in a Black district. According to Truman biographer David McCullough, in all the months of campaigning, the cheering in Harlem for Truman was loudest of all.

One moment proved prophetic for Robeson. At a Wallace campaign stop on May 20, 1948, Robeson addressed the International Fur and Leather Workers Union convention. Before singing the Langston Hughes poem "Freedom Train," Robeson told the crowd the nation was succumbing to a "kind of hysteria," and he was personally affected by its implications. "I talked to my manager some weeks ago," he told the audience. "And he said, 'Paul, in your going around defending labor, fighting for Wallace, you have no more concert career.' I said, 'Tell me, I am interested: How did you figure that out?' He answered, 'Nobody will book you.'"

Chapter Seven

I

HOSTILITY DEFINED THE AMERICAN REACTION to the World Congress of Partisans of Peace, colloquially known as the Paris Peace Conference. From its opening on April 20, 1949, through its explosive aftermath, the conference was dismissed by the West as the usual communist propaganda, leftists taking their cues from Moscow. A week after its conclusion, in newspapers nationwide, an editorial cartoon circulated depicting a deceitfully contented Joseph Stalin, a toy halo floating over his head, its stem held behind his back by bloodied hands. He stands as a colossus, dwarfing the 1,000-foot-tall Eiffel Tower, his unclasped tuxedo front resembling a soiled bib containing the words, "Paris 'Peace' Conference." He is gluttonous, a world-eater.

At the waist of his stained topcoat are the letters "USSR," and behind the cover of his sinister girth (what the rest of the free world cannot see) is devastation, the wreckage of communism: plumes of smoke, wreckage despairingly titled "Strife." "Famine." "War." "Revolution." The ground underneath his feet is labeled "Asia." Walking away from the Eiffel Tower and Stalin (thus rejecting the conference and the naivete of cooperation with the Soviets) is a nebbish-looking American with pop eyes, a rumpled porkpie hat, and a cigar protruding from his mouth as he cynically mutters, "Who does he think he's fooling?"

The creator was Vaughn Shoemaker, the two-time Pulitzer Prize–winning editorial cartoonist for the *Chicago Daily News* whose syndicated work appeared in hundreds of newspapers across the country. His cigar-chomping creation, John Q. Public, was Shoemaker's enduring contribution to the American popular culture and, in so many of Shoemaker's illustrations, represented the common man.

Shoemaker captured the American sentiment toward the Soviet Union, each element more indicting than the last: Stalin with hands dripping blood, facing the West with an untrustworthy smile, the false halo betraying his true intentions. His sheer size, dwarfing that of the Eiffel Tower, symbolized the looming threat of the USSR over the European continent and Stalin's appetite for more. His enormity obstructing the view of what exists behind him stood as a metaphor for Churchill's Iron Curtain—the hell the Soviet Union is raining on the continent while misguided liberals like Paul Robeson (MI5 referred to him in its files as "rather gullible") still saw him as "Uncle Joe," World War II ally. The smoke hovering over Asia is Shoemaker's metaphorical stand-in for the turmoil in China and Korea, and perhaps the most damning element of the cartoon is the skeptical quotation marks surrounding the word *peace*. Americans, solidified in their convictions, as John Q. Public states, know Stalin is pulling a fast one on an unsuspecting world; he has no interest in peace. Rumors that Stalin is conducting a violent purge of Russian Jews and perceived political enemies across the USSR coupled with Robeson's silence only furthered the belief he was willfully naive about the Soviets.

On January 17, Hoover sent a concerned letter to the FBI's New York office questioning why Robeson was not more tightly surveilled. "While it is realized that existing instructions do not require that a report be submitted periodically on Security Index Card unless the subject is also a top functionary," he wrote, "it is felt that in view of the tense national situation at the present time, a new report should be submitted setting forth the extent of the subject's present activities with the Communist

Party and related groups." In an obvious admonishment, Hoover added that if he was not a security threat, Robeson's security file should be discontinued. Three weeks later, on February 8, the newly motivated New York office reported to Hoover that Robeson planned to sail the *Queen Mary* to Southampton, England, to address the Spanish Civil War veterans from the British International Brigade before traveling across Europe. The next day, February 9, New York sent Hoover an "urgent" communique, detailing Robeson's upcoming schedule and his intention to travel to Europe for most of March and April.

The FBI reported Robeson would address the Joint Anti-Fascist Refugee Committee, one of the many organizations that fought Franco and the State Department designated as "subversive." Hoover did not track Torkild Rieber, the head of Texaco and a Nazi sympathizer who, in violation of federal law, provided oil to Hitler and Franco during the Spanish Civil War when America was supposed to be neutral. But Hoover did spend considerable time watching Robeson and his relationship with Dr. Edward Barsky, the American who had traveled to Spain to assist the Loyalists during the Spanish war as a surgeon, not as a soldier. Barsky had gained widespread admiration for leaving his comfortable post at Beth Israel Hospital in Manhattan, along with 17 medical volunteers in 1937, for the front lines at Jarama. While the FBI surveilled Robeson and Barsky, the latter had been free, pending the appeal of his 1947 contempt conviction for refusing to turn over Joint Anti-Fascist documents to the House Un-American Activities Committee. Barsky would lose his appeal and be sent to prison for five months. The celebrated writer Ernest Hemingway, who covered the war, raised money for Barsky's family and legal defense. Hemingway wrote to a confidant, "Eddie's a saint. That's where we put our saints in this country—in jail."

In April, Robeson arrived in Paris as a headliner. The famous mystery writer Dashiell Hammett attended, as did W.E.B. Du Bois, the venerable intellectual dean of Black America. Pablo Picasso met Robeson at Paris-Le Bourget airport. Picasso rendered *The Dove*, the official emblem for the conference, and it was his 1937 masterpiece *Guernica* that memorialized the horrors of the Franco coup. Du Bois described

Robeson as "magnificent in height and breadth, weary from circling Europe with song." He would also call the event "the greatest rally for peace this world has ever witnessed." A photo shows Du Bois and Robeson in a hearty greeting, Robeson wearing a three-piece, single-breasted suit. Robeson's presence was one of the dazzling highlights of the event, electrifying thanks to his outsized personality and world-famous reputation.

During his address in Paris, Robeson never said the words that were soon attributed to him, but his protestations did not matter to an America aggressively distrusting of its own citizens. He would maintain to uninterested ears that he was misquoted, distorted in the April 21, 1949, Associated Press dispatch that appeared across the country:

ROBESON: NO NEGRO WILL FIGHT SOVIET

> "I bring you a message from the Negro people of America that they do not want a war which would send them back to a new kind of slavery," Robeson told the Congress. "It is unthinkable," he said, that American Negroes "would go to war on behalf of those who have oppressed us for generations" against a country "which in one generation has raised our people to the full dignity of mankind."

Du Bois recalled the overwhelming response to Robeson, that the "audience rose to a man and the walls thundered. . . . I joined them in wild applause." The *New York Daily News* estimated Robeson spoke in the Salle Pleyel to two thousand delegates from 52 countries. When the conference ended, Robeson continued with his tour of Europe, drawing overflowing audiences: At Forum Hall in Copenhagen, he sang to a record crowd of 16,000. Forty thousand fans greeted him in Stockholm. In Oslo, Robeson attended a May Day outdoor festival where he entertained thousands.

For a time, he remained largely unaware of the effect the Associated Press dispatch was having on American attitudes toward him. From the first time he appeared in the Black press when he was a high school teenager back in 1915 through the thousands of words of songs, speeches, and theater performances, they would be the most important words ever attributed to him.

II

WHEN ROBESON INTENSIFIED CRITIQUES OF Congress for failing to pass even a modest anti-lynching bill in 1946, he and Du Bois grew closer. Du Bois agreed to lend his considerable name to Robeson's efforts. In 1949, Du Bois was 81 years old and blessed with a ferocious energy. He was an American giant, his commitment to the Black story total. The two men were also simpatico in the belief that the Black domestic and international struggles of African people throughout the world could not be decoupled: a sharp, irreconcilable contrast to the domestic-leaning attitudes of the NAACP. Regardless of border, continent, or language, Du Bois saw a oneness in the Black global struggle against white supremacy. Every Black person in the world was affected by racism, exploitation, and colonialism, he reasoned. A failure to understand this essential global interconnectedness and how the wealth inequality of Western capitalism guaranteed the exploitation, Du Bois believed, was to undermine the political leverages and possibilities Black people could achieve collectively. Over the course of his long life, Du Bois would witness the Black American mainstream leadership decouple itself from the global Black struggle.

Paul Robeson was two decades older than Jackie Robinson. W.E.B. Du Bois was three decades older than Robeson. Du Bois was born February 23, 1868, in the Berkshires, in the Western Massachusetts hamlet of Great Barrington, three years after the Confederate surrender and Abraham Lincoln's assassination. His academic accomplishments and scholarly contributions provided a corrective to the prevailing theories of Black intellectual inferiority and limited social contribution. Du Bois was the first Black student to receive a Ph.D. from Harvard. At the University of Pennsylvania, he began research on what would be

The Philadelphia Negro, credited as the first (and groundbreaking) case study of Black life. Du Bois stood on the cutting edge of virtually every political and academic movement that shaped the post-slavery Black journey in America, from his 1903 classic *The Souls of Black Folk* (his 1897 "double consciousness" meditation from *The Atlantic* comprised the first chapter), to his role in the 1906 Niagara Movement that countered the accommodationist strategies of Booker T. Washington, to the founding of the NAACP, to his landmark 1935 work *Black Reconstruction*, which forced a grudging academic reconsideration of slavery and Reconstruction. Du Bois was a living history, overlapping professionally with Frederick Douglass, William Monroe Trotter, A. Philip Randolph, Ida B. Wells, Marcus Garvey, and Harriet Tubman, as well as Washington, Martin Luther King Jr., Malcolm X, *and* Jackie Robinson.

As editor of *The Crisis*, the NAACP's powerful in-house magazine, Du Bois had been organizing Pan-African Congresses (to the disapproval of the United States government) since the end of World War I, had lived through several Pan-African movements, and debated against Garvey and Washington in shaping a nascent Black sensibility toward Africa. In a harbinger of his evolving socialism, Du Bois saw an unbreakable link between capitalism and racism, but Du Bois's independence was legendary. The FBI took notice, having opened a file on him as early as 1942. He was file no. 100–99729–1. A May 1, 1942, synopsis originating from the Atlanta office read, "His writings indicate him to be a Socialist. However, he has been called a communist and at the same time criticized by the Communist Party. Subject favors equality between the white and colored races."

Du Bois and Robeson were not close at the time of Robeson's 1946 clash with Truman, but Du Bois appreciated Robeson's Pan-Africanism. Few American artists were as drawn to Africa as Robeson. For a time, the Black press even took a marginal interest in the anti-colonialist aims of African nations, when the *Pittsburgh Courier* briefly ran a weekly column titled "Africa Speaks."

As a founding member of the Council on African Affairs, Robeson signaled he was not only willing to challenge the American government and its paltry response to anti-Black violence in the United States but indict the U.S. for its international alliances with the European nations who had long dominated Africa. When Truman, in his inauguration speech, said of American ambitions, "The old imperialism—exploitation for foreign profit—has no place in our plans," Robeson countered that the United States fully supported South Africa's apartheid and European colonialism.

While Robeson was consistently portrayed as a communist pawn, supporting Stalin's expansion into Western Europe, he insisted his opposition to capitalism was rooted in the continued exploitation of African resources—an analysis Western intelligence found flimsy. Robeson, according to one British intelligence report, was "rather gullible." Robeson reasoned Africa's riches were the only way a depleted Europe could repay American corporations. A half century later, the American novelist Barbara Kingsolver would write of how average Americans benefited from the Africa that built the American empire: "We were enriched and bejeweled by it. Nearly every married woman I knew wore a diamond taken from African soil. The cobalt in our engines and aircraft, the rubber tires that underpinned our transportation and helped win our wars . . . all this came from a place unmentioned in our history books. This was not an innocent oversight."

Du Bois was activated by the unabated lynching in America—and, in the case of Black veterans, the chilling terrorism of *who* the white mobs were lynching. Du Bois's moment occurred in 1919 while he pored over gruesome images of a Black man lynched in Omaha, Nebraska. According to Du Bois biographer David Levering Lewis, the photo was "taken so soon following the murder that the body still sizzled. The blackened, naked remains, twisted and scabious like a badly burnt pretzel, sank into a pyre heaped up by the grinning white mob at a downtown intersection." The photos confirmed Du Bois's advocacy: his voice could not be that of a detached academic. It was crucial to provide propaganda, context, and outrage.

III

RESPECTFUL OF DU BOIS'S SIZABLE accomplishments, NAACP Executive Director Walter White endured an uneasy relationship with Du Bois, but the NAACP leadership, led by White, Roy Wilkins, and Thurgood Marshall (the lead lawyer of the NAACP Legal Defense Fund), did not extend the same courtesy to Robeson. At one time, they admired him—Robeson was always a willing and an accessible fundraiser for the organization. Now, they saw him as a nuisance whose fidelity to the Soviets could destroy the organization's integration efforts. White's personal belief was that Robeson would harm the movement. Where Du Bois saw value in many voices from all angles pressuring the government to act, White disapproved of Robeson's wildcat strike. He believed in a central voice, and that voice needed to belong to the NAACP.

The NAACP distrusted Robeson's politics. The Black voice needed to be united behind the NAACP, and it needed to be anticommunist. So many of Robeson's own organizations and allies were now official enemies of the state, and organizations on the AGLOSO list jeopardized the tenuous political footholds the NAACP had worked so hard to gain. It was how the organization supported Truman over Wallace. White, Wilkins, and Marshall steered the organization toward the narrow lane future scholars would describe as "liberal anticommunism."

The NAACP and American communists had feuded since the early 1930s, beginning with the infamous Scottsboro Boys trial. When communists led the Harlem march in 1935, protesting Italy's invasion of Ethiopia, the press called it a multiracial rejection of fascism, but the Black press noticed the absence of the Black leadership: the NAACP and Urban League did not participate.

Hostilities reignited during World War II, when the CPUSA muted its criticisms of American racism to avoid jeopardizing the aid America provided the Soviets. The Paris controversy reopened old wounds. The May issue of the *Crisis* featured an editorial, "The NAACP and the

Communists," which primarily focused on projecting NAACP loyalty and a pugilistic tone toward the Soviet Union. "The American Communists are busy stirring disaffection, dissension and unrest in every segment of American life they can penetrate, such as unions, church bodies, youth groups, college campuses, community organizations and Negro groups, including the NAACP," the editorial stated. "The purpose of all of this is *not* to build a better NAACP to fight more effectively for civil rights for Negroes under the American Constitution, using legitimate American methods, but to operate one more front group to confuse and embarrass Americans and the American government in the present contest of ideologies." However, echoing Truman, the NAACP characterized the CPUSA as a shadowy menace infiltrating the Black community, just as American leaders said that communism was infiltrating every strain of American life.

Robeson was a revered figure in the Black community, but Paris provided the moment the NAACP had been waiting on for nearly four years: payback for the Spingarn.

On October 18, 1945, at the Biltmore Hotel in New York, the NAACP awarded Robeson its highest honor, the Spingarn Medal, named after Joel Spingarn, the white, Ivy-educated Republican who was a leading member of the NAACP from the organization's earliest days. The Spingarn was introduced in 1914, "to be awarded for the highest or noblest Achievement by an American Negro during the preceding year or years." Five years later, Spingarn would be a cofounder of the publishing giant Harcourt Brace.

Robeson received the honor, according to the NAACP certificate, for his "distinguished achievements in the theater and on the concert stage, as well as his active concern for the common man of every color, race, religion and nationality." Du Bois, in Europe at the time, did not attend (he had won the award in 1920). Several others sat at Robeson's table: the renowned concert singer Marian Anderson (the 1939 Spingarn winner), the great baritone Harry T. Burleigh, Essie, Walter White,

Robeson's brother Ben (who was an influential pastor in Harlem), and Louis T. Wright (the noted surgeon and 1940 Spingarn recipient). In attendance also were Adam Clayton Powell Jr., Wilkins, and the Black New York City councilman Benjamin J. Davis Jr., himself elected on the Communist Party ticket and who, by 1949, would be on trial and facing more than a decade in prison for being a member of communist leadership.

Honoring Robeson was a massive coup. Estimates of the attendance ranged from 500 to 700 attendees. As toastmaster, Walter White introduced Marshall Field III, the department store heir and publisher, who then introduced Robeson. A year earlier, Field had purchased the venerable book publisher Simon and Schuster and had created *Parade*, a newspaper supplement that would appear in millions of households every Sunday for decades. "A white man can talk of what such Negro pioneering means," Field said in his remarks, "but it is with great difficulty that a white man grasps and appreciates the cost of outstanding accomplishment by an American Negro."

Field adorned Robeson with his medal. Robeson thanked the NAACP and praised the previous Spingarn winners. "I am proud," he said, "to be part of the work they represent." As Robeson pivoted in his comments, he cautioned the audience about the rebuilding of fascism, and, in an obvious nod to the colonial European hierarchies and their presence in Africa, including Western support for South Africa, Robeson warned against the "restoration of monarchies and restoration of their estates to collaborators."

Robeson then presented the Soviet model as an aspirational framework for Black life in an integrated society. "Full employment in Russia is a fact, not a myth, and discrimination is non-existent," Robeson said, adding, "The Soviet Union can't help it as a nation and as a people if it is in the main stream of change."

The attendees were stunned. Walter White was embarrassed, then enraged. Robeson had humiliated him on the NAACP's most important night. Robeson's relationship with the NAACP would vacillate between civil and contentious, but never again would it be warm. Nine days later, it was still news.

> **SPEECH SHOCKS NOTABLES**
>
> **ROBESON LAUDS RUSSIA AT SPINGARN MEDAL BANQUET**
>
> Thirtieth recipient of the Spingarn Medal, annual award for outstanding achievement, presented by the National Association for the Advancement of Colored People, actor-singer Paul Robeson, in his acceptance speech, Thursday at the Biltmore Hotel, shocked his several hundred listeners by voicing frank and pronounced preferences for Soviet principles—economic, political and social.

An example of Robeson's appeal—and the lack of unanimity in the Black community regarding both how the socialist message was being received and the assumed authority of the NAACP—appeared in a gossip item in a Black weekly, the *Michigan Chronicle*, which portrayed the dustup through the lens of the class system, not patriotism. The NAACP had long been known as a pinnacle of Black elitism—a realization of Du Bois's "Talented Tenth"—the best and brightest would lead the race (a strategy Du Bois would come to regret). The NAACP was founded as an interracial organization. Its black leadership was almost exclusively light-skinned; Walter White identified as a Black man, but his complexion was so fair he was often thought to be white. As a child growing up in Baltimore, Thurgood Marshall recalled the adults referring to the aristocratic NAACP as the "National Association for the Advancement of *Certain* People." Robeson maintained his popularity within the Black community, as the column portrayed the NAACP as the snobby Black establishment unable to muzzle the independent Robeson: "Upstanding Harlemites are still all a-twitter at forthright Paul Robeson's acceptance speech praising Russia at the 'too-too' Spingarn dinner."

The FBI was dutifully watching. After the dinner, the New York office placed clippings of the Spingarn dinner news stories, including the

Pittsburgh Courier's front-page write-up and the continuation ("Robeson Lauds Russia"), into Robeson's FBI file.

Traditionally, Black organizations did not spar publicly, fearful of the optics of whites sitting back as a divided Black leadership destroyed one another. Yet, the NAACP launched a calculated full-scale attack on Robeson. The appearance of communist sympathy tainted reputations, Black and white, nationwide, and the NAACP saw itself as particularly vulnerable.

In a sensational 1947 article in *Life* magazine, Arthur Schlesinger Jr. wrote that communists had infiltrated the NAACP. Two weeks before Robeson's Paris remarks, *Life* published an article appearing in the April 4, 1949, issue titled "Red Visitors Cause Rumpus" that accused the federally funded National Council for the Arts and Sciences of being run by communist sympathizers—and began federal scrutiny on defunding the arts. The article contained a photo spread titled "Dupes and Fellow Travelers Dress Up Communists Fronts," which was comprised of fifty photographs of artists and thinkers the magazine accused of backing communist causes, "wittingly or not."

Robeson was not pictured, but the magazine implicated Nobel Prize–winning physicist Albert Einstein, the writer Dorothy Parker, playwright Arthur Miller, and composers Leonard Bernstein, Aaron Copland, and Dean Dixon—the Black, Harlem-raised, Julliard- and Columbia-trained composer. Renowned poet Langston Hughes and Congressman Adam Clayton Powell Jr. were also included in the montage.

The NAACP pondered its strategies. White and Wilkins believed silence might be interpreted as a tacit approval of Robeson and would have weakened the NAACP's leadership position. The State Department was privately pressuring White to criticize Robeson, which he did, straddling the fence between supporting Robeson's right to free speech and questioning his loyalties to the United States.

White also could have issued an expedient denial, forcing Robeson into isolation, but the organization chose the most aggressive strategy: it piled on. In a 1980 interview with Robeson biographer Martin Duberman, the legendary civil rights leader Bayard Rustin recalled personally calling Black leaders to strategize how to isolate Robeson. "We have to prove that we're patriotic," Rustin told Duberman in his landmark 1989 biography, *Paul Robeson*. Though Rustin himself had been a former communist and was viewed with hostility by the FBI, the consensus strategy was to convey to America that Robeson lacked any top-level Black support, to "create a united front to make sure America understood the current black leadership totally disagreed with Robeson." According to Duberman, the group also decided not to confront Robeson to hear his side of the story. "The general theory was that he was being used, and anybody who had to barter with him on these issues was going to end up being used, too, if not by the Soviets, by Robeson himself," Rustin recalled, adding that members of leadership also felt resentment toward Robeson for being provocative but never being around to clean up the ensuing mess.

The coordinated attack began in the May 1949 issue of *The Crisis* in the form of a vicious, unsigned editorial written by Wilkins, which confirmed Rustin's recollection of events and Wilkins's personal animus toward Robeson. Titled "Robeson Speaks for Robeson," the editorial attempted to strip Robeson's voice of credibility with Black people ("Paul Robeson does not represent any American Negroes."), while appeasing the State Department by accusing Robeson of being a communist pawn. It claimed Robeson had long abandoned Black people in favor of white radicals ("Today, Mr. Robeson, if he represents any group at all, speaks for the fellow travelers of Communism and it is well known that these are overwhelmingly white."), which may have come as a shock to MI5, which described Robeson as "strongly anti-white." To *Crisis* readers, Wilkins attempted to sever the man to whom the NAACP had once bestowed its highest honor from his lifelong connection to Black people. ("Mr. Robeson has none except sentimental roots among American Negroes. He is of them, but not with them.")

> Since Mr. Robeson at Paris presumed to speak for American Negroes, it is pertinent to examine into his record of service to his race. How much has he done to help them in their upward struggle? He has inspired them by his singing and given them a "great one" to cite in their briefs for better treatment. But when this inspiration is set down, little is left to chronicle.

The NAACP went so far as to position Robeson's support of African independence as a criticism. "While his people . . . were battling as best they knew how and yelling for help," the editorial stated, "Robeson was writing and talking about Africa."

Following the article, Ben Davis, the communist New York City councilman on trial at Foley Square, wrote Walter White directly, calling the editorial, "One of the most shocking personal attacks upon a great American leader I have ever seen." (A month earlier, Davis had written a letter to *The Crisis,* criticizing the magazine for the "slander" of accusing CPUSA members of exploiting Black issues in its "The NAACP and the Communists" editorial: "It is always shocking to see them slavishly repeated by Negroes who are themselves victims of racist persecution.") One Robeson intimate blanched at Black leadership "crawling on its belly" to prove its loyalty to a country that denied them basic rights. While Thurgood Marshall, Roy Wilkins, Bayard Rustin, and the NAACP top leadership formulated a strategy to attack Robeson, Hoover and the FBI opened files on each of them, including files on Rustin for both his influence and homosexuality.

IV

DURING THE FIRST WEEK OF May 1949, the mortally wounded Progressive Party commenced a "peace tour" of the United States, opposing the North Atlantic Treaty Organization, the new postwar alliance designed to counter Soviet expansion. Trounced by Truman and struggling to survive, the Massachusetts chapter of the party hosted a conference at Mechanics Hall in Boston. Henry Wallace would speak, as would H. Lester Hutchinson, of the British Labour Party, and Michele Guia, the Italian Socialist Party senator. Another speaker, Essie Robeson, titled her presentation, "The Negro and the Peace." Even with Wallace, a former vice president and presidential candidate speaking in a major city and five thousand people in attendance, the event did not receive widespread coverage. The *New England Bulletin*, the Black newspaper out of Hartford, Connecticut, was in attendance.

With Robeson still in Europe, Essie wasted no time criticizing the Black establishment that coordinated against her husband, and she singled out Walter White, questioning the NAACP's authority as much as it had publicly doubted Robeson's. The NAACP and Adam Clayton Powell's Harlem district, she said, may have had the ear of two million people—at best. "Then what about the 12 million un-organized Negroes—the real 'vast majority,'" she asked. "Who speaks for them?"

V

ROBESON RETURNED TO NEW YORK on June 19 for a massive "welcome home" rally sponsored by the Council on African Affairs, at Rockland Palace on 155th Street and Eighth Avenue in Harlem. His reputation was crumbling under the fallout of the Paris Conference, but his comments and Essie's defense of them were long supported by Black history. The question of military service in the face of segregation at home had existed throughout Black political thought since the 18th century, and Du Bois asked the question during both 20th-century world wars. The difference now was the extent to which the Black establishment publicly turned on Robeson.

"We Negroes are Americans and we know it," Essie said in Boston during her response to Walter White, "but our country keeps telling us, time after time, in heartbreaking ways, that we have no rights and privileges as American citizens—except those it chooses to grant when it feels indulgent." In 1838, the Philadelphia antislavery activist Robert

Purvis addressed his audience with a similar rhetoric. "Are we to be thus looked to for help in the 'hour of danger,' be trampled under foot in the time of peace?"

Robeson was greeted at Rockland Palace by 4,500 attendees, including Du Bois, who arrived enthusiastically. The NAACP spent weeks discrediting Robeson, and yet it seemed as if there was no place in Black culture he had not touched. Thirty years earlier, on November 30, 1918, Robeson's Rutgers football team had been shut out by Syracuse, 21–0. After the game, a 20-year-old Robeson came to Rockland Palace to attend a basketball game. In those days, he would play basketball at Rockland to stay in shape. He told the crowd he had played basketball against several local teams, like the Brooklyn YMCA, and returning to the old hall anew made him feel at home.

At the four-and-a-half-hour-long rally, Robeson went on the offensive against the NAACP. With the May editorial in *The Crisis* still fresh, he still felt stung by Roy Wilkins questioning his Blackness. "During the Wallace campaign, I stood on the very soil on which my father was a slave . . . I reflected upon the wealth bled from my near relatives alone, and of the basic wealth of all this America, beaten out of millions of the Negro people, enslaved, free, newly enslaved until this very day. And I defied—and today I defy—any part of an insolent, dominating America, however powerful; I defy any errand boys, Uncle Toms of the Negro people, to challenge my Americanism."

As he had in Europe after Paris, Robeson continued to go where Black leadership would not, coupling the domestic support of European colonialism with the global suppression of Black and brown people around the globe to fund the postwar rebuilding of the West, including intensifying the American war machine. "How can the British, French and other Western European bankers repay Wall Street?" he said. "Only in raw materials—in gold, copper, cocoa, rubber, uranium . . . From where? Why, from South Africa, Nigeria, East Africa . . . Jamaica . . . Guatemala . . . Viet Nam."

A world-class athlete, international singer, Broadway and Hollywood actor, and Ivy League–educated law student, Paul Robeson embodied the range of possibilities like no Black man in the twentieth century had. In a 1944 magazine article, he was called "America's No. 1 Negro." GORDON PARKS, FARM SECURITY ADMINISTRATION—OFFICE OF WAR INFORMATION PHOTOGRAPH COLLECTION (LIBRARY OF CONGRESS)

Robeson's 1942 U.S. debut of *Othello* revolutionized Shakespeare's jealous Moor, and his record-setting Broadway run a year later essentially ended the American practice of white actors playing the role in blackface. FARM SECURITY ADMINISTRATION—OFFICE OF WAR INFORMATION PHOTOGRAPH COLLECTION (LIBRARY OF CONGRESS)

An imposing Robeson at Rutgers. Though the legendary Walter Camp considered him one of the greatest college football players ever, Robeson was later erased from many record books because of his politics. RUTGERS ATHLETICS

Robeson, José Ferrer, and an unidentified *Othello* cast member playing softball in Central Park. Once allies on stage, Robeson and Ferrer were as wary in real life as Othello and Iago. In time, Ferrer would become one of Robeson's fiercest critics for both professional and personal reasons. FARM SECURITY ADMINISTRATION—OFFICE OF WAR INFORMATION PHOTOGRAPH COLLECTION (LIBRARY OF CONGRESS)

Left to right: William Richardson, Commissioner Kenesaw Mountain Landis, and Washington Senators owner Clark Griffith, 1924. As commissioner, Landis held absolute power over baseball for nearly a quarter century. He and Griffith were steadfast in their conviction that the game remain segregated. NATIONAL PHOTO COMPANY COLLECTION (LIBRARY OF CONGRESS)

Two years before the Dodgers signed Jackie Robinson, Robeson was the first Black man ever to address the owners. During that meeting, Rickey may have telegraphed his history-changing plan for Jackie Robinson. ASSOCIATED PRESS/JOHN LINDSAY

The duo that changed history: Robinson would refer to Branch Rickey as "the father he never had," while Rickey's conservative political views would be the driving force that led Robinson to testify against Paul Robeson publicly. NATIONAL BASEBALL HALL OF FAME AND MUSEUM

Robinson's 1947 debut would electrify a nation while simultaneously strengthening the belief among team owners that the arrival of Black players would send the game into financial ruin. NATIONAL BASEBALL HALL OF FAME AND MUSEUM

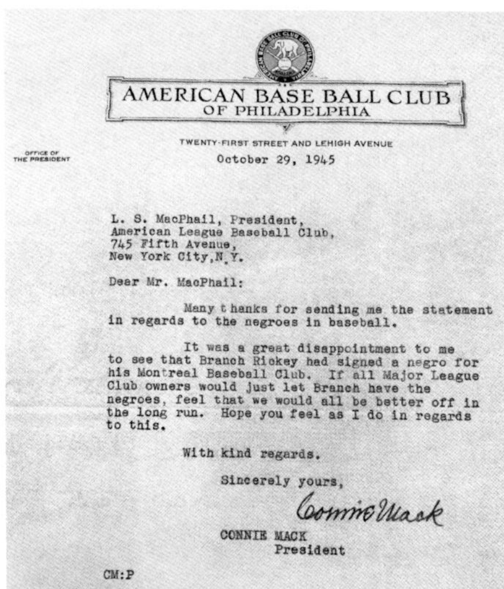

AMERICAN BASE BALL CLUB
OF PHILADELPHIA

OFFICE OF THE PRESIDENT

TWENTY-FIRST STREET AND LEHIGH AVENUE

October 29, 1945

L. S. MacPhail, President,
American League Baseball Club,
745 Fifth Avenue,
New York City, N. Y.

Dear Mr. MacPhail:

Many thanks for sending me the statement in regards to the negroes in baseball.

It was a great disappointment to me to see that Branch Rickey had signed a negro for his Montreal Baseball Club. If all Major League Club owners would just let Branch have the negroes, feel that we would all be better off in the long run. Hope you feel as I do in regards to this.

With kind regards.

Sincerely yours,

Connie Mack

CONNIE MACK
President

CM:P

History positioned Robinson's arrival as a singular triumph, but owners privately saw the move as the deepest personal betrayal. A private letter written by Philadelphia A's owner Connie Mack underscored the institutional hostility that awaited Robinson. NATIONAL BASEBALL HALL OF FAME AND MUSEUM

Frustrated by the indifference of the Truman administration, Robeson announced a national anti-lynching campaign while speaking on the steps of the Lincoln Memorial—angering Black leaders, who believed Robeson's politics would hurt the broader civil rights movement as Cold War tensions rose.

BETTMANN VIA GETTY IMAGES

Truman desegregated the military and was the first president to campaign in Harlem, and in return, the Black vote won him a surprise presidential victory in 1948. But Robeson believed Truman cared more about Black votes than Black voters.

BETTMANN VIA GETTY IMAGES

Truman's 1949 inauguration was the most expensive and ostentatious in the nation's history at the time: a military parade posing as an inauguration for one purpose—for the U.S. to signal its military might to the USSR.

HARRY S. TRUMAN PRESIDENTIAL LIBRARY & MUSEUM

The American attitude toward the USSR—and the liberals and progressives like Robeson who believed in cooperation with the Soviets—was summed up by a single cartoon: Stalin and communism were the greatest threat to world peace.

Dickey Front

A founding architect of the NAACP and Black America's greatest academic, W.E.B. Du Bois (*right*) grew disillusioned with the Black establishment leadership he helped create. Like Robeson, W.E.B. Du Bois would have his passport confiscated for nearly a decade as his politics drifted to the left. BETTMANN VIA GETTY IMAGES

Once Robeson admirers, the legendary NAACP brain trust—Walter White (*center*), Roy Wilkins (*left*), and Thurgood Marshall—saw Robeson as a pawn of the Soviet Union. They worked with the state department to distance him from mainstream civil rights issues, only to see anti-integration forces turn around and question the loyalty of Black organizations. LIBRARY OF CONGRESS/CORBIS/VCG VIA GETTY IMAGES

Jackie Robinson stood at the center of baseball's desegregation, but it was Rachel Robinson who was in a powerful partnership with her husband. For all of Jackie's competitive fury, it was Rachel's quiet diplomacy that restored Robinson's name as essential to baseball history. NATIONAL BASEBALL HALL OF FAME AND MUSEUM

A light moment on a heavy subject. Pressured by Rickey to testify, Robinson denounced Robeson on July 18, 1949—a decision Rachel would later say was fueled by Robinson's seeing America as "my country, right or wrong." PHOTOQUEST/GETTY IMAGES

Although much of white America hailed Robinson as a hero for testifying against Robeson, the Black community was not unanimous in their support of Robinson, where he was accused of being in far over his head as a pawn of segregationists. *BALTIMORE AFRO-AMERICAN*

Following Robinson's testimony, an effigy of Paul Robeson hangs from a farming vehicle as a warning to Robeson not to appear at his scheduled concert in Peekskill, NY. When he arrived, Robeson was greeted by an angry mob and a burning cross. BETTMAN VIA GETTY IMAGES

Two concerts. Two riots. As the anti-Robeson protestors pulled concertgoers out of their cars, local police did little to quell the violence. Much of the Black establishment responded to the attacks on Robeson and his fans with silence. CHARLES HOFF/*NEW YORK DAILY NEWS* VIA GETTY IMAGES

A legend at his apex. A champion and now baseball's most valuable player, Jackie Robinson, in 1949, added the title of American hero to his name. Yet, five years after his signing, more than half the teams in baseball still had not integrated. NATIONAL PORTRAIT GALLERY, SMITHSONIAN INSTITUTION

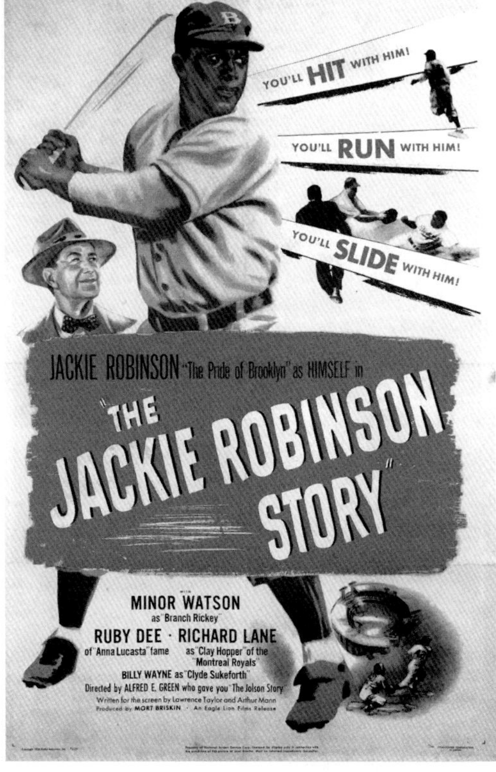

Robinson played himself opposite Ruby Dee, but the film was less a biopic of his remarkable life and more a vehicle for Branch Rickey's and the nation's battle against communism.

Branch Rickey was the mastermind behind baseball's integration and Robinson's testimony. A hardline conservative and anti–New Dealer, Rickey saw Paul Robeson's international fame as a threat to American influence around the world. ROBERT RIGER/GETTY IMAGES

The most exciting play in baseball: Jackie Robinson stealing home. While Robinson's play changed the game, the slow pace of change intensified his disillusionment with baseball. NATIONAL BASEBALL HALL OF FAME AND MUSEUM

Americans were obsessed with the fear of domestic subversion, and communism was a powerful subtext in films and television. In a paranoid time, the theme grew in power: No one was exactly who they seemed.

No unelected government official ever held as much power as Ruth Shipley, who for nearly three decades decided which Americans would be granted passports. For eight years, she denied Robeson's right to travel, along with many other liberal Americans she considered "subversive."

An explosive final showdown in June 1956 between Robeson and HUAC ended with an aging, defiant Robeson being cited for contempt, but the influence of the committee, after nearly twenty years of attacking American citizens, was waning. ASSOCIATED PRESS

Because Robinson wasn't performing as well as he did at his peak and they were tired of his frequent rages, the Dodgers traded Robinson to the rival New York Giants, but Robinson, in turn, decided to retire at thirty-seven. Despite Robinson's exemplary triumphs, three teams—the Phillies, Tigers, and Red Sox—never integrated during Robinson's career. NATIONAL BASEBALL HALL OF FAME AND MUSEUM

After eight years of being denied the right to travel, a smiling Robeson leaves for England in 1958, following the Supreme Court's ruling that it was unconstitutional to deny passports based on political beliefs. Robeson would leave the country for nearly five years, and W.E.B. Du Bois, also freed to travel, would never return to the United States. ASSOCIATED PRESS

As the civil rights movement intensified, segregationists discredited integration as part of a communist plot. Jackie Robinson and the Black leadership distanced themselves from Robeson to prove their loyalty to America, only to be called communists a decade later. BETTMANN VIA GETTY IMAGES

A last smile. Robinson would be voted a first ballot Hall of Famer in 1962, but his relationship with the Dodgers would be forever strained, and he would respond to the game's lack of front-office integration with a decade-long estrangement from the sport. NATIONAL BASEBALL HALL OF FAME AND MUSEUM

Freed from baseball, Robinson went headfirst into the civil rights movement, surveying terrorist campaigns of the Ku Klux Klan. Simultaneously, conservative political alliances disintegrated as the party moved more to the right and remained uncommitted to expanding civil rights.
STEVE SCHAPIRO/CORBIS VIA GETTY IMAGES

Stricken by diabetes, the death of Jackie Robinson Jr., and a sport and country that had not lived up to its ideals, a fifty-two-year-old Robinson reflects. Sixteen months later, he would be dead of a heart attack. NATIONAL BASEBALL HALL OF FAME AND MUSEUM

Paul Robeson in Moscow. Largely reclusive following his return to the United States in 1963, the FBI still continued its surveillance of him until 1974, two years before his death in 1976. AFRO AMERICAN NEWSPAPERS/GADO/GETTY IMAGES

Robeson's admirers called him "the tallest tree in the forest." Since 1999, Paul Robeson has stood, for posterity, at 4502 Chestnut Street, West Philadelphia. COURTESY OF THE AUTHOR

For a man who had been battered by White and Wilkins and members of the Black press as a pawn of Moscow, he returned fire at the NAACP—it, too, was also a pawn, but for the segregationists and colonialists responsible for the worldwide Black condition. "What a travesty is this supposed leadership of a great people, and in this historic time when their people need them the most," Robeson said. "How Sojourner Truth, Harriet Tubman, Fred Douglass must be turning over in their graves at this spectacle of a craven, fawning, despicable leadership able to be naught but errand boys, and at the lowest level . . . let them get their crumbs from their Wall Street masters."

The FBI trailed Robeson, reporting to Hoover that Harlemites offered no reaction to his motorcade as it passed, the suggestion being Robeson possessed no following among Black people. Even where Robeson seemingly enjoyed his strongest support, the Bureau argued that no one cared.

VI

A WEEK AFTER THE ROCKLAND Palace rally, the *San Francisco Examiner* published an above-the-fold editorial titled "An Undesirable Citizen," which stated (in all caps) that "IT CANNOT BE SAID THAT PAUL ROBESON WAS DENIED THE BENEFITS OF AN AMERICAN EDUCATION . . . AND FOR ALL THIS, PAUL ROBESON DESPISES HIS COUNTRY." Robeson himself had never argued the *Examiner*'s point, one repeated in embittered editorials nationwide. "And I say to *The New York Times* that personal success can be no answer," he said at Rockland Palace. "It can no longer be a question of an Anderson, a Carver, a Robinson, a Jackson, or a Robeson. It must be a question of the well-being and opportunities not of a few, but for all."

It was America—and not his talent, his critics said—that had given him the opportunity to live a successful life. For more than two decades, he stood as the symbol of American possibility, especially for the Black underclass. Now, by criticizing America, Robeson had, in the minds of his detractors, betrayed America, not only with his lack of patriotism but also his lack of gratitude. The triumphant *Othello* debut in Cambridge now felt distant. He *owed* America, the *Examiner* argued. The *Lincoln Evening Journal* penned an editorial, "Paul Robeson: Tragic Dupe," expressing anger that Robeson no longer sounded like a credit to his race. "The old Paul Robeson was one of those who best served his people's cause. The new one is a tragic dupe."

Three days after Paris, a similar editorial ran in the *Salem News*, a newspaper in tiny Salem, Ohio.

PAUL ROBESON, OPPRESSED

> The speech made by Paul Robeson to the Communist-backed world peace conference in Paris last Wednesday was so bitter against the United States that the speaker's countrymen can only wonder what lies behind such feeling.
>
> Paul Robeson at the age of 51 has had a full life. Before he took up agitation for the communist revolution, he had been acclaimed as a great athlete, a great actor, and a great concert singer.
>
> We are not arguing that all colored people have had the same opportunities as Paul Robeson. Few white people have had them, and fewer yet have had his outstanding ability. We are saying Paul Robeson is not an oppressed colored person and never has been; that many colored persons in the United States have risen above oppression when they have encountered it; and that for Paul Robeson to pretend that this is not so in the United States is a grievous disappointment to every person who has tried to be decent and fair dealing with the Negro minority. His bitter speech to a Communist-sponsored gathering in Paris needs to be answered—preferably by spokesmen of his own race who are ashamed of his prejudice.

The instruction in that final sentence—to find someone Black to refute a Black voice—had been feverishly in the works. While the editorial pages traded volleys and most of the mainstream public stewed, anti-Robeson forces privately mobilized. In the weeks following Paris, the public outcry could be heard in every pub, newsroom, and backroom around the country, but no official action had yet been directed at Robeson. Then, on July 8, the request from the little *Salem News* that Black people publicly counter Robeson was accommodated by the House Un-American Activities Committee and its chairman, the Georgia Democrat John Stephens Wood, who had found his man.

BALLPLAYER TO REFUTE SLUR ON RACE

> The House Un-American Activities Committee has invited Baseball star Jackie Robinson to "give the lie" to Singer Paul Robeson's comments on the loyalty of American Negroes.
>
> Robinson, and other prominent Negroes, have been asked to testify next week, starting Tuesday. Chairman Wood (D-GA) told reporters: "I think the purpose of the hearings is to give the lie to statements made by the singer Paul Robeson that American Negroes wouldn't fight in the case of a war against Russia."

Wood told reporters the genesis of the hearings came from "certain Negro leaders" who volunteered to go on record against Robeson. The following day, reporters caught up with Robinson at Ebbets Field, where he said he would fight any American adversary because "I want my kid to have the things that I have," and added, "I'll be very glad to tell the reporters how I feel."

The Committee set the hearings for July 13–18, officially titled "Hearings Regarding Communist Infiltration of Minority Groups." Unofficially, the purpose of the hearings was for Black people to show their loyalty to America.

The newspapers referred to Robinson as HUAC's "star witness." Days before, Robeson sent a letter to Robinson with the intention of clarifying his distorted comments in Paris and to prevent two of the most famous Black men in the nation from publicly clashing for the enjoyment of segregationists who despised both. Robinson did not respond.

Book Two

The Un-Americans

Part Three

Enemies

(1949–1952)

Chapter Eight

I

BLACK AMERICANS SWEARING LOYALTY TO America exemplified both the times and Du Bois's twoness. Paul Robeson called it insulting. Alvin Stokes worked two years to create the moment, cultivating the Dodgers to deliver Robinson to Washington by appealing to Branch Rickey's anticommunism—his version of the game's integration had to be protected. Robeson in Paris provided the news cycle, and Black people paraded in front of the government under oath to prove they could be trusted was sensational enough to catch the entire nation's attention.

Stokes's boss, J. Parnell Thomas, had mastered the theatrical blueprint, turning the lives of American citizens into white-hat, black-hat drama. Thomas, the anti-New Dealer who saw FDR's social programs to steady America out of the Depression undermining American capitalism, gained significant currency denigrating liberalism through anticommunism. The Hollywood Ten and Alger Hiss investigations in 1947 and 1948, respectively, gave HUAC and Thomas nationwide cachet—but his star was brief. A *Miami Herald* editorial once described him as a demagogue who "splashed his smears" with "careless energy," and by 1949, after being convicted for payroll fraud and heading to prison, the *News* noted Thomas's comeuppance. After flaying open the lives of private citizens, Thomas was "No longer the attacker, but the attacked."

HUAC relied on the emotional theater—exposure and contrition—but Stokes had yet to secure a substantial victory. Here was his chance. Eighteen months earlier, on January 2, 1948, in a secret meeting at a Harlem restaurant, Stokes met Arthur Mann with the intention of cultivating Robinson. He did not know Robinson's politics, and neither, at the time, did the Dodgers. His 1944 trial for refusing to agree to segregating seating in the Army made national news, but that was the extent of his known political profile.

Before even discussing an appearance with Robinson, Mann laid out to Stokes the parameters for securing Robinson. First, Robinson's appearance had to appear voluntary. Secondly, Robinson had to be allowed to speak his mind independently. Third, Robinson must not affiliate himself politically.

Five days after the meeting, Thomas announced to the press and during a radio address HUAC would be holding hearings into communist infiltration of Black organizations within the month to reveal the findings of Stokes's nine-month undercover investigation. Thomas tantalized reporters that the hearings would involve big names—the boxers Joe Louis or Jersey Joe Walcott, perhaps. Maybe even Paul Robeson.

The papers never mentioned Robinson by name, but Rickey privately instructed Mann to make Robinson available to the committee. The Dodgers were training in the Dominican Republic in the spring of 1948, and Mann told Stokes Rickey would fly Robinson to Washington. Ultimately, the hearings never took place, likely because Thomas was kicked off the committee, and the Republicans lost the 1948 midterms, reducing Stokes as a priority. After nearly two years, Stokes's hearings were dead.

Eighteen months later, Robinson saw the value in testifying. However risky, it provided an opportunity to display his patriotism and erode Du Bois's omnipresent twoness. America was a land split in two: *America* and *Black America*, and here was an opportunity to bridge the distance. Domestically, Robinson understood the racial dynamic could be complicated, but in the case of the Soviets, to him it was not. The communist threat was a threat to the nation, which meant it was a threat to him. Robinson believed he was entitled to a complete interest in his country, even if through discrimination his fellow citizens were responsible for denying him his full share. Rachel Robinson knew her husband well and understood the contradictions gnawing at him. He had been wounded by America, but the United States remained *his* country, still the land of his birth.

A week before the hearings, Robinson received a telegram from Leslie S. Perry, the legislative representative of the NAACP's Washington bureau, urging him to reconsider. The relationship between Robeson and the NAACP may have been frosty, but both held HUAC in disdain, even as Walter White, Thurgood Marshall, and Roy Wilkins aggressively attempted to establish the organization's anticommunism with the FBI. Perry sought clarity from Robinson: Did the committee reach out to him? Was he subpoenaed? Did Robinson, like so many Americans trying to avoid the committee's career-destroying glare, volunteer to appear? The distinctions were critical. If HUAC would brazenly target a figure as prominent as Jackie Robinson, the NAACP needed a forceful response. If Robinson had chosen to speak to the committee on his own, he risked being used by the Committee against his own interests. "As you know, over the years we have been critical of this committee's methods, activities, procedures, personnel and orientation," Perry cabled Robinson. "Would appreciate opportunity (to) consult with you prior to testimony if you decide to come. Please wire collect."

No known surviving correspondence exists between the two men, but it is unlikely Perry and Robinson ever connected, for Branch Rickey and Arthur Mann were orchestrating Robinson's participation.

II

THE JACKIE ROBINSON WHO ACCEPTED Chairman Wood's invitation to appear before HUAC was not the same man who three years earlier had joined the Dodgers farm team in Montreal, doubt affixed to his every gesture, agreeing to Rickey's demand he allow himself to be harmed as a condition of employment because it was his responsibility to future generations of Black people. Debating his prospects, always a euphemism for whether or not he could succeed in the white man's game, was no longer a question. By the end of June 1949, Robinson was hitting .366—best in the National League. He was the National League's top All-Star vote-getter. He became the first Black player to play and start in an All-Star game. Robinson was a superstar unleashing the full suite of his awesome talent.

Concurrently, he was constantly hounded by segregation. Robinson was reminded by Rickey, teammates, and daily insult that these indignities were his burden, absorbing them, his contribution, but the effects mounted and could not be remedied. Segregation had stolen his youth and the effortless beauty that once made him the greatest athlete in the country, and it was that physical beauty, kinetic and temporary, that time treated so mercilessly. Robinson had easily lost 10 years of his professional baseball career, and now the bill was coming due. The price for being a 28-year-old rookie was being a rapidly aging 30-year-old in just his third season.

Everything was simply harder. Weight was a constant issue, a source of ridicule. Following his rookie season, Branch Rickey sent him a scale as a Christmas gift—a reminder to stay motivated, but also exposing a personal vulnerability. To get him in shape, Durocher made him run laps under the merciless Florida sun wearing a rubber sauna suit—"the fat suit," the ballplayers called it—during the spring of 1948. Periodically, Robinson would try to joke about it, but he was very sensitive to being overweight. Earlier that year, *New York Daily Mirror* beat writer Gus Steiger described Robinson in print as "waddling" after a ground ball. The next day, Robinson lashed out at Steiger with obscenities. Embarrassed, Robinson arrived to camp in 1949 eighteen pounds lighter. In a year, he would be diagnosed with Type 2 diabetes.

Quitting had once been a daily thought, but the future depended on his success—or did it? Integrated teams won pennants in both of Robinson's first two seasons, but the rest of the league did not follow.

On Opening Day 1949, only seven Black players had ever played in the league, and six played for either the Dodgers or Cleveland. On June 8, 1948, Dan Dodson of the La Guardia Committee again contacted the Yankees. Larry MacPhail was gone, but George Weiss remained. The persistent investigator told Weiss his failure to integrate was unacceptable. "It would be extremely awkward for this committee . . . to intercede a second time," Dodson wrote, "for it would be difficult to justify your lack of action here in this, the beginning of the fourth year since the demonstration started that Negroes could be integrated into Baseball."

Weiss responded with an attack, dispatching longtime Yankee Stadium superintendent Charley McManus to investigate Dodson. In a memo to Weiss on team letterhead, McManus called Dodson a communist. "He is colored, a teacher at N.Y.U. on sabbatical leave and very much on the pink side." McManus then described Dodson to Weiss as "a louse."

Because it was the white game and he was an unwelcome visitor invited only by Branch Rickey, Robinson agreed to bear the taunts of teammates and competitors. While his forbearance made for great historical theater, it exacted the heaviest toll on the man. When Rickey's arbitrary prohibition expired in 1949, a new chapter commenced: Jackie Robinson as angry Black man. Once he was allowed to confront his tormentors, many of Robinson's allies were no longer sympathetic. They preferred the defenseless martyr. When Robinson complained to the press in 1947 and 1948 about the hostility he faced, he was derided for being soft, crying to the press, unable to handle the rough edges of the real man's game. In 1948, no player had been hit by more pitches than Robinson, a telling but misleading statistic for it did not track the number of times he got out of the way.

When Robinson behaved like an average ballplayer—coarse, competitive, belligerent—the same people who saw him as oversensitive *still* believed he was oversensitive, but now he was too quick to anger, reacting disproportionately to every slight, taking his liberation too far. According to Dodger pitcher Carl Erskine, a Robinson ally and longtime friend, Rickey came to regret granting Robinson the freedom to retaliate. Approaching the subject directly with Robinson at the end of 1949, Rickey told Robinson he was "worried" about his attitude, that he argued too much, and was losing friends for his "tendency to step high"—a euphemism for being "uppity." Rickey would tell Robinson to return to his 1947 approach and accept the abuse without retaliation. This time, Rickey was offering Robinson advice, not delivering a mandate.

During one intersquad scrimmage in early 1949, a rookie named Chris Van Cuyk (brother of Johnny Van Cuyk, whom the Dodgers touted over Robinson in 1947) threw at Robinson's head twice in the same at bat, and the two nearly came to blows. Under normal circumstances, a rookie throwing consecutive beanballs at an established teammate would have produced a serious, in-house rebuke, but the incident was escalated to Happy Chandler's office.

The commissioner issued a lecture-threat, imploring Robinson to be the bigger man; he was too important to be baited by a nobody. (Van Cuyk wouldn't make the team and only played 44 career big-league games.) Robinson inferred Chandler's words differently: the game was free to brutalize him, but only his behavior would be policed. An editorial in *The Sporting News* reinforced his suspicion:

> **THE JACKIE ROBINSON SITUATION**
>
> The Commissioner pointed out to Robinson that he was not just another ballplayer, but that he was the standard bearer for a whole race and that any trouble in which Jackie might become involved would give serious setback to efforts to bring more Negroes into the major leagues.
>
> From the camp of the Dodgers comes word that, having become established as a fixture, with a $20,000 contract, Robinson has forgotten his color and his mission and is showing aggressiveness he hitherto had curbed.

Three weeks before Robinson was scheduled to testify, the Dodgers destroyed the Pirates 15–3 at Forbes Field. Robinson tortured Pittsburgh, getting three hits, including a double, with three runs scored. In the seventh inning, he faced former teammate Hugh Casey, who was already salty the Dodgers had scored ten runs in the inning. Casey threw high and inside. Robinson attempted to bunt. Casey drilled him in the leg on the next pitch. The benches nearly emptied.

There was history. Casey was one of the 1947 Dodgers who initially refused to play with Robinson. In his book *The Era*, Roger Kahn recalled a scene at a poker table. Losing badly, Casey turns to Robinson and says, "Jackie, man! Am I in lousy luck today! Got to change my luck, boy. Back home in Georgia when my poker luck ran bad, Jackie boy, I'd jes go out and rub me the tits of the biggest, blackest nigger woman I could find." With that, Kahn reported, Casey leaned over and rubbed Robinson's head. History would largely forgive these incidents, preferring to emphasize Robinson's unqualified successes and not the effect of absorbing humiliation, lampooning the Hugh Caseys and the everyday racism Robinson suffered as merely cartoonish and unrepresentative of common American attitudes.

III

WHEN WORD THAT ROBINSON PLANNED to testify against Robeson became public, telegrams poured into the Dodgers' offices. On the same day, the NAACP's Leslie Perry cabled Robinson, so too did Mr. and Mrs. John Hester, of 4114 South 25th Street, Omaha, Nebraska. "We are stunned by newspaper announcements you plan to testify before House Un-American Committee criticizing Paul Robeson's fine statement against Jim Crow in America," the telegram read. "We beg of you, don't be a tool of the enemies of first-class citizenship to destroy the unity of the Negro people on this vital issue."

Robinson leaned toward declining the invitation, but he held Branch Rickey in childlike reverence, and the more Rickey convinced him that testifying against Robeson was part of his responsibility, the more Robinson felt he could not say no to the man who gave him his historical importance—and signed his paychecks. Robinson had his own reasons for testifying. Branch Rickey believed racism would be overcome by excellence, but the game still hadn't embraced integration. It hadn't held up its end, but Jackie Robinson was the most recognizable Black face in America, and he felt an obligation to hold up his.

The conflicts persisted: Robinson saw no advantage in being pulled into a geopolitical vortex of which he was not an expert. He was, after all, Jackie Robinson, American inspiration. To the people who supported integration, many of whom revered Paul Robeson also, Robinson's journey had been restorative, not divisive—but Rickey was insistent, believing he had found in Robinson the perfect parry to Robeson.

Rickey was insistent, but Robinson believed deeply in the potential of America, and, like most Americans, saw communism as the enemy. Allowing Robeson's words to go unchecked might increase the difficulty of the journey for Black America. In that spirit, he headed to Washington.

The Hearings Regarding Communist Infiltration of Minority Groups opened Wednesday, July 13, 1949, at 10:30 a.m. in Room 1301, an expansive setting in the New House Office Building, reserved for high profile events that transformed government monotony into grand theater. The day before, at a muddy Ebbets Field, the National League committed five errors and lost the All-Star Game 11–7 to the American League. Seven Dodgers were on the roster, including first-time All-Star Jackie Robinson, who doubled and scored three runs.

Washington, DC, was abuzz, carrying the nervous, anticipatory air of a heavyweight fight. Robinson was scheduled to appear the first day, which explained the grandiosity. Film cameras and photographers lined the broad hallways; Alvin Stokes basked in his big moment. Getting Robinson to testify was a coup for Stokes, the committee, and the entire city. Washington was not part of a National League city, so here was a chance to steal a glimpse of the great Jackie Robinson in person. Advocacy groups, such as the NAACP, now had an opportunity to test the city's rigid segregation laws—and expose their hypocrisy: Robinson in the nation's capital defending the great freedoms afforded all Americans, without a single hotel willing to admit him as a guest.

The grand opening never came. Wood's opening announcement was that Robinson needed to reschedule, with Wood misspeaking by referring to Robinson as "one of the witnesses subpoenaed to appear," when Robinson's acceptance, by all accounts, had been voluntary. That Wood had used the word "subpoena" for Robinson evoked anew Leslie Perry's concern that Robinson had been secretly forced to testify.

Wood granted Robinson's postponement. He would appear Monday, July 18. With his absence, a national event shrank to a mundane exercise in bureaucracy, the drollery of government work and its witnesses, monotony, and endless paper trail of exhibits. Without Robinson's star power, the energy evaporated. Much of the media and the photographers left a cavernous hearing room, exposing a small proceeding. Alvin Stokes's grand opening, for the moment, had fizzled.

Unofficially framed as a loyalty test of Black Americans, the hearing was undercut when General Dwight Eisenhower, the most revered military man in the Western world, unequivocally testified to the loyalty, performance, and professionalism of Black soldiers: ". . . you have an historical record which provides irrefutable proof of the loyalty of our Negro troops," Eisenhower wrote, ending his statement by telling the committee nothing in the postwar years "leads me to believe that our Negro population is not fully as worthy of its American citizenship as it proved itself to be on the battlefields of Europe and Africa."

Alvin Stokes testified first, telling the committee he had given "special attention to Communist attempts to infiltrate, control and dominate Negro organizations and to recruit, capture, and control outstanding Negroes and others for service in the Communist movement." He then failed to report any Black organizations under communist threat, including the NAACP, whose membership included Benjamin Davis, currently on trial at Foley Square for being part of the leadership of the CPUSA, and several high-profile political liberals. Stokes then claimed "one-tenth of one percent of the Negro population" to be members of the Communist Party. Stokes further diminished the urgency that even within that miniscule number, "many of whom I am sure would be found loyal to the United States in a real moment of crisis." For two years Alvin Stokes has positioned himself as the undercover agent who had scoured the country for subversion of Black institutions, only on his grand stage to produce nothing of substance that would survive beyond the next day's newspaper. His golden moment was over.

Unable to deliver the promised threat, only one purpose remained: attack Paul Robeson. The second speaker of the morning, Rabbi Benjamin Schultz, spoke of the communist "conspiracy" of "inciting Jews, Negroes and other groups against America." "The Jackie Robinsons are typical of the Americans of Negro extraction, and the Paul Robesons are not typical," he testified. "We persons of Jewish blood—note I say Jewish blood; no person of Jewish faith has any sympathy with communism—we persons of Jewish blood have our Paul Robesons also, but with us, too, the Jackie Robinsons are in the majority."

Without Robinson, the remainder of the hearings were removed to the cramped and dingy confines of Room 226 in the old House building. As he did in the morning session, Frank Tavenner, the HUAC general counsel, gave way to Stokes as the main interrogator. The first witness of the afternoon session was George Hunton, executive director of the Catholic Interracial Council of New York, who, like Schultz, clearly followed the script of pitting Robinson against Robeson ("In my judgment the hiring of Jackie Robinson improved the racial attitudes of hundreds of thousands of sports lovers in this country") and had much to say about "the commies."

> MR. STOKES: Are you now or have you ever been a member of the Communist Party?

MR. HUNTON: I'm glad you ask that question. Of course I am not, first because I regard myself as a good American, and that would preclude anyone sincerely from becoming a member of the Communist Party.

Black publisher Thomas W. Young repeated Roy Wilkins's May attack on Robeson in *The Crisis* by responding to Ohio Democrat John McSweeney that "Mr. Robeson is now so far out of touch with the Negro's thinking and his everyday emotions that he can no longer speak authoritatively about or for the race."

MR. MCSWEENEY: Do you, as a representative of your people, know of any other country in the world which would recognize the splendid talent of Mr. Robeson more than America, and any country which would compensate that voice more than America?

MR. YOUNG: My experiences are limited. I would not be qualified to say whether or not some other country might, but I will say I think this country has generously recognized his talents and rewarded him for them.

MR. MCSWEENEY: That is all.

It only got worse. Lester Granger, the Black executive director of the Urban League, opened the second day of testimony. Wood was no longer present at the hearings, nor was any other committee member, except McSweeney, who presided.

Granger had long resented Robeson—the two had appeared at events together over the years—and used his testimony to both suggest the afternoon was unnecessary ("Let me make it very clear from the outset that I consider that the extent of Communist influence among our Negro population has been grossly exaggerated, not only by spokesmen for the Communist Party, but also by gullible and fearful protectors of the status quo in politics") and to make clear he considered Robeson merely a pawn.

MR. MCSWEENEY: Were you at the Robeson homecoming rally?

MR. GRANGER: No. I knew what was being said in advance and saved the time.

The most outrageous testimony came on the second day, courtesy of Manning Johnson, a paid federal informant and former Communist Party member in the 1930s. Interrogated by Tavenner, Johnson said communists had planned an "armed insurrection" in the South to create a "Negro republic." Johnson testified that Robeson "wants to be the Black Stalin among Negroes." Johnson told the committee he had not "one iota of doubt" that Robeson was a communist, that it was "regrettable that such a man has sold himself to Moscow," and that Robeson planned to "ride into power on the broken backs of Negro Leaders who are good Americans."

IV

CIVIL RIGHTS ADVOCATES NEVER GOT the chance to discover how Washington hotels would treat Jackie Robinson. On the morning of July 18, the day before her 27th birthday, Rachel flew with Jackie to Washington. Over the weekend, Robinson tormented the Cincinnati Reds, a team that would succumb so completely to communist hysteria, it would change its name from "Reds" to "Redlegs" for five years. Early drafts of Robinson's address to HUAC, co-written by Rickey and Arthur Mann, exist in Mann's donated papers to the Library of Congress, but in no exact sequence. One version could be titled the "I Like It Here" speech. Aspirational in tone, the text leaned on America's boundless potential. ("It was only 85 years ago that slavery was abolished in this country," one passage read, "and ways of life do not change overnight.") The violence against Black citizens and Jim Crow laws and the culture of the South are phrased as mere annoyances. Robinson testifies that racial equality is a national standard:

> I cannot speak for others. I do know that the trend in this country of ours today is toward full and complete equality for all who live in it and love—equality without regard for considerations of race or color. Legally this equality has been a fact for many years. Today, social equality is more than a mere concept.

This version, which appears to be edited in pencil by Rickey, does not mention Paul Robeson, the Soviet Union, or Russia by name. In tone, the draft resembles Truman's inauguration speech from months earlier, espousing the virtues of the United States, casting the American ideal, faults and all, in deep contrast to the world's dictatorships. The final section of the draft reads:

> Whole nations of people in totalitarian lands today are headed toward slavery. We have come a long way from it in the past 85 years. Utopia may still be far off—we may never attain it—but it comes closer as opportunity increases and horizons broaden. I like it here.

Two additional versions followed, both likely collaborations by Mann and Rickey. Neither were satisfactory, especially to Rachel. Jackie Robinson was optimistic about America, but Mann's and Rickey's uncritical prose ran counter to Robinson's life experience, as a civilian, as a soldier—and certainly as a Black man. Robinson would forever be loyal to Rickey, but two white men crafting his comments was unacceptable to Rachel Robinson. For assistance, the couple turned to Lester Granger.

Granger was a familiar figure. A year earlier, in February 1948, Rickey and Robinson received the Urban League's annual Two Friends award, which each year, on President Lincoln's birthday, recognized the impact of interracial cooperation. Jackie, Rachel, and Granger worked on the final draft that was submitted in advance to the committee. The papers would say several members of the Black establishment had a hand in the speech, and Granger would write to Rickey that he was "miffed" he did not receive solo credit for crafting Robinson's remarks. "How small can a group be—or am I stouter than I think!"

Jackie and Rachel arrived in Room 226, Jackie wearing a tan, single-breasted suit, Rachel a dark, professional skirt. He sat at a small rectangular table, alone, a thin microphone before him. In later years, Rachel would say she mouthed the words of his statement silently to herself as her husband spoke, the best proof that she contributed to and approved of his final draft.

The main event had finally arrived. Over the previous two sessions, Robinson had been preceded by Stokes, whose benefactor, J. Parnell Thomas, was heading to federal prison; by Schultz, accused by the New York Board of Rabbis in 1947 of having in his rages against communism used "the smear technique of the scandalmonger, a technique entirely inappropriate for a rabbi"; by Granger, a Robeson nemesis; and by Manning Johnson, the paid informant who in later years would admit to lying under oath, often proudly, to criticize the NAACP for "going too far" in its pursuit of integration, and, eventually, be discredited by the FBI.

Apart from the moderate Granger, the week showcased demagoguery recast as patriotism—and now Jackie Robinson, at the behest of Branch Rickey, had joined their association. When he testified, Granger framed Robinson's dilemma as much as his own. "Authentic Negro leadership finds itself confronted by two enemies on opposite sides," Granger told the committee. "One enemy is the Communist who seeks to destroy the democratic ideal and practice which constitute the Negro's sole hope of eventual victory in his fight for equal citizenship. The other enemy is that American racist who perverts and corrupts the democratic concept into a debased philosophy of life. In opposing one enemy, Negro leadership must be careful not to give aid and comfort to the other."

Robinson adjusted his notes before him into a small stack. The Democrat Burr P. Harrison, descendant of one of the leading members of the Virginia slaveholding aristocracy dating back to before the Revolutionary War, presided over the hearing in place of Chairman Wood, who was absent with the flu. Like Wood, Harrison was a leading segregationist who publicly opposed anti-lynching legislation and school integration.

Unlike the previous witnesses, Robinson made clear he was an unenthusiastic participant who had been urged to refuse the invitation to appear. ("And so it isn't very pleasant for me to find myself in the middle of a public argument that has nothing to do with the standing of the Brooklyn Dodgers in the pennant race—or even the pay raise I am going to ask Mr. Branch Rickey for next year!")

"So you'll naturally ask, why did I stick my neck out by agreeing to be present, and why did I stand by my agreement in spite of advice to the contrary," he said. "It isn't easy to find the answer, but I guess it boils down to a sense of responsibility."

Robinson differentiated himself from the previous witnesses, Granger included, by not searching for a fertile space to grovel before the committee, but to tell it communism was not the primary obstruction in Black American life:

> The white public should start toward real understanding by appreciating that every single Negro who is worth his salt is going to resent any kind of slurs and discrimination because of his race, and he is going to use every bit of intelligence such as he has to stop it. This has got absolutely nothing to do with what Communists may or may not be trying to do. And white people must realize that the more a Negro hates communism because it opposes democracy, the more he is going to hate any influence that kills off democracy in this country—and that goes for racial discrimination in the Army, and segregation on trains and buses, and job discrimination because of religious beliefs or color or place of birth.
>
> And one other thing the American public ought to understand, if we are to make progress in this matter: The fact that it is a Communist who denounces injustice in the courts, police brutality and lynching when

> it happens doesn't change the truth of his charges. Just because Communists kick up a big fuss over racial discrimination when it suits their purposes, a lot of people try to pretend that the whole issue is a creation of the Communist imagination. But they are not fooling anyone with this kind of pretense, and talk about "Communists stirring up Negroes to protest," only makes present misunderstanding worse than ever. Negroes were stirred up long before there was a Communist Party, and they'll stay stirred up long after the party has disappeared—unless Jim Crow has disappeared by then as well.

Robinson's critique, exceeding Granger's own testimony, confirmed that he and Rachel had taken ownership of the speech. Granger may have been in collaboration, but he did not write Robinson's words for him. If there was a signature of Granger's handiwork in Robinson's testimony, it could be found when Robinson finally addressed Robeson directly:

> I've been asked to express my views on Paul Robeson's statement in Paris to the effect that American Negroes would refuse to fight in any war against Russia because we love Russia so much. I haven't any comment to make on that statement except that if Mr. Robeson actually made it, it sounds very silly to me. But he has a right to his personal views, and if he wants to sound silly when he expresses them in public, that's his business and not mine. He's still a famous ex-athlete and a great singer and actor.
>
> I can't speak for any 15,000,000 people any more than any other one person can, but I know I've got too much invested for my wife and child in the future of this country, and I and other Americans of many races and faith have too much invested in our country's welfare, for any of us to throw it away because of a siren song sung in bass . . . We can win our fight without the Communists and we don't want their help.

Throughout his drafts, including the final one, Robinson largely avoided direct discussion of Robeson. The committee called on Robinson to testify for the raw meat of an attack, words the *Congressional Record* and the newspapermen could spread across the country and give the hearing purpose. Robinson had not exactly cooperated, using virtually the entirety of his prepared statement to indict the American racial order that stood in existence long before Robeson arrived in Paris, an order that had shaped Robeson long before the Communist Party existed and before Jackie Robinson was born.

Robinson brought a rare skepticism to the controversy, being one of the few critics to question the veracity of his Paris statement. His attack on Robeson ("a siren song sung in bass") sounded more like the words of an adversary than from Robinson, who had not previously said a negative word publicly about Robeson before the hearings. The battle between Robeson and Black leadership, however, preexisted and would continue into the next decade.

Robinson took questions from the committee and headed to National Airport, but not before photographers snapped photos of him and Rachel walking along Pennsylvania Avenue, which seven months earlier served as part of Truman's inauguration route. On his arrival back in New York, Robinson resumed his role as the best player in baseball with a triple, a run scored, a walk, an RBI, and two stolen bases in a 3–0 shutout of the Cubs.

Jackie Robinson had defended America, but which America had he protected? While virtually all of the national coverage reprinted his "siren song sung in bass" dig at Robeson and another at the communists ("We can win our fight without the Communists and we don't want their help"), his criticisms of police brutality, lynching, and the lack of due process in the court system, basically his critique of the American system, did not make the morning editions.

The day after, New York Republican Pat Kearney, a veteran of both world wars, immediately recommended Robinson for the VFW's gold medal for "Good Citizenship," but only because he stood up against Robeson. The most recognizable Black man in America had publicly denounced Robeson, which signaled to the rest of America that Paul Robeson would not be protected by the Black establishment. Kearney told the Associated Press that Robinson had proven he was a "good American . . . compared to statements of another member of his race."

For three days, Paul Robeson was the subject of a hearing he did not attend and was not subpoenaed to attend. He had not provoked nor pursued a confrontation with Robinson, stating publicly and privately he had no quarrel with Robinson. Robeson would often say he felt sorry for Robinson, who was clearly conflicted, obligated to Branch Rickey and the mounting societal weight to stand against communism—understood by most Americans to be mankind's greatest threat. Robeson had already been affected by the darkening shift of the country directly. When he quipped to the fur workers union during the Wallace campaign a year earlier that his politics had cost him his career, it was more than a clever remark to rouse the crowd, but a reference to a grim conversation with Bob Rockmore, his manager, who told him his concert appearances, record contracts, and other business offers had nearly dried up completely, voided long before Robinson arrived in Washington.

Robinson was not the catalyst for Robeson's market toxicity, but his testimony energized Robeson's enemies. Jackie Robinson enamored himself with the nation's most extreme anticommunist factions, such as the VFW and American Legion, who saw themselves on the front lines of a domestic war. After he and Rachel left Washington, Jackie returned to a pennant race, unaware of the legal and extralegal violence his testimony was about to unleash.

Chapter Nine

I

IN THE DAYS AND WEEKS following his takedown of Robeson, Jackie Robinson was lauded as a national hero. Eleanor Roosevelt praised him and the committee while distancing herself from Robeson, a man she once greatly admired. A photographer from *Life* magazine arrived in Queens and took portraits of the Robinsons—Jackie, Rachel, and nearly three-year-old Jackie Jr.—sitting on the front stoop of their home as part of an impromptu photo shoot buttressing Jackie's all-American credentials: the ballplayer as patriot and family man in his new house on a tree-lined, integrated street.

The Hartford Courant urged readers curious about "what Americanism is" to read Robinson's testimony "verbatim." A Kentucky newspaper editorial lamented Robeson's bitterness because "his achievements in art and athletics did not bring with them immediate and complete social acceptance," while commending Robinson for confronting his country's shortcomings with optimism, choosing "to look at the positive rather than the negative side of the American race picture." There was even talk a movie on Robinson's life might be in the works.

Lester Granger moved quickly to assuage any fears Robinson's testimony had been a terrible mistake. The day after, Granger typed on makeshift National Urban League stationery a two-page letter congratulating Robinson. Addressed "Dear Robbie," Granger wrote,

> *Together with hundreds of thousands of other Americans in New York and throughout the country, I was inordinately proud when I picked up the papers last night and this morning and read the reports of your appearance before the House Committee on Un-American Activities. I don't need to tell you what impression you made on the public generally.*

Granger wrote that Robinson "stated the case for the American Negro in such a way as to send it around the world in quarters where no other such expression would have received any notice at all. This should be a matter of great pride to you and your wife, even while you realize that there will be sharp criticism and some under-hand attacks coming from left-wing or uninformed sources." Confirming Robinson's overwhelming support, Granger told Robinson he "circulated for five hours among bars and grills, sidewalk groups and neighbors and friends. It was remarkable that in not one single case did I receive from any person to whom I talked anything but praise for the way you expressed yourself."

In a simplistic attempt to contrast the two men, a July 20 *Minneapolis Star Tribune* editorial titled "Jackie Robinson Speaks" described Robeson as a man who "does not think much of his country," and Robinson as one who "burns with a sense of indignation over the injustices which unthinking Americans heap upon his race. But Robinson feels a profound sense of loyalty to his country." The paper concluded, "When Robeson looks at the American doughnut, he sees only the hole of prejudice and discrimination. When Robinson looks at it, he perceives not only the hole, which he thoroughly despises, and the encircling substance which he greatly respects. That substance is America's heritage of freedom and opportunity, and more and more the Negro is possessing it. Jackie Robinson knows this. Paul Robeson chooses to ignore it. That is why Robinson retains an abiding faith in the American system, while Robeson, blind to the progress of his race, turns in bitterness toward Russia."

• • •

The same day, the Robeson-led Council of African Affairs (already deemed subversive by the attorney general's office) issued a press release indirectly referencing Jackie Robinson, which in part read,

> The loyalty of the Negro people is not a subject for debate. I challenge the loyalty of the Un-American Activities Committee. This committee maintains an ominous silence in the face of the lynchings of Maceo Snipes, Robert Mallard, the two Negro veterans and their wives in Monroe, Georgia, and the violent and unpunished murders of scores of Negro veterans by white supremacists since V-J Day . . . To destroy this threat our people need the aid of every honest American, Communist and non-Communist alike. Those who menace our lives proceed unchallenged by the Un-American Activities Committee. I shall not be drawn into any conflict dividing me from my brother victim of this terror.

The release referred to the murder of two Black men in Wood's home state of Georgia: the 1946 murder of Snipes, a Black World War II veteran shot twice in the back in Taylor County for voting in the 1946 Democratic primary election, and Mallard, killed in Toombs County after ignoring local warnings against voting in the 1948 Presidential election. Edward Williamson, member of the Ku Klux Klan, was acquitted after claiming he shot Snipes twice in the back in self-defense, while Mallard and his wife, Amy, were surrounded in their car by more than a dozen hooded Klansmen. On November 20, 1948, Mallard was shot and killed by a bullet fired through his driver's side window. One newspaper reported the general sentiment in Toombs County was that Mallard "must have asked for it." An all-white, all-male jury acquitted the men indicted for Mallard's killing in less than 25 minutes.

Amid Robinson's cross-country applause, Robeson had remained quiet—just as he had in the month leading up to Robinson's testimony. He resurfaced two days after the hearings, calling a press conference at the Hotel Theresa. The *Daily Worker* appeared, as did the Black *New York*

Age and *Baltimore Afro-American*. No mainstream, white press outlets attended.

He spoke for two hours. He had never contacted Robinson to persuade him from testifying, he said. Nor, he said, did he desire to be a "Black Stalin," as the professional informant Johnson accused. "All I want to do is sing and act." Robeson said the Associated Press quoted him inaccurately in Paris. "The statement I made before the Paris Peace Conference has been distorted. I am not interested in war, but in peace, and here's what I said at the conference: It is unthinkable that the Negro people could be lured into any kind of war especially against the Soviet Union, where former colonial people have complete equality . . . If we were to go to war today, we'd be fighting for . . . that one percent of America that exploits the other ninety-nine percent."

Robeson alternated between coy and restrained, contained and antagonized. He jousted with the writers, aware of their intention to goad him into attacking Robinson ("I am not going to permit the issue to boil down to a personal feud between Jackie and me. To do that would be to do exactly what the other group wants us to do. Let's not fall for anything like that."), but nor did he allow the moment to pass. Robinson's appearance must, he said, be seen in the context of what HUAC had been for the eleven years of its existence, and which Americans HUAC—and by extension Jackie Robinson—was ultimately serving. Robinson's utility was neither vexing nor complicated to Paul Robeson: Robinson had allowed himself to be manipulated by some of the most fervid anti-Black, right-wing entities in the country.

If Lester Granger believed Black support of Robinson to be unanimous, he was not reading the *Baltimore Afro-American*. Two days before Robinson's testimony, the newspaper published the most severe admonishment of Robinson titled, "Drop That Gun, Jackie," which levied two criticisms at Robinson. The first warned Robinson he was letting himself be a pawn. The second was even more pointed: He was just a ballplayer who was out of his league on the subject matter.

DROP THAT GUN, JACKIE

Jackie Robinson says he is going to Washington to appear before the House Un-American Activities Committee this week. He has been invited to call Paul Robeson a "liar."

Yes, we know Jackie will fight. He fought in the last war and is a good American.

And so is Paul Robeson a good American and despite the fact that Jackie is one of the finest athletes in the nation, he cannot begin to fill Paul Robeson's shoes.

When Jackie Robinson talks about the things he has gained, he is thinking about himself.

When Paul Robeson said he is not willing to fight against Russia, he is not thinking about himself. He is not thinking about Russia.

He is thinking about millions of colored people in the South who can't vote, who are terrorized by mobs at the least provocation, and cannot get a decent job or decent education.

Our advice to Jackie Robinson, as much as we admire him, is that he put away his pop gun and put on his baseball uniform. He is more a credit to us as a baseball player than a politician.

Accompanying the editorial was a cartoon depicting him as an unworthy novice on the trail of a great prey. Tracking enormous footprints that read "Paul Robeson," the caption beneath an overmatched, adolescent-looking Robinson carrying a rifle twice his size read, "The leading player in the National League is only a tyro as a big-game hunter."

In his remarks at the Theresa, Robeson stated that Robinson had done a "disservice" to Black people, "because it helped the Un-American Committee." "It should be clear that Robinson, by appearing before this committee, has performed a profound political act that has aided those who would enslave the Negro. He erred too in stating to this committee that the Negro didn't need the help of the Communists.

The Negro needs the help of all—Communist and non-Communist. But it does not need the aid of a man who once called the Ku Klux Klan an American institution."*

II

SATURDAY, AUGUST 27, 1949. Still feted as a national hero, Robinson would again share the headlines with Robeson. Dan Burley of *The New York Age* reported a bombshell: Branch Rickey was actively trying to trade Jackie Robinson.

> **JACKIE OUT, SAM IN FOR BROOKS??**
>
> Branch Rickey of the Brooklyn Dodgers has his ears wide open for the best offer for his star second baseman, Jackie Robinson, the New Age learned exclusively this week following a highly secret meeting of some 40 representatives, Negro and white, called to "talk this thing over."

The "highly secretive" meeting found its way into the newspaper, and the details were as stunning and revealing as Rickey's 1947 conclave when he offended Black community leaders with his broadside before Robinson had even played his first game. This time it was more of the same: Rickey accusing the "lower classes" of Black fans of "whiskey drinking" and "foul language" at Ebbets Field and an even more uncomfortable revelation: Rickey, who often referred to himself as "color-blind," believed he needed to make a move because the Dodgers risked being "too Black," a move that might include trading Robinson. According to the *Age*, Rickey feared the Dodgers had reached a "saturation point" of Black players, where, the newspaper reported, "associate

* Robeson was referring to committee chair John S. Wood, but the quote is actually attributed to Congressman John Rankin, the proudly segregationist Mississippi Democrat.

club owners might accuse him of maintaining an 'Uncle Tom's Cabin' at Ebbets Field."

Rickey, who told the public Robinson would be treated on merit, privately told the group he could not pay Robinson more than twice the salary of his highest-paid white player, "no matter how great a star he turned out to be."

Rickey's thought was to trade Robinson to make room for Sam Jethroe, the former Negro League player tearing up the International League for Montreal, as Robinson once did. Robinson and Jethroe were two-thirds of the trio that infamously worked out in 1945 for the Red Sox.

That Rickey would consider trading Robinson, who at the time was the favorite for the National League MVP, was illustrative of his cold viewpoint toward players, even Robinson, and, given Robinson's deference toward Rickey, underscored the power imbalance that existed between the two men regardless of the warmth of their personal relationship. For his entire life, Robinson would always refer to Rickey as "Mister Rickey."

No other papers picked up the story, but it did result in a move. Jethroe was sold to the Boston Braves, where he would win National League Rookie of the Year the next year. Robinson, already disappointed by the slow process of integration, received yet another glimpse into the mindset of the Lords—and into that of Rickey, whose disdain for Black customers was a constant. The league did not have many Black players because they did not want them, and Rickey would only sign the best players, but only to the point of maintaining a white hierarchy.

Sharing the headlines with Robinson that Saturday morning was Robeson, who headed to a fundraising concert in Peekskill, New York, a former Underground Railroad stop that had traditionally been friendly territory. Roughly 35 miles north of Manhattan in Westchester County, Peekskill was a summer enclave of camps and bungalows for working-class Jews and union members since the 1920s. Robeson appeared in a Hudson Valley town in each of the previous three years before large and appreciative crowds.

As Helen Rosen, one of Robeson's closest confidants, described it, 1949 was the year Robeson became "notorious." Peekskill reflected a schism common to many vacation towns that dotted America: populated seasonally by big city political progressives, while the year-round residents leaned far more conservative. The VFW and American Legion had been targeting Robeson since the end of the war, and largely inflamed by the local paper, the Peekskill *Evening Star*, word of his appearance put the entire town on high alert to his presence.

The concert was sponsored by the People's Artists Committee, a left-wing music collective whose members included the folk singer Pete Seeger, who was also scheduled to appear. The proceeds went to the Harlem branch of the Civil Rights Congress, another of Robeson's organizations deemed subversive by the Justice Department. As the date approached, rumors of violence intensified. The local American Legion and VFW posts organized a parade of 500, with a convoy of cars, to disrupt the concert site. During the week, the *Evening Star* stoked the locals.

Robeson's presence alone did not account for the heightened tensions. Three days before the concert was to be held, the USSR announced it had successfully exploded an atomic bomb. The four-year nuclear weapons monopoly the Americans held since the end of the war was over. Communists were taking power in China, and now the United States was no longer the world's sole nuclear power. "Chapter by chapter with the atomic bomb, the Soviet Union has almost everything in the military field that the United States has. The pace of the Soviet atomic armament has been amazing," reported the *Buffalo News*. "The change in the structure of Soviet military power is, of course, of tremendous importance. For years, Russian land power, the army, had to make up for the Russians' lack of the atomic bomb. Now, the Soviet Union has both, the strongest land power, and the atomic bomb."

Robeson arrived in Peekskill from Grand Central Station the day of the concert and had heard enough to anticipate trouble. Helen Rosen and her son John met Robeson at the train station along with Syd Danis, a union organizer, as added protection.

As the two-car convoy crested the ridge, protesters had already ringed the concert site. Near the stage, a burning cross illuminated the evening sky. The parade of veterans had reached the picnic ground, and picketers had attacked the concert site. Some protesters threw chairs on the stage; piles of lawn chairs were set afire. Others overturned cars. At least one vehicle blocked the road, backing up traffic and allowing rioters to pull concertgoers out of their cars. Newspapers reported 13 concertgoers injured, including one stabbed and in critical condition. "I hardly knew my way to the concert grounds and certainly the others didn't either, but as we approached closer and closer, you could hear the shouting and the noise and some screaming," Helen Rosen recalled. "And as we got even closer, we saw broken glass on the way. There were these women in summer dresses lined up with children and piles of stones, which they were throwing at us."

Robeson never reached the stage, which had been destroyed by rioters before the concert had begun. Helen Rosen and her son John, along with Danis (and Robeson in the back seat) managed to drive out of the grounds without being harmed. At a bridge near the picnic grove, protesters met another round of concertgoers, pelting them with rocks and sticks as they attempted to flee the scene. No one was arrested.

3-HOUR RIOT RAGES AT PAUL ROBESON CONCERT

13 STABBED AND CLUBBED IN OUTBREAK

PEEKSKILL, N.Y., AUG. 27

Marching veterans battled a Paul Robeson concert crowd in a fierce three-hour riot tonight and at least 13 people were reported beaten, stabbed, or bruised.

The heated battle broke out when a parade sponsored by Veterans groups clashed head-on with concert-goers on a dirt road outside a wooded picnic grove where the Negro singer was scheduled to perform.

The injured, Peekskill Hospital reported, were beaten with "rocks, clubs—anything they could get their hands on."

"Our objective was to prevent the Paul Robeson concert and I think our objective was reached," Milton Flynt, commander of the Peekskill Post of the American Legion explained to reporters. "Anything that took place after the organized demonstration took place was entirely up to individual citizens and cannot be blamed on the patriotic organizations."

Days later, at the urging of the author Howard Fast, Helen Rosen and her husband, the noted surgeon Dr. Sam Rosen, opened their vacation home in nearby Katonah to outraged Robeson supporters, who formed The Emergency Committee to Protest the Peekskill Riot. The committee accused the local authorities of negligence in failing to protect the concertgoers and called on New York Governor Thomas Dewey, to investigate who initially declined to do. Representative Vito Marcantonio, the same Marcantonio who years earlier had pressed Landis to integrate before Robeson addressed the Lords, accused law enforcement officials of willful negligence. The committee told reporters that concert organizers had requested police protection days in advance and were assured the concert would receive a police presence. When the riot began at approximately 7:30 p.m., organizers said only two police officers were present, and no assistance arrived until roughly 10 p.m., leaving concertgoers exposed to violence for two and a half hours. After a night of deliberation, frustration, and anger, the committee agreed to hold a second concert for Robeson in Peekskill a week later. Robeson, in New York at the time, did not need convincing. He had resolved to return to Peekskill—the athlete in him defiantly rising to challenge.

Peekskill was becoming a national referendum. For years the country's mood had grown increasingly anti-communist as an economic philosophy. With the United States and the Soviet Union having the bomb, tensions were high. The attacks in Peekskill added the element of physical violence. Americans, increasingly conditioned to distrust one another, were being encouraged to mob violence.

For someone perceived as anti-American, Robeson believed in American principles and willfully placed himself in danger. Instead of hating his country, he demanded to be protected as an American in a just society, which led him to believe he could return to Peekskill.

His defiance was often received as a combination of arrogance and naivete, arrogance in his belief that he was somehow immune to the powerful international forces that were shaping the world around him and naivete in his romantic view of class struggles. Around the country, *naivete* was a word affixed to so many Americans who said they had once believed in the communist experiment. On June 15, 1949, a month before Jackie Robinson's testimony, Frank Oppenheimer, brother of the famed nuclear physicist J. Robert Oppenheimer, appeared before the HUAC and testified to Chairman Wood that he had been a member of the Communist Party in 1937, but he always remained loyal to the United States. "The contention here," according to a Midwestern newspaper editorial a day after Oppenheimer's testimony, "is that it utterly is impossible for a native American to be a communist and at the same time be loyal to his country."

In the *Daily Mirror*'s August 29 coverage of the Peekskill riots, the paper informed its readers that Robeson had "asked for it." On August 30, back in New York, Robeson appeared before an overflowing crowd of 3,000 at the Golden Gate Ballroom in Harlem to confront the line of attack most insulting to him: the questioning of his commitment to Black people. Robeson had agreed to a series of interviews with Dan Burley of *The New York Age*, where he would circle back to the same theme. "I'm in the headlines and they're saying all manner of things about me such as 'enemy' of the land of my birth, 'traitor' to my country, 'dangerous radical' and that I am an 'ungrateful' cur. But they can never say that I am not 100 percent for my people." While onstage with Ben Davis and Vito Marcantonio, Robeson addressed the crowd at the Golden Gate Ballroom. Robeson looked backward, connecting to the historical lineage of Black American protest in the tradition of figures like Frederick Douglass and Harriet Tubman. This was evident when *Othello* opened in Cambridge and the NAACP attacked him following his remarks in Paris. Robeson shaped the Black dilemma in diasporic terms: while Jackie Robinson criticized him at the behest of American legislators, Robeson saw Black people around the world—in Africa, the Caribbean, and South America—suffering under the same global disenfranchisement as Black people in the United States.

The second Peekskill concert was set for Sunday, September 4, at the Old Hollow Brook Country Club, a defunct golf course of sloping fairways pockmarked by sand traps that was located four miles outside of town. United Press International set the stage days before the concert with a story headlined, "ROBESON TO SEE FLAGS," reporting that war veterans invited fellow vets from five states to arrive and "wave thousands of American flags in Paul Robeson's face." Westchester County mobilized its entire police force to the golf course and the route out, some 700 officers. Robeson assembled his own security team, an interracial cadre of burly union men, standing arm in arm to protect the stage. At the Golden Gate Ballroom, Robeson said the audience attendees would defend themselves if the police would not, which was interpreted by the press and Westchester County law enforcement as a threat: Robeson was returning for a fight. The morning of the concert, buses lined up in Manhattan to transport concertgoers, who brought piles of baseball bats for protection, to Peekskill. Reporters were told by several people boarding the buses that they were heading north to Peekskill to "go fishing." The *New York Daily News* estimated the concert crowd to reach 15,000. The newspaper referred to attendees as "Robesonites."

That morning, a four-paragraph story appeared quietly in the *Daily Worker* under the headline "Jackie Blasts Mob Attack," in which Robinson clearly recognized the pattern of organized violence in Peekskill resembled a racial attack more than a political one. "I think those rioters ought to be investigated and let's find out if what they did is supposed to be the democratic way."

"The Star-Spangled Banner" played at 2 p.m. Pete Seeger sang. The concert was interrupted by periodic jeering. Sticks and rocks were thrown onstage as Robeson performed, while members of the American Legion and VFW and other protesters attempted to drown out Robeson's singing with chants of their own. Robeson sang "Go Down Moses" and "Song of the Warsaw Ghetto." At roughly 3:30 p.m., the concert ended with Robeson's classic rendition of "Ol' Man River." Robeson was placed into one of several cars whose passenger windows were covered with blankets.

During the first incident, the veterans prevented the concert from happening. This time, they transformed the golf course into a trap. As the buses began heading toward the long, narrow one-way strips of road leading out of the grounds, protesters began stoning the exiting vehicles, pulling concertgoers out of their cars when possible. The performers and concertgoers were allowed to attend, but not allowed to leave.

Rioters scoured the stuck cars, looking for Robeson. Robeson, although eager to confront the mob, was urged by his security detail to lie flat on the car floor, covered by a blanket. Protesters eventually discovered his car, but they could not pull Robeson out of it, so they settled for stoning the front windshield. *The California Eagle* reported a police officer used his baton on Robeson's windshield and shouts of "Lynch the big, black niggar" [*sic*] could be heard from a CBS broadcast recording of the disturbance. According to witnesses, the police watched impassively as rioters stoned the stationary automobiles.

The next day, an 80-point headline screamed across six columns of the *Detroit Free Press*:

THE SECOND BATTLE OF PEEKSKILL

ROBESON RIOT HURTS 60

ROCKS RAIN INTO CROWD AT CONCERT

3,500 VETERANS AT ANTI-RED OUTBURST

PEEKSKILL, NY (U.P.)—At least 60 persons were injured Sunday when anti-Communist demonstrators attacked cars and buses leaving a concert by Paul Robeson, Negro baritone and advocate of Communism.

A barrage of stones and pop bottles greeted the 12,000 to 15,000 Robeson supporters when they drove away from the scene of the concert, an abandoned golf course outside Peekskill, about 40 miles north of New York City.

III

PEEKSKILL BECAME A ONE-WORD SYMBOL of resistance against the perceived communist menace, the good Americans standing up for American values, and the collective acceptance of violence as a tool to suppress dissent. Helen Rosen would remember being called "nigger lover," "dirty commie," and "dirty Jew" during the attacks. "I really had no notion of it. I didn't know that there was that kind of organization in a small, dusty town like that," she said later. "I knew about the Birchers. I certainly knew about the Klan, but I didn't realize that it would be unleashed in so furious and personal a way, and we were very worried about Paul's safety at that point."

Neighbor was now pitted against neighbor. The seven-month combination of Truman's inauguration address, Robinson's testimony, and the USSR detonating an atomic bomb convinced veterans they were protecting the country from internal subversion, even if it meant attacking fellow Americans. In storefront windows, makeshift signs, and newspaper editorials alike came a refrain that symbolized the new

American conscience from the tiny hamlet that even found its way on to bumper stickers: "Wake Up, America. Peekskill did!"

Did Robeson believe the crowd would kill him? Over the years, he would speak affirmatively about his life being in danger, but, like many Americans, Robeson often believed life-threatening lawlessness was relegated to the Jim Crow South. It is unlikely he believed he would be murdered in Peekskill, New York, 40 minutes from Harlem. He had entrusted his safety to the New York State police and local officials. Following the riot, Robeson now reminded reporters that violence knew no region.

The front page of the September 7, 1949, issue of the *York Daily Record*, featured a photograph from Peekskill of Eugene Bullard, the son of Georgia slaves who had served in World War I. In the photo, a bloodied Bullard balances on one knee, struggling to his feet. Bullard fought in both world wars, part of the storied legacy of African Americans who fought under the French flag in the Great War because white Americans refused to fight alongside their Black countrymen. Heavily decorated after his French service, Bullard would fight in World War II for France after the 1940 German invasion. For his bravery and wartime service, Bullard would be knighted by the French government, but in Peekskill, in the country of his birth, Bullard lay bleeding on the ground while the riotous group of veterans, the New York State Police, and local Westchester County law enforcement stood over him watching. Though the NAACP petitioned Governor Dewey to investigate—and, in a rare moment of support, Robeson nemesis Roy Wilkins condemned the attack—Robeson's association with Peekskill reduced the outrage the Black press showed for the violence and for the Black attendees beaten at both sites.

Robeson used his energy to address the indifference to violence against Black Americans, predicting the coming of state-condoned mob lawlessness. Rule of law was breaking down, he said, but for Black people, it was merely a continuation of the lynching and extralegal tactics already being inflicted on them. "Where will be the next Peekskill?" he asked rhetorically in an interview with *The New York Age*. Four days after the second concert, 150 white residents in Los Angeles attacked two white families who had sold homes to Black buyers. Dueling letters to the editor in a New Jersey newspaper illustrated the national schism. "You no longer have the confidence and respect of the patriotic people of this country . . . Have a care, Paul. If you should realize your wish and live in Russia, you would lose your freedom to criticize and to make disparaging observations," wrote a reader from Robeson's hometown of Westfield. Another reader took the counter position. "In the Army . . . we were taught that fascists in America, in order to gain power, start first on the Communist, and call everyone who opposes them a Red. They then proceed to persecute minorities, be it political, national, or religious . . . They do in the name of democracy, with the American flag draped over them."

Three days after the second concert, a preliminary report of Dewey's official inquiry by Westchester Country District Attorney George Fanelli concluded there "was absolutely no police brutality" committed by law enforcement. The report acknowledged 200 injured and seven overturned cars was the byproduct of local teenagers agitated by Robeson, not the veteran's groups who had promised in advance to disrupt the concert. The conclusion of the report—and an ensuing grand jury investigation—was that law enforcement was to be commended for showing restraint against communist agitation. Robeson filed a $2 million lawsuit against Fanelli, Westchester County Sheriff Fred Rusco, and two veterans groups.

When Robeson addressed Landis in 1943, he preemptively admonished the owners against attempting to pit him against Black publishers. Their struggle was his, he told the Lords. Less than six years later, with America unleashing itself against him, he remained on the offensive, but much of the Black newspaper establishment felt he only had himself to blame. A scathing, nearly full-page column in *The Future Outlook*, a Black newspaper out of Greensboro, North Carolina, appeared the same day as Fanelli's report. "Any person of his stature and notoriety who goes around and makes the remarks that he has, and even goes as far as to denounce his own country to the point of even going to war on the side of Russia, deserves to get the licking of his life. Paul Robeson, through the blessing of God, was endowed with one of the greatest singing voices in the world . . . So what does Paul do? He gets lined up with the commies and voice, or no voice, Paul is now one of the most hated men in this country."

The Black Dispatch, a Black newspaper based in Oklahoma, reflected a common pattern of support: in contrast to the established *Chicago Defender* and *Pittsburgh Courier*, many smaller, less-affluent outlets did not pander to the times and abandon Robeson. "Paul Robeson is an indictment of the American pattern of living," the paper stated in an editorial published six days after the second Peekskill riot. "His presence here in America is evidence that our prated democracy is a sham and a pretense. Instead of attempting to set Paul Robeson in order, we should be doing some basic work on the house and the environment in which he lives."

Legendary folk singer Pete Seeger's most haunting memory about the second Peekskill concert was the throng of adults, all white and grim-faced, standing next to waist-high pyramids of stones. Some of the piles were as tall as the grade-school children standing next to them. The mob sprang into action—mothers, fathers, and children—adult and little arms hurling the rocks at cars exiting the grounds. The protesters attacked, Seeger observed, with the approval of the state and local police who were on-site presumably to maintain order. "When my wife and I got home, we rinsed the broken glass out of the heads of our babies," he said. "Inside the car we found two rocks which had come through the glass. I later cemented them into our fireplace." Seeger rejected the premise that good, upstanding locals peacefully opposed Robeson, while a few roughnecks got out of hand. Given the chance, Seeger believed, Paul Robeson's countrymen in that picturesque little town would have killed him.

A burning cross awaited Robeson when he arrived for the first concert. Two effigies of Robeson—one hanging by a noose—were burned in Peekskill during the second concert. At the second Peekskill riots, war hero Eugene Bullard was beaten while law enforcement watched, and the loudest, most influential Black voices in the nation remained largely silent about both incidents.

The California Eagle was an exception. In a prescient editorial, Charlotta Bass stated what Black leadership refused to acknowledge because of its fear of being associated with Communism: Cross burning was a tactic to terrorize Black people, not a traditional response to communism. "Robeson being the only Negro not afraid to speak out against what he and all know are undemocratic practices against Negroes such as segregation, discrimination and the full enjoyment of civil rights, becomes the target. It's Robeson today. It could be Jackie Robinson or Walter White tomorrow."

Chapter Ten

I

THERE WAS NO ANNOUNCEMENT ROBESON'S world had shifted, just as there had been no warning when he destroyed the Naval Reserves that day at Ebbets Field, alerting the sports world he was a new force. It just simply began happening: Paul Robeson's name, once ubiquitous, started disappearing. In New Brunswick, where he was his school's most famous alumnus, Robeson's name could not easily be found within the pages of the Rutgers record books. Walter Camp's legendary All-America Teams in 1917 and 1918, featuring Robeson, now listed ten-man teams. The nascent College Football Hall of Fame—ironically located on the Rutgers campus—intentionally omitted his name from the nominating process. The chairman, *Boston Herald* columnist Bill Cunningham, said Robeson was ineligible because of his "communist affiliations," and thus did not "measure up in carrying his weight in life."

Each new component of his erasure quietly formed a new, disturbing whole. Plateau Hall, the magnificent concert hall in Montreal where Robeson was performing when news broke of Jackie Robinson's signing, no longer listed him as one of its notable past performers. In 1951, the *Amsterdam News* listed the recent winners of the NAACP's Spingarn Medal, except for 1945—the year Robeson won it. That same year, sportswriter Christy Walsh published a mammoth history of the top college football players from 1890 to 1950. The book, *College Football and All-America Review*, boasted on its cover "Scores of 72,061 games. More than 100,000 Lettermen. 514 All-Americans." Walter Camp once called Robeson the greatest football player he'd ever seen, but Robeson was erased from the book.

In 1952, 1954, and 1955, the legendary poet Langston Hughes, himself under attack by HUAC and anticommunist forces, sacrificed Robeson to save himself, removing Robeson's name from three of his popular children's volumes on influential Black Americans. Hughes biographer Arnold Rampersad later wrote of the poet's contribution to the erasure of Paul Robeson: "In his books, to preserve his career and certain sources of income, he had compromised his principles in a way that would distress many of his friends and admirers."

In 1993, the Pulitzer Prize–winning historian and journalist David Halberstam published the bestselling book *The Fifties*, a sweeping, 800-page history of the pivotal decade. From the rise of the postwar, American consumer class to the Cold War and budding civil rights movement, no aspect of the decade would go unmentioned. Yet, Paul Robeson's name does not appear once.

For most of his life, he was "Big Paul," recipient of accolades and ovations, America's No. 1 Negro. When Robeson played Othello in 1943, Ed Sullivan wrote emphatically of Robeson, the influential symbol. Less than five years later, and eighteen days before the newspaperman would launch a television show that would change the trajectory of television, Sullivan had reached a disappointed conclusion. "Instead of helping his people, Robeson has failed them," Sullivan wrote in his June 2, 1948, "Little Old New York" column in *The Daily News*. "It is most unfortunate, it is even tragic, that he has dissipated his strength by swinging so far to the left that liberals who have been deeply concerned with the task of aiding his race have been compelled to abandon him."

The mob at Peekskill targeted his body, the newspapers his sense of self and reputation, and the VFW his wallet, harassing any venue booking Robeson into canceling him. Black leadership contributed. "In 1954," Pete Seeger recalled, "the Oberlin College chapter of the

NAACP told me, 'We wanted Robeson to come and sing for us last year, but we were told by the National Office that they would revoke our charter if we did so.'"

In June 1950, the State Department cancelled his passport, denying his freedom of movement and crippling his international voice and earning potential. The government also denied Robeson entry into Puerto Rico, Guam, Hawaii, and Alaska—U.S.-controlled territories American citizens were routinely permitted to visit *without* a passport. While newspaper editorials and veterans groups loudly advocated the ungrateful Robeson leave the country, his government would not allow it.

The FBI never issued the arrest warrant for Robeson that J. Edgar Hoover desired, but it had entered its second decade of surveillance of him. His FBI file contained anonymous tips offering potentially damaging information to Hoover. One such note arrived on December 5, 1949. Addressed to Hoover, it read, "If you want something on Paul Robeson, the Negro singer, he visits a white girl at 22 East 89th Street, NYC apartment. Calls her his secretary. He goes up in a self-service elevator, don't know what floor." The note contained no further information or context, but the implication that Robeson was potentially involved in an interracial relationship was incriminating enough. Approving of a society willing to deputize itself against its own neighbors, Hoover sent form letters to citizen patrols, thanking them for their vigilance. In response to the tip on Robeson, Hoover responded: "I have received your letter . . . and sincerely appreciate your interest in bringing your observations to my attention. During these critical times it is important that all loyal citizens call to our attention matters affecting the national security of our nation."

America had entered a terrifying new phase. Suspicion disguised as patriotism hovered over every meaningful component of American life, reverberating beyond politics and the workforce, seeping into the popular culture: films, television, books, and even comic books. At the movies the science fiction themes of aliens mirrored American. The shape-shifters, body snatchers—characters all rooted in the fear of domestic subversion—were metaphors for a frightened, angry people: no one could be trusted to be what they seemed. The specter of the Soviets made it difficult to publicly criticize the rightward momentum of the country, but beneath the hysteria was a clear political strategy to attack liberal politics, progressivism, and labor, which had long extended to suppressing Black civil rights. The word itself, *communism*, was the most dangerous weapon in America, and, like many powerful entities, Rickey used it to attack his enemies. Three months before Robinson's testimony, baseball's reserve clause, the rule that prohibited free agency and bound a player to one team for life, was challenged by a little-known infielder named Danny Gardella. Speaking at an April luncheon in Baltimore, Rickey attempted to turn the public against Gardella, and he knew exactly what tactic to use.

RICKEY CLAIMS COMMIES SEEK BASEBALL RUIN

> Branch Rickey said today baseball's reserve clause is opposed by persons of "avowed communistic tendencies" and he drew immediate fire from the men challenging him in the courts . . . Gardella's attorney, Frederic A. Johnson, quickly answered the charges.
>
> "Rickey has had dictatorial powers so long he doesn't recognize the true principles of American life."

Danny Gardella was attempting to practice free-market capitalism, perhaps the most American of economic concepts. For it, Branch Rickey called him a communist. A Midwestern newspaper, offended by the Red Scare tactic, responded with the headline, "If You Oppose the Reserve Clause, Know What That Makes You?—Guess."

Rickey was attempting a ploy Hollywood had perfected. As executives actively purged the film industry of suspected communists, one influential weapon was the newsletter *Counterattack*. Bankrolled by powerful international business interests, such as the anticommunist Alfred Kohlberg, and staffed by several former FBI agents (most loudly by Theodore Kirkpatrick), *Counterattack*'s stated mission was to give readers "facts to combat communism." Kohlberg was a vocal member of the establishment who believed U.S. nongovernmental organizations advising American policymakers—such as the Institute for Pacific Relations (IPR), of which Kohlberg was a member—were filled with communist sympathizers and led to Mao's communist takeover in China. Kohlberg likely felt vindicated by the conviction of key IPR member Alger Hiss. In a November 1944 memo to the IPR Board of Trustees, Kohlberg's top recommendation was, "Fire all the Reds, because the truth is not in them." In the summer of 1950, Branch Rickey paid $24 for a year's subscription.

Counterattack made no distinction between communism and progressive politics, often tarring political adversaries with the portmanteau *commugressives*, a pithy attack, but also an important reveal: anticommunism was often just an assault on liberal politics that had nothing to do with the Soviets, as Rickey had shown by his attack on Danny Gardella.

Counterattack advocated for the Republican political agenda, urging subscribers to support Nixon's Subversive Activities Control Act, which overwhelmingly passed in the House but died in the Senate in 1948. The June 1948 issue of *Counterattack* accused Eleanor Roosevelt of being the "honorary head of a Communist front," led not by her politics—the newsletter assured its readers the former First Lady was anticommunist—but by her naivete, her inability, the newsletter stated, "to resist a humanitarian appeal." The same issue referred to Robeson as "the Communist Paul Robeson." *Counterattack* was accompanied by *Red Channels*, which focused on the entertainment industry. The 213-page booklet named 151 purported subversives working in the entertainment industry.

HUAC had once carried a certain tinge of disrepute, for government interference in the private lives of citizens felt like a dangerous overreach, but now, positioned as protecting America against perceived subversives, the committee gained an uncomfortable air of prestige.

II

SIX WEEKS AFTER THE SECOND Peekskill attack, Robeson's close friend Ben Davis and several other members of the Communist Party leadership were sent to prison—Judge Medina's last laugh at Robeson. Anti-immigration attitudes have always percolated just under the skin of American life. The Alien and Sedition Acts of 1798, nearly as old as the Constitution itself, maintained a robust political utility. As world war and nativism spawned the Smith Act of 1940, the Cold War offered fresh opportunities for additionally restrictive legislation—the Internal Security Act of 1950, the brainchild of Nevada Senator Pat McCarran established prison terms for suspected communists and the right to deny passports to anyone affiliated with a communist organization.

The bill broadened deportation grounds to cover political ideologies and tightened visa quotas for entry into the country, which the government used to restrict immigration from countries predominately in Africa and the Caribbean. *Daily Worker* reporter and Harlemite Claudia Jones, who joined the Communist Party in the 1930s because of its support of Black rights following the Mussolini invasion of Ethiopia, was imprisoned several times and, ultimately, deported under the Smith and McCarran Acts. When her home country, Trinidad and Tobago, refused her reentry, Jones agreed to be deported to Great Britain.

Stephen Weschler, a young Army soldier stationed in Europe, did not admit he had been a member of the Party as a left-leaning college student at Harvard. Fearing discovery—and possibly a lengthy prison sentence—Weschler abandoned his military post in 1952 and defected from the Army, swimming across the Danube into Soviet-controlled Austria. Weschler would change his name to Victor Grossman and relocate to East Berlin, never returning to live in the United States.

Two years later, in January 1954, at the University of Minnesota, a front-page scandal broke when Barbara Roehrich, a former communist, testified before the Subversive Activities Control Board in Washington that she had associated with as many as 200 to 300 communists—possibly even 500. Roehrich accused University of Minnesota teaching assistants, Jules Chametzky and Eugene Bluestein, as well as her Black ex-husband (additionally scandalous to those who believed communists were indoctrinating young white women to engage in interracial marriage), and several others of being communists. Her testimony set off hysteria on campus, until the university concluded Roehrich had falsely accused Bluestein and Chametzky. Roehrich accused Betty Mae Sunne, who worked at the Labor Youth League. Sunne was an unapologetic member of the Minnesota Communist Party and, over the following years, responded to HUAC with tenacity, fighting the legality of anticommunist legislation in the courts, eventually taking the right to appear on the ballot as a Communist Party candidate to the Supreme Court.

In left-wing circles, the McCarran Act was often called "the concentration camp law." Truman vetoed the bill, but the president was no match for the anticommunist movement he helped foster. Congress easily overrode his veto, and the McCarran Act became law. Using the World War II framework that enabled Japanese American internment camps, the McCarran Act empowered the president to detain "subversives." Barely five years after the Holocaust, Americans advocated for the imprisonment of its own citizens. McCarran's anticommunist crusades was rewarded in 1948, when Las Vegas named its airport after him.

For decades, the United States had used the Passport Division as a weapon against dissent. During World War I, the government denied the Black, muckraking journalist Ida B. Wells a passport for publicizing the lynchings of Black Americans at home while their fellow Americans fought for freedom in Europe. Even as W.E.B. Du Bois began coupling American segregation with the worldwide Black struggle, the government made it difficult for him to travel. Passport issuance was both procedurally mundane and, when weaponized, vital in curtailing a freedom Americans took for granted.

Few people, if any, in the history of the American government possessed as much unchecked power as an obscure, career bureaucrat named Ruth Shipley, chief of the passport office. Shipley was 43 when she was named head of the Passport Division in 1928, during the Coolidge Administration, and had been working for the government for 20 years. She was Maryland-born, Methodist, and the only daughter of Rev. Robert Alexander Bielaski. Shipley's grandfather, Alexander, was born in the Russian Empire, in Minsk, in what is modern-day Belarus. After joining the Polish army at 20 years old, Bielaski was shot in the face with a musket ball while defending Warsaw in a battle against the Russians. Bielaski settled in Maryland in 1832, joined the Union army in 1861, and died in battle just seven months into the Civil War. Her older brother, Bruce, was one of the original members of the Bureau of Investigation (renamed the Federal Bureau of Investigation in 1935) and was named its second chief in 1912, twelve years before Calvin Coolidge appointed J. Edgar Hoover as chief. Her uncle, Oscar, played big-league baseball for five years and was both an inaugural member of the 1876 Chicago White Stockings (renamed the Cubs in 1904) and rumored to be the first Polish major-leaguer. Oscar Bielaski was teammates with Cap Anson, the man long credited throughout history as one of the chief architects behind the exclusion of Black players from the game in the 1880s.

While each was more publicly prominent, her grandfather, brother, and uncle would not carry as much power as the unknown, unelected Ruth Shipley. Ostensibly reporting to the Secretary of State, Shipley was the most powerful woman in America, given the sole discretion to unilaterally grant, deny, and revoke the passports of American citizens. For nearly three decades, no American traveled without Ruth Shipley's approval.

Though the Passport Division office was comprised of more than 200 employees, Shipley was said to have reviewed every passport application personally, leaving applicants at the mercy of her personal preferences and partisan politics. She answered to no committee. Her decisions were mercurial, final, and not subject to legal appeal.

As a favorite of Pat McCarran, Shipley had been one of the silent architects of the McCarran Act. Her Cold War influence was comprehensive. Shipley had targeted Americans of left-wing views and was suspicious of Black Americans, whether or not those views stemmed from their political activity. She preferred privacy and rarely agreed to interviews. A 1941 newspaper profile described her as "softhearted and hardboiled . . . gentle and feminine, with soft gray hair."

In the 1950s, Shipley denied passports to not only Robeson, but also left-wing writer Howard Fast, Pulitzer Prize–winning playwright Arthur Miller, the quantum chemist Linus Pauling, the artist Rockwell Kent, and psychiatrist Walter Briehl. Both Kent and Briehl, like Robeson, refused to sign the noncommunist affidavit and sued the State Department. *California Eagle* publisher Charlotta Bass, who was one of Robeson's greatest supporters in the Black press, was barred from travel by Shipley, and in 1951, Shipley deemed the old lion, Du Bois, who had been traveling the world since the 19th century, a "foreign agent" for his broad critiques of the American system and revoked his passport. In August that same year, Shipley denied Robeson's son, 23-year-old Paul Robeson Jr., a passport to attend a conference in Berlin. In confirming the denial of Paul Jr.'s, passport, Shipley imperiously told the Associated Press, "No further comment is necessary." Shipley was a key, unseen foot soldier in America's rightward shift, often serving a Cold War political agenda instead of a constitutional one.

When Shipley retired in 1955, at the mandatory age of 70, she was lauded by new Secretary of State John Foster Dulles for "refusing passports to applicants whose prior actions indicated that the proposed travel would be inimical to the best interests of the United States."

The opportunistic Wisconsin junior senator Joseph McCarthy pushed Republicans to campaign on subversion, liberal, New Deal politics as un-American. William F. Buckley, the rising new voice of the conservative movement, warned against "the enemy within." Bea Lumpkin, a devoted member of the Party, whose brothers-in-law often provided security for Paul Robeson, and met Robeson in 1948 while he campaigned for Henry Wallace, recalled a story a coworker told her about that period. "The government illegalized us. She told me, 'Once, I was fired from five different jobs in two weeks.' When you have young children. You know what it means when the foreman walks up to you and says, 'You're wanted in the front office,' and I asked her, 'What did you do?' And she said, 'Nothing. My job is still there.' Can you imagine the courage of knowing if you walked into the office you're going to be fired, again? I think of all the tens of thousands of Party members who withstood such threats."

In a column titled "Making America a Police State," the left-wing journalist I.F. Stone referred to the McCarran Act as "intended to make it unsafe to question the status quo . . . to give America our own slick, chrome-plated version of Fascism." The American Civil Liberties Union, stalwart defender of free speech even for the American Nazi Party and the Ku Klux Klan, was so fearful of the taint of being un-American, it agreed to rid its ranks of suspected communists. Monitoring the beliefs of private citizens ran counter to the organization's entire mission of upholding constitutional principles, and yet it quickly succumbed to the national mood, investigating its own employees.

Good, right-thinking Americans responded passively, personally appalled but convinced of the strength of their institutions. They believed the Constitution would support their outrage and the country would make it through this dark period. They believed in the First Amendment, that the courts would differentiate between the innocent and the guilty, and that common sense would prevail. As the accusations intensified, and thousands of Americans lost their careers and reputations, the nation remained largely disbelieving that the anticommunist climate was recklessly destroying lives. That was just an overreaction—the United States simply didn't *do* those things.

New days produced new headlines. The Oscar-nominated actor John Garfield, star of the 1930s and 1940s, appeared in Room 226 before HUAC in 1951, refused to name names, and immediately landed on the Hollywood blacklist. Among others, Orson Welles; Du Bois's wife, Shirley Graham; conductor Dean Dixon; and Robeson's *Othello* co-stars Uta Hagen, José Ferrer, and Margaret Webster were all named in *Red Channels*. In 1952, in her second full year of acting, the young Oscar-winning actress Lee Grant would be blackballed from Hollywood for the next 12 years. Government interrogation without due process became mainstream, and average Americans adjusted with the times, adopting a new attitude: Only the guilty had something to fear.

III

ROBESON FOUND COMFORT IN a close-knit circle of friends and his unwavering commitment to labor and community, while also focusing on the courts. After the first appeal of his passport cancellation was denied, Robeson and his team of lawyers would navigate the labyrinthian thicket of passport law. (One of Robeson's lawyers, Leonard Boudin, the famed left-wing attorney and brother-in-law of I.F. Stone, would one day represent Daniel Ellsberg against the federal government over the Pentagon Papers.) In March 1952, Robeson sued Dean Acheson, the Secretary of State. Five months later, Robeson lost the case because of a semantic sleight of hand. Boudin argued the State Department unconstitutionally denied Robeson a passport, but since his passport had expired the previous year, the court countered that no valid passport existed for the state to deny—the government could not refuse Robeson a document Robeson did not possess. The Passport Office did not deny him a passport; they simply chose not to renew it. Robeson's lawyers were told there was a fast way to resolve his situation: he could sign the noncommunist affidavit that was required under the Smith and McCarran Acts. Robeson refused.

The relationship between Black America and communism was comparable to that of its relationship with another organization coming of age during the same postwar period: the Nation of Islam. The Nation's membership never reflected more than a small percentage of the nation's Black, and overwhelmingly Christian, population. Yet few Black people could argue with the Nation's sharp critique of Black life as an underclass—or the power of the organization's ascending new spokesman, Malcolm X. When the white mainstream demanded "respectable" Black leaders to denounce the Nation, many complied, but with delicate, carefully worded statements. Too much truth existed in Elijah Muhammad's indictment to enthusiastically counter it without appearing to be a pawn for the very forces responsible for Black disenfranchisement and its deadly, accompanying violence. Black criticism of the Nation of Islam instead focused on optics and tactics—Malcolm X's uncompromising rhetoric and the wisdom of self-imposed segregation versus the risks and hopes of integration—and not the substance of their arguments. Many Black Americans approached leftist political movements similarly: few actually joined the Communist Party, and even fewer favored the USSR in U.S.-Soviet geopolitics or the Comintern ambition of a global communist revolution, but large numbers silently appreciated the Party's support for Black issues neither Republicans nor Democrats would champion.

In the Black community, career opportunities were always perilous. In Hollywood, a hostile industry, combined with the pressure of the times, threatened the few avenues that did exist. *Counterattack* was a fringe operation, but its impact reverberated far beyond its circulation given its high-level connections. *Counterattack* could kill careers—and did. CBS followed the federal government in instituting loyalty oaths at the network.

A method to isolate Robeson was to threaten the livelihoods of anyone associated with him. *Red Channels* went after Robeson's old friend Lena Horne, who by then was a well-known and elegant singing star and actress. Nothing in Horne's background suggested she attempted to overthrow the government. Her activism centered around civil rights, and, like Robeson, forcing Hollywood to create dignified screen roles for Black actors. In the fall of 1951, the *New York Journal-American* unsuccessfully attempted to have her removed from Ed Sullivan's show.

Hoover had been tracking Horne since at least 1947, largely along the lines of her many associations with Robeson and her public criticism of American segregation. The Bureau listed her as file 100–353031. Horne never joined the Party but shared the same racial anger and grievances as Robeson. In a stroke of paternalism, the FBI considered Horne incapable of her own independent thoughts on American racism: the Bureau concluded she was not a communist but was controlled by Robeson.

During a string of performances at the Copacabana in the late summer of 1948, FBI Special Agent John J. Manning filed a report to Hoover that Horne was merely "'window dressing' by many communist fronts who depend on her appearance at their functions to attract many known Communists and sympathizers to the cause of the negroes for better rights and improved working conditions." Manning wrote that Horne was not "very well informed regarding the true background of various political and racial movements within the United States," and was "under the complete domination and influence of Paul Robeson."

Louis Budenz, a former managing editor of the *Daily Worker* who turned FBI informant and expert witness, told agents Horne had been a "concealed communist" since 1945, and that was enough to make her toxic. She would spend years privately negotiating with various anti-communist power brokers to spare her career. If Horne was to work again, she would have to fulfill two requirements: beg for it and admit she had been duped by Robeson.

For Black artists, Robeson was the giant he had been since the 1920s. Supporters called him "The Great Forerunner" and "The tallest tree in the forest," but now they risked their careers by mentioning his name. "The first time I met Paul Robeson was right after he sang at a concert hall, and I stood by the door of the auditorium and I could feel his magnetic energy coming through his voice," recalled the film and stage star James Earl Jones, who, inspired by Robeson, had also played Othello. "It rocked my body. I could feel a rocking of my body."

Canada Lee, the former boxer who had chosen to enter the theater after being inspired by Robeson's 1924 performance in Eugene O'Neill's *All God's Chilluns Got Wings*, made the blacklist in 1949 after appearing in FBI documents during the Judith Coplan espionage trial. Less than a week before Jackie Robinson's testimony, Lee was hounded by headlines claiming that he was a communist. "I am not a Communist or a joiner of any kind," he said. Aware of the trap, Lee saw through the weaponizing of the word *communism*. "Call me a Communist and you call Negroes Communists." His protestations had no effect. Job opportunities evaporated, but, like Lena Horne, there was a way out: he had to publicly denounce Robeson. The influential Hollywood gossip columnist Walter Winchell wrote Lee had agreed to disparage Robeson before a veterans group in Peekskill. Lee denied the charge and unsuccessfully demanded its correction, even after contacting Winchell directly. Lee then took to sending letters to the editor to newspapers across the country, indirectly supporting both Paul Robeson and Jackie Robinson.

"As everyone must know by now, I am for complete democracy and for the Negro in terms of his participation in this democracy," he wrote. "His right to act, sing, speak, or play ball without mob violence any place in these United States."

Money grew tighter. Robeson estimated his annual income dropped from $104,000 to roughly $2,000. In December 1952, he was awarded the Stalin Peace Prize and the $25,000 cash prize that went with it. The State Department denied his request to receive his award in person. In America, Robeson was attacked for accepting the award. In a wire story that appeared across the country, José Ferrer, Robeson's 1943 *Othello* co-star, attacked Robeson directly.

FERRER ON ROBESON

> Any American who accepts an award from the Soviet Union today does a tremendous disservice, not only to his country, but to the cause of peace around the world. . . . In the case of Paul Robeson, his action of

> accepting Stalin's so-called "peace prize" seems to me to be particularly reprehensible because he is doing almost irreparable harm to his own race and grave harm to the cause of all Negroes.
>
> He pretends to be their spokesman, and he is not. I do not believe that Paul Robeson has anything fundamentally in common with Ralph Bunche, Marian Anderson, Joe Louis, Dorothy Maynor, Jackie Robinson, and other Negroes who are winning the uphill battle for Negro rights.
>
> Nor does he have very much in common with the Negro soldiers in Korea, who are helping to fight the battle for freedom against Communist aggression and dictatorship.

Ferrer's criticism of Robeson drew national praise, and his mentioning of Jackie Robinson underscored the impact of Robinson's testimony. Ferrer was lauded for standing up for American values by standing up to Robeson, but Ferrer had an additional reason for antipathy toward Robeson: Robeson had been having an affair with Hagen during their *Othello* run. Hagen for years believed she and Robeson might marry.

IV

WEEKS BEFORE THE STATE DEPARTMENT invalidated his passport, Robeson traveled to Chicago for the National Labor Conference for Negro Rights. He was under siege, but eyewitnesses marveled at his energy as he echoed themes from *Native Land*: America was in the middle of an anti-labor, right-wing authoritarian takeover, convinced "communism" was a smokescreen.

The government did not want him talking about how America treated its Black citizens, especially to anyone in Africa, where anti-colonial sentiments were at an all-time high, and Southeast Asia, where Vietnamese were fighting French colonialism. Robeson in his remarks highlighted both. British MI5 and the State Department confirmed Robeson's voice and appeal was a growing nuisance. According to author David Caute, "the racial dimensions and the campaigns for African independence" comprise the bulk of Robeson's MI5 file, and, in the United States, Robeson's attorneys were told his passport difficulties were because "his frequent criticism of the treatment of blacks in the United States should not be aired in foreign countries—it was a 'family affair.'" Initially, the government said Robeson signing a noncommunist affidavit would end his confinement, but it now requested an additional condition for his passport restoration: he must agree not to give politically oriented public speeches on foreign soil. He must, essentially, agree to be silenced. In response, and much to the embarrassment of the State Department, Du Bois and Robeson called on the United Nations to condemn American racism.

Black leadership still did not support him. While it was true the organization held animosity toward Robeson, the NAACP simply saw no upside in antagonizing the State Department. In 1944, in the midst of a court-martial, Jackie Robinson requested the NAACP intervene on his behalf. It refused. The organization was on even shakier ground internationally. Its mission centered on domestic issues, and did not include anticapitalism or anticolonialism. Yet, the most important reason Robeson lacked support from Black leadership was far more basic: Black people needed equal treatment under the law *and* to be seen by the white majority as equally committed to America, to have their deeds respected as patriotic with room to share the privilege of being American in their hearts. Jackie Robinson testified against Paul Robeson out of a sense of responsibility, which was shorthand for this sense of patriotism. The enemy of the State Department should also in theory be the enemy of Black Americans, a difficult, if not impossible, duality internationally, where the United States and Soviet Union battled to win over resource-rich third-world nations. Africa further complicated Du Bois's twoness. Black organizations centered on proving themselves worthy and loyal, domestically and internationally, and that meant rejecting Du Bois's Pan-Africanism and not risking violation of the Smith and McCarran Acts. That meant collaborating with the State Department—not challenging it.

V

FROM CHILEAN POET PABLO NERUDA to Frantz Fanon, Black radical politics were powerful world influences. Robeson, Du Bois, Mary McLeod Bethune, and other Black Americans saw a political oneness with Africa and anticolonialism. To counterbalance that influence, the State Department employed a two-pronged strategy: expose Africans to a wider range of successful, America-friendly Black celebrities and launch an African misinformation campaign against Paul Robeson.

Nearing the 1952 All-Star break, the United States Information Agency (USIA), the global propaganda arm of the State Department, saw possibilities in baseball. Baseball had been an effective tool during America's occupation in Japan after the war. The State Department suggested a series of international baseball games, including one in Egypt and one in northern Africa, featuring none other than Jackie Robinson.

The USIA had been sending Black jazz musicians overseas on "goodwill missions" since the 1940s and saw value in utilizing Black athletes to place a soft public face on the hard realities of Black American life. The confinement of Robeson and Du Bois to the United States created a special kind of urgency, and, for the second time in three years, Jackie Robinson would be a key piece of a government plan to offset Paul Robeson's.

Originally the brainchild of Harlem Globetrotters owner Abe Saperstein, the idea was for the Dodgers to play the Cleveland Indians in a "World Tour" of baseball following the World Series. Both teams were important: Cleveland and Brooklyn were the first two teams to integrate America's game—and even seven years after Robinson's signing, the only two willing to treat Black players as a permanent, legitimate talent source. In 1952, Cleveland and Brooklyn had the highest number of Black players combined—a symbol of the integration the game quietly discouraged. The State Department told Walter O'Malley it would provide financial sponsorship. Robinson, already one of the most famous names in the sport, was an even more valuable ambassador following his HUAC testimony—certainly his appearance would draw attention from Robeson. Secretary of State Dean Acheson told Walter O'Malley baseball's racial diversity contained enormous value internationally. The *Tampa Bay Times* was more succinct: "The teams were selected because of Negro players. Their presence will be great anti-Communist propaganda."

The tour never happened. Logistical issues (and O'Malley not receiving the money he wanted) killed the project, but not only was Robinson very nearly again in opposition to Robeson, but he was also a handshake from selling to the world the false pretense that baseball proudly espoused the "democratic principles" of integration when he himself was increasingly disillusioned by the game's unenthusiastic response to hiring Black players.

Still, the USIA believed it had discovered a winning formula: Black athletes could be sent around the world to counteract Robeson—and communism. A year earlier, the great boxer Sugar Ray Robinson, never known for his political opinions, attacked Robeson with what appeared to be significant outside coaching from the government. Returning stateside following a five-fight tour of Europe, Robinson was depicted by newspapers as angry that Robeson was besmirching his country. On the story was Charles Einstein, a 24-year-old reporter for the anti-communist, Hearst-owned International News Service who would one day become a well-known San Francisco sportswriter, ghostwriter, and confidant of the great Willie Mays.

ROBINSON, BACK FROM EUROPE, RAPS PHONY STORIES BY REDS

NEW YORK, Jan. 3 (INS)–Welterweight champion Sugar Ray Robinson, back from an all-victorious tour of Europe, blames the Communists for spreading stories about racial discrimination in the United States.

The lithe 147-pound titlist, who arrived back from Europe yesterday . . . reacted angrily when asked about discrimination.

BLAMES ROBESON

> "Those people," he snapped, "are capitalizing on statements made by Paul Robeson. Robeson speaks for himself and not the American Negro. He certainly doesn't speak for my race.
>
> "If the things the Communists say are true, I wouldn't be in the position I'm in today. America provides opportunity for everyone regardless of race, creed, or color. If you have the ability in America, you're a success."

While Sugar Ray disparaged Robeson, the USIA office in Ghana suggested a propaganda piece on Robeson that appeared sympathetic but intended to damage him further be strategically distributed across the continent. A month later, the February issue of *Ebony* hit newsstands with a profile titled "The Strange Case of Paul Robeson," written by Walter White. Given the frosty relationship between the two, the seven-page spread satisfied the USIA's mandate and White's revenge for being embarrassed by Robeson at the Spingarn dinner six years earlier. "There have been innumerable contradictions which have characterized Robeson's obvious groping for a political and economic philosophy," White wrote, "which are understandable only to him and possibly a psychologist."

As with the Paris Conference aftermath, the NAACP could have chosen silence. It did not. Months after Walter White's *Ebony* feature, the November 1951 issue of *The Crisis* carried the headline, "Paul Robeson—The Lost Shepherd" under the byline Robert Alan:

> A few short years ago, Negro Americans were proud to point to Paul Robeson as another example of the fallacy of the "white supremacy" myth. From concert platform, from behind theatre footlights, from speaker's rostrum, his voice served as constant reminder of the heights his people have risen through sheer ability.
>
> The Paul Robeson whom Moscow now parades before the world is not the same man. And all but a handful of America's 15,000,000 Negroes are quick to point out the difference.

> They see no similarity between Paul Robeson, American, who overcame the obstacles of discrimination to win world acclaim for his artistic accomplishments, and Paul Robeson, Moscow's No. 1 Negro, who spouts Communist propaganda as wildly as Vishinsky.

The article was intended to soil Robeson's international reputation, especially when distributed in Africa—the same continent the NAACP attacked him for focusing on instead of domestic issues two years earlier. In addition to calling him "Moscow's No. 1 Negro"—a sharp jab at his previous adulation—the story featured the names of well-known Robeson antagonists: Walter White, Lester Granger, and Max Yergan, a Robeson ally on the Council of African Affairs turned hardline anticommunist. A footnote at the bottom of the article's first page revealed that even the byline was false: Robert Alan, the footnote read, "is the pen name of a well-known New York journalist."

Behind much of the campaign was J. Edgar Hoover. Over the years, the postal service had confiscated copies of *The Crisis* to prevent its American readers from seeing its contents. Now Hoover had arranged to have the issue in which Black leadership criticized Robeson reprinted and distributed throughout volatile African countries. The article attempted to sound compassionate toward Robeson, but it ultimately maintained a consistent thesis: he was the Soviet agent who had lost his way, forfeiting his title as a reputable figure of the race.

The NAACP and State Department were badly mistaken in believing an anti-Robeson would sway the rising young leaders of the anticolonial movement—the opposite was true. Nelson Mandela in the South African resistance, Jomo Kenyatta in Kenya, Patrice Lumumba in the Congo, and India's Jawaharlal Nehru were all solid admirers of Du Bois and Robeson, and, like their heroes, were under heavy surveillance from Western intelligence agencies themselves. Nehru would refer to Robeson as "Uncle Paul." The scholar Sterling Stuckey saw the shunning of Robeson and Du Bois a great and underappreciated blow to Black people. "With Robeson and Du Bois effectively isolated, their people for the first time in history were led by men with no recognizable interest whatever in Africa," Stuckey wrote in 1973. "Thus occurred a great break in historic consciousness, a rending from the roots of blackness."

The Cold War resembled a chess match, an everchanging cast of kings and pawns. The United States and Soviet Union fought for control of the chessboard, which was to say, the world. Robinson, Robeson, and Du Bois had been kings, crowned by the Black community who idolized them, but who were the pawns? Robeson supporters believed it was Robinson, allowing himself to be used by HUAC that July day in 1949, a champion to the segregationists who would not shake his hand. The NAACP, and much of the country believed, it was Robeson, the former for setting back Black progress by conflating civil rights with communism, the mortal enemy of his country—Americans were currently fighting communists in the unforgiving mountains of Korea. Robeson and Du Bois suspected it was the entire Black leadership itself, the Walter Whites and Roy Wilkinses, who appeased the very government agencies—Hoover's FBI and the State Department, among others—that were also surveilling them, did not trust them, and would, in the very near future, accuse them of the same subversiveness that was destroying Robeson's livelihood. The furious Malcolm X saw Black America as the pawn, constantly willing to be used by their country in exchange for an acceptance from whites as equals that would never come.

VI

HIS OPPORTUNITIES DIMINISHED, ROBESON TURNED to writing. Partnering with Du Bois in November 1950, the two detainees launched *Freedom*, a monthly newsletter named after *Freedom's Journal*, the first Black newspaper in the United States, founded in 1829. The flag of Robeson's new venture contained the quote, "Where one is in chains, all are enslaved." The publication featured Robeson's standing column titled "Here's My Story" and essays by Du Bois. Another member of the staff was a gifted 21-year-old writer named Lorraine Hansberry.

Certain of the political motives communist hysteria masked, Du Bois wrote in the inaugural issue of *Freedom*, "Have we been invaded? Has anyone dropped an atom bomb on us? . . . Is our business failing and our millionaires disappearing? . . . Is there any sign that the United States of America is victim or can be victim to a foreign power? No! Then of what are we afraid . . . unless it is of ourselves."

America supported apartheid South Africa. Robeson was further angered in May 1951, when Truman announced American military aid to Franco's Spain, the fascist former ally of Hitler and Mussolini. Along with Rockwell Kent and 238 others, Robeson signed a petition to Truman calling aid a "betrayal."

Within the tumult, Robeson would reflect and find periodic oases. In the November 1951 issue of *Freedom*—the same month the NAACP published its broadside against him in *The Crisis*—Robeson penned a wistful column in his installment of "Here's My Story." In it, he drifted backward to reflect on his grand successes. Robeson noted his final baseball game; a victory over Princeton, the bitter home of his childhood, would be his last in a Rutgers uniform. "We won, 6–1, and I have a little gold baseball as a precious memory."

Robeson would think fondly of Rockland Palace, but his essay revealed the persistent strains of the daily fight. Under the full weight of his country's ire, Robeson's prose suggested he was weakening. "I'm back at Rockland Palace, at another level, having gone through a kind of spiral, still fighting for the dignity of my people, but fighting harder; saying that time is short."

The start of 1952 brought a new year, new losses, and a deepening sense the government had no intention of ever letting Robeson leave the country. He now referred to himself as a political prisoner. He received an invitation to perform at Denman Auditorium in Vancouver on February 1 before nearly 3,000 members of the International Mine, Mill, and Smelter workers. Two weeks before the concert, on January 17, the State Department announced it would prevent Robeson's attendance, even though Americans were permitted to drive into Canada without a passport and Canadian officials were not restricting his entry. Five days later, a federal judge dismissed the $2 million lawsuit Robeson filed against Peekskill town officials and the veterans groups for the riot.

Both Robeson's team and the union officials expected the Vancouver concert to happen. They were wrong. The United States had no jurisdiction in Canadian affairs, but when Robeson attempted to cross into Canada, the U.S. border patrol prevented him from leaving the country. Robeson remained in America, and, over a long-distance telephone-radio hookup, he performed a 17-minute concert.

The final indignity occurred in New York, when Robeson dined with friends at the famous Red Rooster in Harlem. Jackie Robinson's teammate, Don Newcombe, also happened to be in the restaurant, three weeks before his army induction. When Robeson stopped by Newcombe's table and offered a handshake, one news account reported that Newcombe recoiled and shouted at Robeson, "I'm joining the Army to fight people like you." The two heavyweights nearly came to blows—Robeson was 6 ft., 3 in., 250 pounds, and Newcombe was 6 ft., 4 in., 220 pounds, and 28 years younger. Another news story described Newcombe's reaction as less hostile, but the result was equally insulting to Robeson. "At that instant, lumbering Newk jumped up and shouted, 'I don't want to meet you. I don't want anything to do with any Communists. If the Dodger bosses hear about me hanging out with you, they will get the wrong impression.'"

Robeson, although ready to fight, quickly let the confrontation go. Essie did not. Newcombe to her was no different than Walter White, Lester Granger, and Roy Wilkins, another Black public figure doing the bidding of the white establishment while framing Robeson as the enemy. "It is astounding, if true, that Newcombe could say to Robeson, 'I'm joining the Army to fight people like you.' In the first place, it has been reliably reported that Newcombe isn't 'joining' the Army, but has been drafted," Essie wrote in a letter to the *Baltimore Afro-American*. "I cannot imagine why Newcombe wants to fight people like Robeson. Does Newcombe think Robeson is responsible for having kept him out of big-league baseball for so many years?" she asked. "Does he think Robeson is responsible for making him and the majority of the Negro people live under segregation and discrimination and persecution? All I can say is Don Newcombe had better begin to talk and think for himself if he ever wants to be more than a pitcher."

Part Four

Recognition

(1950–1969)

Chapter Eleven

I

IN JACKIE ROBINSON, BRANCH RICKEY created a figure new to American politics: the Black anticommunist. Robinson had not requested the role and was not always an enthusiastic participant, but no one at his fame level had ever occupied such a unique, yet schizophrenic space: the Black man celebrated for upholding the values of a segregated society through the rejection of communism.

Rickey received plaudits for enlisting such a high-profile soldier in his Cold War fight, and his coterie of anticommunists showed their appreciation. John Bricker, the Republican senator and former governor of Ohio, sent Rickey a positive *New York Post* article. Bricker was an anti–New Dealer who shared the Republican ticket with Dewey that lost the 1944 election to FDR, but not before calling the president of twelve years who steered the country through the Depression and World War II a "communist front." Rickey wrote to Bricker, "It was really quite an experience for Jackie to testify before the Un-American Activities Committee and I, too, think he did a good job . . . Thank you for the clippings. I was amazed at the editorial comment, and I hope the boy has made a collection of such clippings."

A day before the first Peekskill attack, the final installment of Robinson's nationally syndicated *Brooklyn Eagle* serial appeared with the headline, "Robeson Has Wrong Outlook." The column publicly interrogated what motivated him to testify against Robeson. In his as-told-to column, Robinson reflected on his own journey, both the conflicts ("The unhappy days in Pasadena, the Army captain who wanted so bad to destroy me because I was a Negro, the hoots and jeers of a few prejudiced guys in the grandstands.") and the uplifts ("Colonel Bates and how he stuck up for me at my court-martial. About all the guys on the Dodger team and how they rooted for me to become a success."). Robinson revealed a degree of complexity, the complete embodiment of twoness, an enlisted man of wavering confidence redoubling his faith in America:

> I have never met Paul Robeson.
>
> Let me say that I think he is a very talented man with the wrong outlook on life.
>
> I want to ask him a question . . . Can you sit down in Russia and say the head man's a louse?
>
> No. Not unless you want to play centerfield in the Siberian League.

Robinson referred to the boxes of letters he'd received after his HUAC appearance as proof of America's superiority. "I can show them to you," Robinson wrote. "In Russia, I don't think they would get through the mails." Many of these salvos carried the stilted handiwork of ghostwriters (and the heavy influence of Branch Rickey) but were largely an accurate reflection of his views. Robinson would curiously ignore Robeson's central grievance that was also certainly his own: in America, where you could sit down and call the head man a louse and receive your mail without government interference (or so Robinson thought, unaware of what Albert Burleson had done to the Black press), Black people were being murdered for exercising their right to vote. For being successful. For not being successful. For being rich. For being poor. For looking at a white person the wrong way. For not looking at them at all. Two days after Robinson's column was published, a burning cross awaited Robeson in Peekskill.

The day of the second Peekskill concert, eleven hundred miles south of where Robeson would again be attacked and about 30 minutes west of Cairo, Georgia, where Robinson was born, the small town of Bainbridge, Georgia, made national news when an affluent Black man was murdered on his own property by a group of trespassing whites.

> **NEGRO KILLED BY GUN BLAST**
>
> *HAD TOLD WHITES TO LEAVE HIS PLACE*
>
> Four or five white men a well-to-do Negro farmer ordered away from his fish pond shot him to death with rifles and shotguns, Sheriff A.E. White reported Saturday.
>
> Mr. White said the body of Hollis Riles, 53, was found riddled with 13 buckshot and propped against a tree. He quoted a witness as saying the Negro was cut down by gunfire as he fled for his life.
>
> Mr. White said he believed the slaying was pre-meditated murder. He explained that four months ago, Mr. Riles's home was blasted with shots from an unidentified automobile after he tried to keep white men from fishing in his pond.
>
> The Negro was owner of a 200-acre farm.

Why couldn't Robinson find common ground with Robeson on their mutual grievance of white vigilantism against Black citizens? Communism, as the NAACP had long insisted, was a disqualifying factor, but the answer also lies in the power of Branch Rickey, to whom Robinson was completely devoted, even though Rickey was willing to trade him following what would be an MVP season. In January 1950, the newly minted NL MVP Robinson sat down with *The Sporting News* heir J.G. Taylor Spink, where he praised the full influence of Rickey. "When I was scheduled to go to Washington to testify before the House Committee on Un-American Activities, Mr. Rickey urged me strongly to go, and nothing but good came out of it for me and my race." When the interview appeared in the February 1, 1950, issue, Robinson told Spink of Rickey's financial support of his charitable endeavors, that "no other man means as much to me as he does." After Robinson completed his praise of Rickey, Robinson asked Spink, "Do you understand now, Mr. Spink, how easy it will always be for me to do what he asks?"

II

RICKEY WASTED NO TIME CAPITALIZING on Robinson's increased popularity. The rumors were true, after all: A motion picture based on Robinson's life *was* being shopped around Hollywood. Rickey dispatched Arthur Mann to California. Robinson effusively told *The Sporting News* how much "good" the picture would do. Rickey immediately saw the value of a Robinson portrayal to the Dodgers—and to himself—in a charged political climate. Eagle-Lion, a British-American distributor whose biggest American hit was 1948's *The Red Shoes*, would release the film. Robinson would play himself, while Ruby Dee, a young theater actress born in Cleveland who was raised in Harlem and attended Rev. Ben Robeson's church at the Mother AME Zion Church—the oldest Black church in the city—accepted the role of Rachel. Just as Paul Robeson gained fame from his roles in Eugene O'Neill's works, Dee gained prominence from her performance in *Anna Lucasta*, adapted from O'Neill's Pulitzer Prize–winning *Anna Christie*. Minor Watson, the veteran stage and character actor, played Rickey—but only after Rickey torpedoed Arthur Mann's scheme to play his boss. Though he had never appeared in a movie, Robinson's playing himself would charge the film with a certain star power and an instant publicity coup. With a meager budget of $300,000, its principal photography wrapped in less than a month.

Two days after the 1947 World Series, Eagle-Lion had signed Robinson to play himself in *Courage*, which was to be produced by longtime filmmaker Benjamin Stoloff and producer Jack Goldberg, who produced several films made primarily for Black audiences. The two worked on the materials with Robinson and a script with Lawrence Taylor, but the film never materialized. The studios wanted the film to feature a white man teaching Robinson how to be the man and ballplayer he would become—a condition Robinson rejected.

With anticommunism rising in favor, Eagle-Lion revived the Taylor script to exploit the demand for so-called "pro-American" films. With Taylor's script resurrected, he and Mann would share screenwriting credits. Mann would also be billed in the credits as the film's technical supervisor, guaranteeing Rickey's control of virtually every portrayal in the film. Rickey was so sure the film would further his interests, he even allowed the producers to use both the authentic Montreal and Brooklyn Dodger uniforms, while opposing team uniforms would bear no names.

The Jackie Robinson Story premiered in New York on May 16, 1950. It would not be a baseball film, but one of several propaganda films designed to reflect and reinforce the anticommunist mood of the country, Hollywood cleansing itself of its left-wing politics by giving HUAC a heroic sheen. The film's opening voice-over ("This is the story of a boy and his dream, but more than that, it is the story of an American boy and a dream that is truly American.") is less about Robinson and more about Robinson providing the vehicle for Rickey's anticommunism—and foreshadowing an attack on Paul Robeson. The film balances each diluted example of racism that shaped Robinson's early life with benevolent whites on call to reassure audiences whenever reality threatens the picture. Rickey instills upon Robinson that he cannot fight back against the hostility he will face, lest the integration effort fail. Just as Robinson's indictment of American racism during his HUAC testimony was not publicized, Robinson's biopic omitted his 1944 court-martial, where he refused to move to the back of a public bus, even though the humiliation and trial had been a defining moment in his life. The film provides space for Robinson and Rickey's shared Christianity ("Any time you have a real problem," Robinson's mother, played by Louise

Beavers, says, "Listen to God a while."), as both symbolic of their faith and a direct repudiation of the Communist Party's outlawing of religion.

In taking dramatic license over the final five minutes of the film, Robinson is approached by HUAC at the end of his triumphant rookie season in 1947, not midway through 1949. It is there, in the dugout after the Dodgers clinch the National League pennant, where Rickey tells him appearing before the committee is his responsibility to his country.

> JACKIE ROBINSON: By the way, Mr. Rickey. There's something bothering me. About that invitation to Washington. Do you really think I should go?
>
> BRANCH RICKEY: Yes, Jackie, I do. To Washington. To the Senate. To the House of Representatives. To the American people. You've earned the right to speak. They want you to speak about things on your mind. About a threat to peace that's on everybody's mind, Jackie. Now, you can fight back.

For more than 77 minutes, the name "Paul Robeson" is never mentioned, but his specter dominates the film. The word *communism* is not mentioned, though communism is clearly the "threat to peace that's on everybody's mind," and, by implication, so is Robeson. The film intercuts a shot of the U.S. Capitol with Robinson testifying before fading into an image of the Statue of Liberty. Robinson's humility before the committee comes off as an obvious response to Robeson. ("I can't speak for 15 million people. No one person can.") The film also truncates Robinson's dig at Robeson by deleting the infamous coda, "a siren song sung in bass." Under oath, Robinson said, "But I and other Americans of many races and faiths have too much invested in our country's welfare, for any of us to throw it away because of a siren song sung in bass." In the film, Robinson says, "But I'm certain that I and other Americans of many races and faiths have too much invested in our country's welfare to throw it away or to let it be taken from us." Having Robinson recite what he said under oath would have meant acknowledging he was appearing only in opposition to Robeson.

"The Committee on Un-American Activities" is not mentioned by name. The most enduring and personal portion of Robinson's 1949 testimony, his indictment of American racism, police brutality, and inequality, is not addressed, nor is the racial discrimination he fought. Fidelity to Robinson's life was not the goal. The purpose was to elevate HUAC. Beyond its anticommunism slant, the film's message suggested life could be difficult, but American racism was merely a nuisance that could be overcome by hard work, good intentions, and white benevolence.

III

IN THE SUMMER OF 1951, Branch Rickey was contacted by Dr. James Fifield Jr., pastor of the First Congregational Church of Los Angeles and founder of Spiritual Mobilization, a religious organization fortified by major corporations and described by its literature as a "16-year nonsectarian crusade for freedom in America." Months earlier, Rickey had lost his power struggle to Walter O'Malley, who had purchased Rickey's share of the Dodgers. He was out, but, with some sly maneuvering in concert with Pittsburgh owner John W. Galbreath, he immediately took over the daily operation of the Pirates. Fifield contacted Rickey at his new offices at Forbes Field.

An early forerunner to today's right-wing evangelical political blocs, Spiritual Mobilization coalesced around the philosophy that free-market capitalism and Christian libertarianism were foundational concepts to an American life being threatened by FDR's social programs. The New Deal, Fifield preached across the country, was the first step toward socialism, then communism. Spiritual Mobilization would respond to the New Deal by dedicating itself to return "Christian values" to the government and schools. The United States needed to remind itself it existed "under God," a phrase Fifield would use to great effect.

To commemorate the nation's 175th birthday, Fifield and other leaders of Spiritual Mobilization formed The Committee to Proclaim Liberty, a steering group organizing events across the nation that asked

Americans to "give thanks to God for liberty." Taking its name from a passage in Leviticus 25:10, the committee's "founding committee" would contain 56 names, a symbolic nod to the 56 original signers of the Declaration of Independence. The Committee was well-financed and star-studded, represented by industries ranging from hospitality (hotel magnate Conrad Hilton) to automotive (General Motors President C.E. Wilson and Chrysler Corporation President B.E. Hutchinson), politics (former President Hoover and General Douglas MacArthur), education (Brown President Henry Wriston), and Hollywood (Paramount Pictures Vice President Y. Frank Freeman, Cecil B. DeMille, Bing Crosby, and Ronald Reagan).

Looking to add baseball to the list, Fifield invited Rickey to join the Committee. The two men would be simpatico in their values: two anticommunist, anti–New Dealers committed to linking free markets—the same free market concepts Rickey denied the players—to Christian evangelism. On May 31, 1951, Rickey wired Robinson a two-sentence telegram via Western Union:

> *I AM ACCEPTING MEMBERSHIP ON THE COMMITTEE AS REQUESTED BY DR. FIFIELD. I HOPE YOU WILL WIRE HIM ACCEPTANCE.-BRANCH RICKEY.*

Less than a month later, when committee coordinator James Ingebresten wrote to Rickey soliciting a financial donation, two new names appeared on the founding committee masthead. One was Branch Rickey. The other was Jackie Robinson.

Effectively sponsored by Rickey—constrained by his HUAC appearance and the demands of his former employer and lifelong mentor, to whom he owed so much—Jackie Robinson would be the only Black person among the 58 members. There is no surviving evidence that Robinson was actively involved in much of the organization's activities beyond lending his name, but Jackie Robinson's name stood alongside some of the most rabid, right-wing elements of the country.

The Jackie Robinson Story depicted HUAC as the true protector of

American freedoms. As did the right-wing actor John Wayne, who, in 1952, would produce and star in the anticommunist propaganda film *Big Jim McClain*, which contains a scene panning across HUAC members and staffers, from John Wood to Frank Tavenner, accompanied by the voice-over, "Undaunted by the vicious campaign of slander launched against them as a whole and as individuals, they have staunchly continued their investigation, pursuing their stated belief that anyone who continued to be a communist after 1945 is guilty of high treason."

Anti-liberalism cast as anticommunism dominated the screen. As *Big Jim McClain* played on screen, Canada Lee, Ruby Dee's co-star in the 1944 play *Anna Lucasta* and blacklisted by Hollywood unless he agreed to attack Robeson, died suddenly at 45, his physical ailments exacerbated by the emotional pressures of the blacklist. John Garfield, whose career was also finished by the blacklist, died of a heart attack twelve days later. FBI files were created on Ruby Dee and her husband, Ossie Davis, for being suspected communist sympathizers after expressing anger following the 1953 federal execution of Julius and Ethel Rosenberg. On the stationery of the Sands Hotel in Las Vegas, Lena Horne wrote a letter to anticommunist power brokers, begging forgiveness for being naive about the communists, hoping it would save her career—but did not name names against Robeson. "I have heard it said many times that he influenced me sympathetically toward communism," Horne wrote. "This I must emphatically deny."

Robinson's reviews were kind. He was a novice who, in the word of one reviewer, "was no Spencer Tracy." He was treated much kinder than the film itself. ("The film is a peculiar concoction of mediocracy, corn, sentiment and sincerity.") The *New York Daily Mirror* saw through the film's pretense as a Robinson biopic ("There is little insight into the conflicts of his life.") for what it was: Branch Rickey's statement on Robeson through Robinson. "The picture makes clear that though communist propagandists exploit the treatment of the Negro, Jackie Robinson's fighting heart and talent were recognized because he had faith. A final scene shows him before a senate committee deprecating

Paul Robeson's Russia-loving statement that the Negro has no love or patriotism for the U.S."

The film served its purpose—as did Robinson in the moment—first on Capitol Hill, and then in Hollywood, as HUAC, McCarthy, *Counterattack*, and *Red Channels* led a purge through the movie industry.

If the Lords felt betrayed when Rickey signed Robinson, the coalition of liberal, progressive, socialist, and communist voices who first supported integration, and then specifically Robinson, could not hide their disappointment in his role in the second Red Scare. *Daily Worker* columnist Lester Rodney, one of the loudest of Robinson supporters, offered a scathing encapsulation of this chapter of Robinson's life. *The Sporting News* reprinted an excerpt of Rodney's film review.

COMMIE VIEWS OF JACKIE

> Whether Robinson, who knows better about the facts, is happy with this script, we don't know. He lent himself once to the purposes of the worst enemies of the Negro people and the American people as a whole—the infamous Un-American Committee. Although he later did condemn the Peekskill violence, that couldn't undo the damage of his spotlighted Washington recital before the KKK-infested group of witchhunters. . . . To make a picture which will put this fascist-minded group in a favorable light on the screen will be, for Robinson, compounding his mistake of Washington, D.C. No two ways about it.

IV

ROBINSON TURNED 35 IN JANUARY 1954 and the body stopped cooperating. He was a utility man in 1953 when the Dodgers fielded their greatest team, playing wherever the Dodgers needed him: 76 games in the outfield, 44 at third, and only nine at second base. On September 22, at Ebbets Field, Robinson even started at shortstop for the first and only time in his big-league career. He was still dangerous, an All-Star for the fifth straight year, but far closer to his retirement than his prime. Even some reviews of *The Jackie Robinson Story* criticized Robinson's weight in the film—no rookie could be that out of shape. Second base—his position—now belonged to a young Black phenom named Jim Gilliam.

He was fortified by Rachel, and there were three kids now—Jackie Jr., Sharon, and now David—but Jackie Robinson grew increasingly isolated professionally. He was unprotected. Rickey was gone, as was his favorite manager, Charlie Dressen, who called Robinson the best ballplayer he'd ever had. Dressen loved Robinson. The new manager, Walter Alston, did not. Walter O'Malley was never a true advocate, and Robinson's devotion to Rickey made closeness between himself and O'Malley impossible. O'Malley was not personally invested in Robinson as a man, nor was he receiving credit in the historic triumph of integration. Where the nation saw a pioneer, O'Malley and Alston saw a faded star who could not move as he once did and did not impact the game for seasons at a time as he once could. Most irrevocably beyond performance, Robinson reminded Alston and O'Malley of Rickey's greatest success, not their own.

Three days after Thanksgiving, November 30, 1952, Robinson appeared on *Youth Wants to Know*, a Sunday morning television show for young adults on NBC. A young woman in the audience asked Robinson if he believed the Yankees were against integration. Robinson replied, "Yes."

A firestorm ensued. Yankees general manager George Weiss professed outrage, even though the Yankees' racism was the biggest open secret in baseball. Weiss was never shy about voicing trepidation about integration's potentially negative effects on attendance, and, most pointedly, the Yankees were the richest, most successful team and barely scouted Black players. They didn't need them. As an example of Robinson's vulnerability, his response created a surprising alliance: the creaky baseball establishment and some key members of the Black press agreed: Jackie Robinson had grown *too* loud. The *Courier*'s Wendell Smith tempered his crusading with a column in January 1949, stating few Black players were ready for the majors. *The Sporting News* reprinted the story, adding an editorial cartoon depicting Branch Rickey and Bill Veeck in the jungle, wearing safari hats, lamenting a "scarcity of game." Robinson, Doby, and Satchel Paige are all trapped in bamboo cages hanging from palm trees.

The game had tired of Robinson's opinions. Integration was an honorable goal, but Robinson was striving for something less agreeable—equality. *New York Daily News* writer Dick Young told Robinson his HUAC appearance had made him arrogant. "Ever since you got back from Washington," Young told him, "you've got a swelled head." The papers said Robinson was now the highest-paid Dodger at $50,000 per season, but that wasn't close to being true. According to the data cards the league kept on each player at the time, Robinson earned $39,750 in 1952, and accepted a pay cut to $38,750 in 1953. For the first time in his career, the Dodgers offered him to the rest of the league, placing him on waivers in June and September of 1952. Proving Robinson still had value, nine teams claimed him, including the Red Sox, Braves, Phillies, and Rickey's Pirates, but the Dodgers pulled him back both times.

His frustrations sparked perplexity and resentment: he was rich and living better than most Americans, Black or white, so why was he so upset? Robinson saw his own successes as secondary to the overall Black condition—a position Robeson had taken two decades earlier—and as he prepared for his seventh season more vulnerable than ever before, he was reaching another conclusion: for all his pioneering, baseball did not really want Black players at all.

On Opening Day, 1953, nearly eight years after Robinson's signing, more than half of the 16 big-league teams still had not fielded a single Black player. Connie Mack never wanted Black players and said so—but neither Branch Rickey nor the press corps exposed him. Even Rickey, in his fourth year in Pittsburgh, had not yet integrated the Pirates, amplifying a remarkable revelation: Branch Rickey initially had no intention of integrating the game with an American.

In a stunning interview with Pittsburgh journalist Davis J. Walsh in 1955, Rickey explained his original intention was to integrate the game by subverting segregation, not by challenging it. "Now, it wasn't a matter of wanting to solve the race problem in this country—I can deal with that in due time . . ." Rickey told Walsh. "I spent better than $25,000 investigating it, had a scout in Cuba and Puerto Rico and particularly in Mexico only to find out at the end of two years that the best negro players in the world were right here in the United States and then came my inquiry at that point." In a game the State Department said represented American democratic values, Branch Rickey intentionally bypassed American players, hoping to sign a Mexican or Black Latino who could play the regular season on a work visa and then be returned to his home country.

"I think it's telling that when Rickey came to the Pirates, he was in no hurry to bring in any African American players to integrate or upgrade our team," recalled the Pirates Hall of Fame outfielder Ralph Kiner. "Nobody ever mentions this when assessing baseball's 'Great Emancipator.' I never had an African-American teammate until I was traded to Chicago."

Both Rickey and history would continue to repeat his version of integration, the chestnuts about merit and fairness and avenging Charley Thomas. However, Rickey was always contemptuous about the Negro Leagues, once telling the La Guardia Committee that Negro League teams were run by "racketeers" and did not deserve compensation.

Rickey's contempt did not end with the Negro Leagues. Just as he admonished Black community leaders in Brooklyn in the weeks before Robinson's 1947 debut, and again in 1949, he recalled for Walsh his concern that Black behavior would incite white ticket buyers. "The one I dreaded the most was the acceptance of the player—the kind of acceptance of the player by the negro race itself . . . mass rooting for him and that could be inflammatory, antagonistic and arouse, solidify a great number of the white folks who initially had doubt about the advisability of the move anyhow."

V

THE DEEPER AMERICA MOVED INTO the 1950s, the more Robinson's arc began to mirror Robeson's, another set of footprints on the continuum. If Robinson could not speak freely, he would create the outlet he sought. Like Robeson and Du Bois with *Freedom*, Robinson founded *Our Sports*, a magazine targeting Black sports fans and billed as "The Negro's Own Sports Magazine."

Unwilling to be silenced, Robinson had *Our Sports* pick up where his appearance on *Youth Wants to Know* left off. The July 1953 issue featured a banner headline on the cover that read "Are the Yankees Anti-Negro—Here's the Lowdown."

The story was written by *New York Post* sportswriter Milton Gross, the rare white reporter to cover integration consistently. One paragraph in particular echoed Robeson in Paris: "Jackie straights out many a curve ball when he is at bat . . . but his words only had the effect of making the pot boil over! This happened largely because the news services, making capital of everything Jackie says or does, speedily spread his off-the-cuff remarks all over the country, to some degree misconstruing them."

Gross diligently quoted a performatively outraged Weiss, the man who once said he would not inflict on white fans the indignity of sitting next to Black people. Weiss relied on old tropes: the Yankees were only interested in merit. The team would only consider players competent enough to play and would not yield to outside agitation (common code for the communists). And, of course, the sinister line of thinking that would endure throughout American life: Black people expected handouts, and the Yankees would not accommodate them. "We have no intention of giving them any edge. But neither will we give ground to special pressure. We'll hire a Negro, but only if what he can do will show in the standings of the clubs. Not for profit or exploitation. That," said Weiss, "is our position now. It has always been our position."

Gross followed the pattern common in integration stories, carefully analyzing the Yankees' institutional racism as the most difficult, vexing issue, while allowing the organization ample space for its unchallenged public denials. Gross erred on the name of a top Black Yankee prospect, mistakenly referring to Elston Howard as "Howard Elston." In 1955, two years after the article appeared, and 10 years after Rickey signed Robinson, Howard became the first Black Yankee—and Weiss had nearly traded him to the White Sox before his Yankee debut.

For all of Weiss's protestations, under the subhead "Obvious Race Hatred," Gross relayed an anecdote of the Yankee scout who declined signing both—the white lefthander who would go on to win the American League MVP in 1952 for the lowly Philadelphia Athletics, and the great Willie Mays—and for his poor judgment be demoted to traveling secretary. Ridiculed one time too many for missing on a player of May's caliber, Gross quoted the unnamed traveling secretary after Mays hit two home runs in the first game of a July 22, 1951, doubleheader against the Reds: "I don't care what he did today or any other day," the unhappy traveling secretary said. "I got no use for him—or any of them. I wouldn't want any of them on a club I was with. I wouldn't arrange a berth on the train for any of them."

Robinson stood on the precipice of a new, uncertain phase for him, once again the end of something. Jackie Robinson, the aspirational hero, the symbol of racial progress, the alternative to Paul Robeson, had been uncomplicated. He protected the mainstream view of American values—how the country saw itself—even as the FBI monitored death threats against him. In 1954, President Eisenhower gave Branch Rickey and James Fifield a victory in their quest to combine church and state, adding the words "under God" to the Pledge of Allegiance and to American money. In May, the Supreme Court's *Brown v. Board of Education of Topeka* decision struck down the 58-year-old law upholding Jim Crow segregation, and many of the very people who lauded Jackie Robinson for defending the nation against Robeson now mobilized to protect themselves and their children against his. The NAACP during this period cut a curious figure, undisputably heroic. For decades its approach to segregation shaped through deed and demeanor by Thurgood Marshall, resembled that of a grim lumberjack—chopping at the sequoia of unequal education through the courts with a professional monotonousness until the tree finally fell. In all of its history, the NAACP would enjoy no greater triumph than *Brown*—a vindication of the organization, its tactics, and the people it represented while simultaneously actively contributing to harming Paul Robeson through its cooperation with the State Department. Playing his part in Du Bois's twoness, to be seen as American both individually and in representing the organization as adversarial to segregation but loyal to America, Marshall's FBI file contained several instances of him attempting to ingratiate himself to J. Edgar Hoover, offering in advance to add anticommunist rhetoric to his upcoming speaking engagements. In response to the *Brown* legislation, Mississippi lawmakers countered with legislation of their own that designed to ensure their kids would never share classrooms with Black children. Other Southern states would follow, defying the courts, setting the stage for the unified resistance that would bond the South, accompanied by a mantra that would shatter Jackie Robinson's entire belief in America: "Integration is Communism."

Chapter Twelve

I

THE EPONYMOUS TERM "McCARTHYISM" SEEMED fitting for the man who cast a pall over the country, and yet remained curiously incomplete in capturing the scope of the times. Joseph McCarthy was not an era, but a comet, exploding onto the national scene in 1950, scalding American politics, and, within five years, authoring his own spectacular, public downfall. By 1957, McCarthy was dead.

The name endures as unmistakable shorthand, but the second Red Scare long predated and far outlasted McCarthy. If one person symbolized its entirety and carried the scars to prove its destructiveness, it was Paul Robeson. On the morning of June 12, 1956, Robeson arrived in Washington for one final showdown with his government.

When Robeson arrived at the caucus room in the Old House Office Building to confront his old foe, the House Un-American Activities Committee, he was 58 years old, gray marching relentlessly through thinning hair. He was entering his 11th year as an outcast, essentially the entirety of the postwar years. "Peace time" for him had been anything but. There had been so many fights. When Robeson quipped in 1948 that his outspokenness was ending his career, his prescience likely eclipsed even his imagination.

Nearly six years to the day Ruth Shipley declined to renew his passport, Robeson resembled a relic of a previous time—domestic subversion was being replaced by civil rights and school integration as top line issues. Robeson was still a great physical presence, but he wore glasses now. The vibrant, formidable frame sank more frequently and required additional energy to recover from its valleys. He was wearing down.

At the time, the July 1949 hearing appeared to be just another loud note in a violent, summerlong cacophony, but Jackie Robinson's testimony revealed an uncommon stamina. It had endured, hastened the nadir of Paul Robeson's professional life, and as he arrived to the setting where Robinson once sat, it would be the arena for its epilogue.

Robeson still fought in the courts, but he faded as an injustice, as if his issues had already been settled. They had not. There were movements. "Let Paul Robeson Sing" was a rallying cry. Neruda's "Ode to Paul Robeson" was a classic, but much of the common sentiment concluded Robeson deserved all he had received. He had never admitted to being a communist, but he was admittedly a socialist, leftist, supporter of labor. Always labor. Hating the Soviets had become a prerequisite, and because they were not his enemy, Robeson forfeited his rights as a citizen. A year earlier, James Baldwin, an emerging 24-year-old writer from Harlem, had published an essay, "The Harlem Ghetto," in which he laments Robeson allowing himself to be "tricked by his own bitterness."

It had been years since Robeson had received a favorable public ear, but his treatment exposed a country uninterested in something it ostensibly valued: its principles of democracy. Against the Soviet threat, freedom of speech and freedom of privacy were not bedrock principles to be protected as much as they were theoretical abstractions most Americans were willing to table—or surrender completely. *The Daily Telegraph* of London wrote of America's descent into authoritarianism. "Communism, I quite agree, *is* an un-American activity. Paul Robeson, I concede, may well be an un-American activity, too. Unless my reading of American history is quite false, however, I am sure that excessive interference in un-American activities is also an un-American activity . . . Paul Robeson roaming the world praising Russia and damning America is a harmless tribute to American freedom and self-confidence." The article continued, "Paul Robeson penned passport-less in Washington becomes a symbol of America's supposed insecurity and lack of faith in her own ideals. Why not let him roam?"

II

THREE YEARS INTO APARTHEID, South Africa moved to strip 50,000 Black citizens of their voting rights. The government announced it would adopt a racial classification system and mandated all citizens carry identification. On May 7, 1951, Sailor Malan, a white South African World War II hero, protested the government, leading a torchlight rally of 18,000 through the Johannesburg city square. Over the loudspeakers, Robeson protégé Lorraine Hansberry would write, was the voice of Paul Robeson. In America, U.S. District Attorney Leo Rover justified Robeson's confinement in one passport hearing by referring to him as "one of the most dangerous men in the world." The USIA responded by enlisting Black athletes around the globe as Cold Warriors with a message: there were more worthy Black Americans to admire than Paul Robeson.

"DIPLOMATS IN SHORT PANTS"

BOOST U.S. IN FOREIGN NATIONS

For the Negro athletes who have won laurels in America and who are now touring free world countries as good will ambassadors under the terms of the Smith-Mundt Act, it's an apt name.

Officials here point proudly to huge turnouts in such countries as Africa and India as testimony to the athlete's success in refuting Communist propaganda about the treatment of racial minorities in the United States.

Countering the influence of pro-Communist Negro Paul Robeson, officials point to the pro-American exploits of Whitfield and others,

> including Dr. Ralph J. Bunche, 1950 Nobel Peace Prize winner; Olympic champions Jesse Owens, David Albritton, and Harrison Dillard; Roy Campanella and Jackie Robinson of the world champion Brooklyn Dodgers.

Harold Howland, the State Department official who oversaw the program, said of the Black athletes, "They're not political propagandists, but in a quiet way, they serve as living refutation to Commie lies and distortions about life and opportunity in the United States."

Howland was quoted December 17, 1955. Two events had occurred over the previous four months that spoke to the life for Black people in the United States and Howland called a "Commie lie." On August 28, 14-year-old Emmett Till was kidnapped and murdered in Mississippi for allegedly making a gesture at Carolyn Bryant, a white woman. Till was taken from his bed, shot several times, and dumped into the Tallahatchie River, his teenage body weighed down by a heavy industrial fan. Bryant's husband, Roy Bryant, and his half brother, J.W. Milam, admitted to the killing. Less than a month later, an all-white jury took less than an hour to acquit both.

On December 1, in Montgomery, Alabama, Rosa Parks, motivated by Till's murder, refused to yield her seat to a white passenger, as had been the law for the previous 55 years and as Jackie Robinson had once done, which led to his court-martial. Thirteen days later, Martin Luther King Jr. launched the Montgomery Bus Boycott and the modern civil rights movement.

Two weeks after the Associated Press USIA story hit the wires, on December 30, an almost identical version appeared in the Black press under the byline Marion E. Jackson. Both stories quoted Howland and mentioned the need to neutralize Robeson, but neither mentioned Rosa Parks, Montgomery, or the growing unrest in the Black South following the unpunished murder of a 14-year-old boy, despite it being the biggest story in Black America. The indignities had reached a breaking point, and, in response, the USIA sent Black athletes and entertainers around the globe not to refute communist lies but to shield the world from America's worst truths.

III

IT WOULD BE DIFFICULT TO create a more adversarial atmosphere than the one Robeson encountered June 12, 1956. Robeson did not face the full committee, but a four-member HUAC subcommittee investigating the "Unauthorized Use of United States Passports." Inside the dingy hearing room, they waged the proxy war America had been fighting since Germany's surrender, of the rise of two superpowers and a new world in gestation. Richard Arens, the committee director, was once a McCarthy aide. All four members of the subcommittee, Bernard Keaney of New York, Gordon Scherer of Ohio, Clyde Doyle of California, and the chairman, the Pennsylvania Democrat Francis Walter, had each introduced bills to permanently outlaw the Communist Party in the United States.

Robeson's doctors advised him not to go to Washington. He was recovering from prostate cancer surgery, and intimates feared he was growing increasingly paranoid. The FBI had reported back to Hoover that Robeson had been suicidal and he had suffered a nervous breakdown.

Given Robeson's temperament, testifying was the only option. So much had been taken away, both personally and through what HUAC symbolized, and that demanded a response. Regardless of his health, Robeson wanted no further delays. Whatever else of him had been eroded, the fighter in Robeson remained.

Robeson invoked the Fifth Amendment 30 times over the 60-minute hearing. Repeatedly referencing the "devious methods" communists employed to use the privilege of travel to carry on their "nefarious work," Walter echoed the extralegal reach of Ruth Shipley. "Actual technical membership in the Communist Party," Walter told the hearing room, "is not, therefore, the sole criterion to be used in undertaking to ascertain whether or not a particular individual's activities are in fact contributing to the Communist menace."

The hearing was scheduled to investigate "irregularities" in Robeson's passport, but, in reality, the confrontation represented a last stand. For the first time since the war ended, HUAC was vulnerable. During the infamous Army-McCarthy hearings two years earlier that finished him as a public influence, McCarthy had recklessly gone too far, accusing the Army of communist infiltration. After nearly 20 years of hunting its own citizens, HUAC would become the hostile witness of a new discussion: whether the time had come to abolish it.

In the moment, the committee focused on, at long last, getting Paul Robeson.

THE CHAIRMAN: You are directed to answer the question of whether or not you have ever known Nathan Gregory Silvermaster.

MR. ROBESON: In answer to that question I invoke the fifth.

MR. SCHERER: The witness talks very loud when he makes a speech, but when he invokes the fifth amendment I cannot hear him.

MR. ROBESON: I invoked the fifth very loudly. You know I am an actor, and I have medals for my voice, for diction.

MR. ARENS: Now, Gregory Kheifets is identified with the Soviet espionage operations, is he not?

MR. ROBESON: Oh, gentlemen, I thought I was here about some passports.

MR. ARENS: We'll get to that in just a few moments.

MR. ROBESON: This is complete nonsense.

The confrontation grew more personal, each side viewing the other as the true enemy: HUAC determined to prove Robeson's subversiveness, Robeson contemptuous of conservative politicians empowered by a government body flaunting its ability to operate outside of the Constitution. Walter and Robeson openly taunted each other.

MR. ROBESON: To whom am I talking to?

THE CHAIRMAN: You are speaking to the chairman of this committee.

MR. ROBESON: Mr. Walter?

THE CHAIRMAN: Yes.

MR. ROBESON: The Pennsylvania Walter?

THE CHAIRMAN: That is right.

MR. ROBESON: Representative of the steelworkers?

THE CHAIRMAN: That is right.

MR. ROBESON: Of the coalmining workers and not United States Steel, by any chance? A great patriot.

THE CHAIRMAN: That is right.

MR. ROBESON: You are the author of all of the bills that are going to keep all kinds of decent people out of the country.

THE CHAIRMAN: No. Only your kind.

Francis Walter had not only been the coauthor of the notorious anti-immigrant McCarran-Walter Act, which lowered immigration limits, strengthened the government's power to deport or deny suspected communists entry into the country, and passed despite Truman's veto. Walter had also helmed the notorious Pioneer Fund, a research center known for its support of eugenics. Once during World War II, Walter sent FDR the bone of a fallen Japanese soldier as a gift.

Scherer, the Ohio Republican, and Arens resurfaced a 1949 article penned by Robeson, most likely ghostwritten, that appeared in Russian media, where he stated, "Moscow is very dear to me and very close to my heart. I want to emphasize that only here, in the Soviet Union, did I feel that I was a real man with a capital 'M.' And now after many years I am here again in Moscow, in the country I love more than any other." As Robeson attempted to contextualize the comment, three times Scherer interrupted him, demanding, "Did you make that statement?"

MR. ROBESON: I would say in Russia I felt for the first time like a full human being, and no colored prejudice like in Mississippi and no colored prejudice like in Washington and it was the first time I felt like a human being, where I did not feel the pressure of colored as I feel in this committee today.

MR. SCHERER: Why did you not stay in Russia?

MR. ROBESON: Because my father was a slave, and my people died to build this country, and I am going to stay here and have a part of it just like you. And no Fascist-minded people will drive me from it. Is that clear?

MR. SCHERER: The reason you are here is because you are promoting the Communist cause in this country.

MR. ROBESON: I am here because I am opposing the neo-Fascist cause which I see arising in these committees. You are like the Alien [and] Sedition Act, and Jefferson could be sitting here, and Frederick Douglass could be sitting here and Eugene Debs could be here.

Mutual contempt laced the afternoon. If the committeemen saw in the hearing a final chance to force him to admit he was a Soviet agent, Robeson recognized the opportunity to leave nothing unsaid. As tensions rose in the circular joust, the committee asked Robeson if he had known Max Yergan, whose bitter falling-out with Robeson and the Council on African Affairs turned Yergan into an anticommunist and friendly government witness.

MR. ROBESON: I invoke the Fifth Amendment. Could I say that for the reason that I am here today, you know, from the mouth of the State Department itself, is because I should not be allowed to travel because I have struggled for years for the independence of the colonial peoples of Africa, and for many years I have so labored and I can say modestly that my name is very

> much honored in South Africa and all over Africa in my struggles for their independence . . . Unless we are double-talking, then these efforts in the interest of Africa would be in the same context. The other reason I am here today is again from the State Department and from the court record of the court of appeals, that when I am abroad I speak out against the injustices against the Negro people of this land . . . That is why I am here. This is the basis and I am not being tried for whether or not I am a communist, I am being tried for fighting for the rights of my people who are still second-class citizens in this United States of America . . . I stand here struggling for the rights of my people to be full citizens in this country and they are not. They are not in Mississippi and they are not in Montgomery, Ala., and they are not in Washington, and they are nowhere, and that is why I am here today. You want to shut up every Negro who has the courage to fight for the rights of his people, for the rights of workers and I have been on many a picket line for the steelworkers, too. And that is why I am here today.
>
> THE CHAIRMAN: Now, just a minute.
>
> MR. ROBESON: All of this is nonsense.

As news of the hearing spread, the sparring returned Robeson to his place within the Black American struggle—the place the Black leadership and FBI sought to deny him. The committee's badgering of Robeson did not resonate with the Black community. The government accused Robeson of lying about Black conditions as a means of promoting communist propaganda, but everyday Black people knew better. Emmett Till was no communist fantasy.

Walter and Robeson resumed battle, and Frances Walter suggested Paul Robeson, whose teammates had once torn off his fingernails to intimidate him into quitting the Rutgers football team, had not experienced discrimination.

THE CHAIRMAN: Now, what prejudice are you talking about? You were graduated from Rutgers and you were graduated from the University of Pennsylvania. I remember seeing you play football at Lehigh.

MR. ROBESON: We beat Lehigh.

THE CHAIRMAN: And we had a lot of trouble with you.

MR. ROBESON: That is right . . .

THE CHAIRMAN: There was no prejudice against you. Why did you not send your son to Rutgers?

MR. ROBESON: Just a moment. It all depends a great deal. This is something that I challenge very deeply, and very sincerely. The fact that the success of a few Negroes, including myself or Jackie Robinson can make up—and here is a study from Columbia University—for $700 a year for thousands of Negro families in the South. My father was a slave and I have cousins who are sharecroppers and I do not see my success in terms of myself. That is the reason, my own success has not meant what it should mean. I have sacrificed literally hundreds of thousands, if not millions, of dollars for what I believe in.

The committee recycled the seven-year-old testimony of Black publisher Thomas Young, who criticized Robeson on the second day of the July 1949 hearings. Throughout the blistering morning, the committee frequently referenced Robinson's appearance, hearings that without his star power were never going to be held.

THE CHAIRMAN: You ought to read Jackie Robinson's testimony.

MR. ROBESON: I know Jackie Robinson, and I am sure that in his heart he would take back a lot of what he said about any reference to me. I was one of the last people, Mr. Walter, to speak to Judge Landis, to see that Jackie Robinson had a chance to play baseball. Get the pictures and get the record. I was taken by Landis by the hand, and I addressed the combined owners of the American and the National Leagues, pleading for Robinson to play baseball like I played professional football.

MR. ARENS: Would you tell us whether or not you know Thomas W. Young?

MR. ROBESON: I invoke the Fifth Amendment.

MR. ARENS: Thomas W. Young is a Negro who is president of the Guide Publishing Co., Inc., publishers of the Journal and Guide in Virginia and North Carolina. . . . I would like to read you his testimony:

"No matter how strongly we may believe it is false, that statement coming from Robeson is not easily disposed of. His own life story is an inspiration to humble people of whom Mr. Robeson now presumes to speak. Mr. Robeson does not speak for the young men who served their country so well during the recent war."

IV

ROBESON'S SENTIMENT IN PARIS HAD altered his life. The U.S. Army, however, knew just how correct Robeson had been. During World War II, the military conducted a series of anonymous surveys across various topics, from the conduct and conditions of the war to soldiers' thoughts on what America would look like once the fighting ended. In 2021, a joint project from Virginia Tech University and the National Endowment for the Humanities made more than 65,000 pages of uncensored responses available to the public. Three handwritten responses reflected the disillusionment of some Black soldiers:

I have seen worse treatment of colored soldiers than they do Prisoners of War. At Fort Knox negro soldier were not allowed to go to swimming pools where Prisoners of War could go. . . . What is democracy? I really don't know. I was refused food in a Army Mess until we went to the back door. Hitler is over here such men as Rankins, Talmadge, Stark and many more senators. What do we fight for. We have to wait for white soldiers to load on the buses at Camp Hood, Texas. Eat at back door eating stands at El Paso Texas.

First Why do the whole Signal Corp have the best training + mostly all that the Colored get is Construction + as a whole no Colored Soldiers wants to fight this War because he don't have any thing to fight for. the White man did not send any help when Italy invaded effrica [Africa] + we don't see why we Should fight to help you be ruler of us. As a hole [whole] even if Germany Won we could not be much worser off then we are now. In the South there are about twice as many negros as anywhere else. does the government do any thing to help there [their] condition. No. then Why Should we do anything to help you?

If the Negro could feel that he was really fighting for Democracy, he would have a much greater incentive. Its pretty tough for a sodlier [soldier] to fight for what he is told to be his country, and be denied the privilege of receiving the benifits [benefits] of some of the important things a democracy has to offer. What will he profit when the war is over? Will the very people against whom he is making war get first preference in jobs? Will he be allowed any real voice in the goverment [government] and how it is run? Will he be fired from the jobs he now holds because he can be replaced by other races although he is qualified. I believe these queostions [questions] are running through the mind of every Negro especially those in the armed services because they have the most at stake. We are supposed to be fighting for freedom of speech. What good is freedom of speech when ears that are deaf is turned upon us. We have a fair proposition to offer but we need fair minded people to listen to it. We do not ask for much, we only ask for what we deserve when we wear the uniform of the United States of America. If these things are denied us then why are we fighting?

Another person knew as surely as the active soldiers—Jackie Robinson. Even as he criticized Robeson, Robinson also wrote in his syndicated column, "Believe me, there wasn't a Negro in the army who didn't wonder—I believe this is true—about which half of the country he was fighting for: the North or the South, or both."

The hearing ended furiously. Robeson was rebuffed by Walter from reading a prepared statement. Robeson rebuked the segregationist Senator James Eastland. Walter threatened Robeson with contempt of Congress. At one point, when Robeson mentioned his father was a slave, both Walter and Scherer invited Robeson to discuss the slave labor camps in Russia under Stalin, since, Walter said to Robeson, "you have such an interest in slaves." Walter then mentioned Ben Davis, who had been jailed with communist leaders at Foley Square. Asked about his association with Davis, Robeson did not invoke the Fifth Amendment.

MR. ARENS: Do you know Ben Davis?

MR. ROBESON: One of my dearest friends, one of the finest Americans you can imagine, born of a fine family, who went to Amherst and was a great man.

THE CHAIRMAN: The answer is "Yes?"

MR. ROBESON: And a very great friend and nothing could make me prouder than to know him.

THE CHAIRMAN: That answers the question.

MR. ARENS: Did I understand you to laud his patriotism?

MR. ROBESON: I say that he is as patriotic an American as there can be and you, gentleman belong with the Alien and Sedition Acts, and you are the non-patriots, and you are the un-Americans, and you ought to be ashamed of yourselves.

THE CHAIRMAN: Just a minute. This hearing is now adjourned.

(gavel)

MR. ROBESON: I should think it would be.

THE CHAIRMAN: I have endured all of this that I can.

(gavel)

MR. ROBESON: Can I read my statement?

THE CHAIRMAN: No, you cannot read it. The meeting is adjourned.

MR. ROBESON: I think it should be and you should adjourn this forever.

V

ROBESON'S TESTIMONY REKINDLED FLICKERS OF public dissent. A published letter in *The Washington Afro-American* attempted to rebuild space for independent thought between Cold War binaries ("I am not a Communist. I am not a leftwinger. I am not a fascist. I am not a Socialist. I am not a Capitalist. I am not a subversive. Upon demand, I will take a loyalty oath, though I disapprove of it. I have nothing to hide. I would welcome an investigation. I am for Paul Robeson."—AN AMERICAN),while Robeson's detractors maintained that he be grateful his father's enslavement did not apply to him ("Imagine anywhere else on this earth where the son of a slave could have risen to the great artistic heights that Paul Robeson enjoyed . . . Paul Robeson should have looked down from his heights and thanked God for this land of opportunity."—AMERICAN LEGION SENTINEL)

Robeson's punchout with HUAC may have been satisfying, but he had not advanced in the battle for his passport. He enjoyed the nascent civil rights protest percolating in the South under Martin Luther King Jr., James Lawson, C.T. Vivian, Diane Nash, James Bevel, and others with great admiration, but another year had passed, and he was not free.

His worldview had met with a certain perplexity, which only heightened over the winter of 1956, when Soviet Premier Nikita Khruschev revealed the extent of Stalin's murderous purges across a thirty-year reign over the country.

Months after the Khrushchev revelations, Arens would corner

Robeson on Stalin during the HUAC hearing. It was Robeson at his least convincing.

MR. ARENS: While you were in Moscow, did you make a speech lauding Stalin?

MR. ROBESON: I don't know.

MR. ARENS: Did you say in effect that Stalin was a great man and had done much for the Russian people, for all of the nations of the world, for all working people of the earth? Did you say something to that effect about Stalin when you were in Moscow?

MR. ROBESON: I cannot remember.

MR. ARENS: Do you have a recollection of praising Stalin?

MR. ROBESON: I can certainly know that I said a lot about Soviet people, fighting for the peoples of the earth.

MR. ARENS: Did you praise Stalin?

MR. ROBESON: I cannot remember.

Just as the 1939 Nazi-Soviet nonaggression pact disillusioned progressives and led to mass defections from the CPUSA, the revelation of Stalin's crimes—murders of political opponents, dissidents, ethnic minorities, and scores of other innocent citizens—shattered the romance of the communist experiment. Lester Rodney, the *Daily Worker* sportswriter who supported Robinson's entry into the big leagues and would write a memoir titled *Press Box Red*, would quit the Party in 1958. As much as any American legislation, confirmation of Stalin's crimes hastened the declining influence of the CPUSA, and the Party would never truly recover. Stalin was, after all, a brutal dictator and murderer who killed innocents, including many people close to Robeson, such as Itzik Feffer, executed in 1952, just months before Robeson accepted the Stalin Peace Prize. Russians called the assassinations of Feffer and other writers "The Night of the Murdered Poets."

Neither Du Bois nor Robeson publicly condemned Stalin, but within the silence was calculated protest. The United States did not recognize its own crimes against the humanity of Black people—the transatlantic slave trade, the hundreds of years of slavery, the murderous legality of Jim Crow, the extralegal killings—because America apologized for nothing. Du Bois would not join as a voice in the criticism of Stalin. "As the battle to the death had been joined between the two superpowers," Du Bois biographer David Levering Lewis wrote, "he saw himself being compelled . . . to espouse the cause of opponents of Wall Street and the Pentagon, even when such advocacy corrupted other ideals of intellectual honesty and humanism." Lewis's translation of Du Bois applied to Robeson as well: he would not allow America to claim a moral superiority it did not deserve. Emmett Till's murder and the 60-minute acquittal of his killers was still fresh, and no one would ever pay for the crime. Whatever dents to his reputation, publicly denouncing Stalin was a bargain Du Bois simply would refuse to take.

Nor would Robeson, even though he had left an obvious two-decade-long paper trail praising Stalin. Three years before his death, Feffer told Robeson the state planned to execute him, and his silence exposed Robeson anew to criticism that he had always been compromised. Upon Stalin's death in 1953, Robeson called him, "My beloved comrade."

> MR. ARENS: Have you recently changed your mind about Stalin?
>
> MR. ROBESON: Whatever has happened to Stalin, gentlemen, is a question for the Soviet Union and I would not argue with a representative of the people who, in building America, wasted 60 to 100 million lives of my people, black people drawn from Africa on the plantations. You are responsible and your forebears for 60 million to 100 million black people dying in the slave ships and on the plantations, and don't you ask me about anybody, please.

Why wouldn't Robeson acknowledge Stalin's crimes? He did not believe America was interested in their suffering. It simply wanted him to admit he was wrong about the Soviets. He had made a calculation.

Even if it exposed his past positions toward the USSR as indefensible, Robeson like Du Bois would not give the United States the satisfaction of claiming itself superior, more virtuous than other nations. It, too, had blood on its hands.

> MR. ARENS: Tell us whether or not you have changed your opinion in the recent past about Stalin.
>
> MR. ROBESON: I have told you, Mister, that I would not discuss anything with the people who have murdered 60 million of my people, and I will not discuss Stalin with you.

Privately, like most radicals, Robeson was devasted. In its surveillance of him, the FBI argued the incontrovertible evidence on Stalin crushed his spirit. Robeson believed in the place whose revolution and promise he had so revered. He had been betrayed by his homeland—and hurt by his second. Sensing the great lion was wounded, Arens in a final attack asked Robeson if his affection for Stalin had diminished.

"That," Robeson told the committee, but in a far softer, less defiant tone, "is a question I will discuss among friends."

VI

TWO YEARS LATER, THE END of the eight-year ordeal appeared quietly in the papers on June 16, 1958, with a single sentence. *The New York Daily News* ran the story on page eight, not on page one, which was so often the public residence of the named names.

> **COURT BARS RED OATH RULE FOR PASSPORTS**
>
> WASHINGTON (AP)–The Supreme Court today stripped from the Secretary of State of power to force a citizen to file a non-communist affidavit in order to get a passport.

> The 5–4 decision was a victory for artist Rockwell Kent and Los Angeles psychiatrist Walter Briehl. Both were accused of having communist ties.
>
> The court simply held that the 1950 Internal Security Act did not give the Secretary of State "unbridled discretion to grant or withhold a passport from a citizen for any substantive reason he may choose."
>
> The court said that Kent and Briehl may or may not be communists but they have "neither been accused of crimes nor found guilty" and "they are being denied their freedom solely because of their refusal to be subjected to inquiry into their beliefs and associations."

A photo of the 75-year-old Kent accompanied the story, with the caption, "Rockwell Kent: *His beliefs are his own*."

For 30 years, Ruth Shipley, encouraged by the Secretary of State, had violated the Constitution. Rockwell Kent and Paul Robeson were two artists living along parallel tracks. Sixteen years older than Robeson, Kent was a renaissance man. He was a great painter of distant landscapes among other talents, and *The New York Times* would refer to him as a "man of multiple skills." In 1944, Kent publicly praised Robeson and would do so again in 1952, calling Robeson "a hero" upon winning the Stalin Prize.

Like Robeson, Kent's politics were anti-capitalist. Like Robeson, he would be considered one of the greatest 20th-century practitioners of his craft. Like so many Americans, he supported Spain against Franco, and for it, the government would surveil him. Like Robeson, he had been a Wallace man. Like Robeson, he was called a traitor. He would often state publicly that he was not a communist and his politics were no one's business. "I'm an American," Kent explained, "who doesn't want his corns stepped on." Like Robeson, Kent had his right to travel denied by Ruth Shipley. Like Robeson's, the government took Kent's passport in 1950.

One of the dissenting justices was Tom Clark, the former attorney general under Truman who, in 1947, created the original list of subversive organizations.

Kent, too, had engaged in a public showdown with the government. In 1953, appearing before the Senate Government Operations subcommittee, Kent would not bow to McCarthy. Like HUAC had treated Robeson, the committee refused to hear Kent's statement. Kent, convinced of the danger to American democracy at the ballot box posed by McCarthy and his followers inside the government, read to the public afterward:

> I am forced to the conclusion that a conspiracy exists for the purpose of overthrowing our Democracy in favor of a Fascist government. I have no hesitancy in charging that this Committee plays an active part in that conspiracy and that its Chairman, Senator McCarthy, is its leader. Moreover, and in view of the forces at the disposal of this Committee, I charge the conspiracy to be one to overthrow our form of government, if need be, by force and violence.

After seven years, Kent had won—but victory brought freedom without introspection on the government's part. Neither the thought leaders who had supported the confinement of Americans for their beliefs nor the everyday Americans who had chosen to surveil their neighbors took time to reflect. The highest court had ruled Ruth Shipley had been wrong, as were the lower courts that rejected Robeson's multiple appeals. Much of HUAC's mission—and the actions and subclauses that had come from the McCarran Act—had been repudiated.

The personal dominoes fell quickly. Kent immediately left for the Soviet Union. Under the same ruling, Du Bois, Robeson, and all others trapped by their government were no longer confined to America's borders. Du Bois and his wife, Shirley Graham, sailed to Europe. The greatest Black scholar the nation had ever produced would never again set foot on American soil.

Though it was not acknowledged stateside as a great injustice, Robeson had won. Even if the Black establishment could not understand why, throughout much of the developing world, Robeson was a hero.

He had spoken for the poor. He challenged an empire on their behalf. His politics were not imperialistic. He was not speaking for the American government but often and usually against it. For it, he was called a "citizen of the world."

A month later, in July 1958, Paul and Eslanda Robeson headed to Idlewild airport and boarded a flight to London, but not before a second appearance at Carnegie Hall. The reception they received when they arrived in London was largely euphoric. "ROBESON IS BACK!" blared one of the tabloids. Captive in his own country for eight years, Robeson was free, determined to resume his life and career. His itinerary did not include a return date.

Nearly a year later, Robeson remained in London. An Associated Negro Press wire story reported that Robeson planned on making London his permanent base, but that one day, he would return to America.

"Nobody," he declared in his deep bass voice, "can take my country away from me."

Chapter Thirteen

I

PAUL ROBESON AND JACKIE ROBINSON would share the headlines one final time. It was above the fold in the *Baltimore Afro-American*, June 23, 1956. Robeson's HUAC showdown was the big story—"WHAT ROBESON SAID"—blared across six columns, accompanied by the sidebar, "Mr. Robeson is Right." Underneath Robeson, the NAACP made an announcement: Robinson would be the 41st recipient of the organization's highest honor, the Spingarn Medal.

Robinson would be celebrated as only the most honored Black Americans had, joining the ranks of Du Bois, Marian Anderson, Ralph Bunche, Thurgood Marshall, A. Philip Randolph—and Paul Robeson—but the announcement proved bittersweet. A year earlier, Walter White, one of Robinson's earliest supporters and, later, major Robeson antagonist, died at 61 of a heart attack.

The announcement celebrated Robinson, but the specter of Robeson lurked. Officially, the NAACP had not excised Robeson from its rolls as had so many institutions, but Roy Wilkins, who succeeded White as executive secretary, certainly did not claim him. In its publicity of the Robinson nomination, the Black press announced Robinson as the first athlete in the organization's history to receive the award, even though Paul Robeson had won the award 11 years earlier and played in the National Football league when Robinson was in diapers. The

Black wire services listed past Spingarn winners, but two names did not appear in their stories: Paul Robeson and W.E.B. Du Bois, one of the original founders of the NAACP and the 1920 Spingarn winner. Due to the scheduling conflicts with the regular season, the NAACP agreed Robinson would be honored after the season, in December.

Robinson played the 1956 season with the knowledge that his time in Brooklyn, and quite likely his time in baseball, was ending. A leg injury suffered in 1955 never improved, and, for the only time in his career, Jackie Robinson (slasher of line drives, possessor of timely power, and batter of a career .313* average) would not, for any day of the season, bat .300. The Dodgers basked in the aftermath of Brooklyn's only championship, finally defeating the Yankees in the 1955 World Series, but with an eye to a future that did not include their most iconic player.

The newspapers wrote openly of how Robinson was unlikely to wrest an everyday position from younger players. Don Zimmer, Don Hoak, and Junior Gilliam were part of the Dodgers' future. Robinson played 10 games in left field, but he was not a left fielder and, at nearly 40, was not a viable option to play 150 games in the outfield. He would have to cobble together a full season of at-bats from multiple positions.

When Robinson would turn back the clock with a performance that reminded the baseball world of who he once was, as he did with a brilliant performance in Game 3 of the 1955 World Series, the writers would craft their stories, unsure if they had seen a final performance, as a reminder to savor the Broadway smash whose run had now entered its final weeks. In August, Robinson was named to the all-time Dodger team, in the same company as old-timers Wilbert Robinson and Dazzy Vance. Even great honors carried the air of a farewell.

---

* For nearly 65 years, Robinson's career average would be .311. In 2020, Major League Baseball announced it would be incorporating Negro League statistics into the Major League averages. Thus Robinson, dead 48 years, increased his career batting average by two points.

Over the offseason, *The Sporting News* speculated where Robinson would play in 1956. The Chicago White Sox were interested. Joe Brown, the president of the Pittsburgh Pirates, who had employed Branch Rickey and Robinson's old nemesis Bobby Bragan (still the manager), said money would not be an issue in obtaining Robinson, if he could still play.

In the first week of January, Robinson addressed a crowd of 300 clergymen at a banquet in West Haven, Connecticut. Described in *The Sporting News* as "graying, and carrying a solid-looking 220 pounds," the implication was not subtle: he was valiant and regal, but aging and heavy, thirty-five pounds over his prime playing weight. In January 1956, free agency was still twenty years away. The only part of his career in a player's control was retirement. "I'm going to try for the Brooklyn infield in the spring. If I am traded, I'd like to remain in baseball, but it would depend on the deal," Robinson told the crowd. "I wouldn't want to be shuffled around just because I'm the property of the clubs. I'm going to make my own decision as to where I'll play, and it will have to be a good deal to make me stay."

When it came to the Dodgers, Robinson appeared more nostalgic, adopting a posture that was certainly difficult for a player of his ferocity and impact: he needed to rely on charity. Robinson was diminished as a player, but the Dodgers were finally champions for the first time in their 74-year history. Perhaps, Robinson said in the offseason, Walter O'Malley and the Dodger front office would show "the old boy"—as he wistfully referred to himself—a little grace. The Dodgers did. Robinson would return for the 1956 season, and then they traded for Randy Jackson, a third baseman—the position Robinson believed he was best suited for. He would not forget the perceived insult.

There was still more baseball to be played. The young Milwaukee duo of Eddie Mathews and Henry Aaron were determined to overtake the venerable Dodgers. For most of September, the two teams would not be separated by more than a game. The Braves held a one-game lead with three to play before blinking. The Dodgers won the pennant by a game. The biggest lead Brooklyn held all season was a mere one and a half games, way back in April. Milwaukee had been the better team all season, but it didn't matter. The old men of the Dodgers were not yet finished.

Once more, the Yankees awaited. Once more, the Yankees won the championship in seven games. In the sixth game, a tenth-inning Robinson single broke a 0–0 tie and forced a seventh game. It was the last hit of Jackie Robinson's career. The Yankees destroyed Don Newcombe, 9–0, the next day to win the World Series. Robinson struck out to end the season.

Alston told reporters he expected Robinson to be back in 1957. Some of the organization's top talent evaluators, like Andy High, believed the team needed to trade Robinson immediately while he still had market value. As the Dodgers landed in Tokyo for a string of exhibition games, Robinson held an impromptu press session at the Imperial Hotel, telling reporters, "I'm 37 years old, but I have no plans at the moment of retiring and will play next year."

Robinson and the Dodgers did not speak until December 13, when two days after receiving his Spingarn Medal (presented to him by another Paul Robeson antagonist, Ed Sullivan), he received a surprise call from Buzzy Bavasi: The Dodgers had traded him to the Giants.

He was stunned. Robinson told Bill Nunn Jr., of the *Pittsburgh Courier*, he was surprised and hurt. To Robinson's home in Stamford, Connecticut, a 25-year-old Willie Mays sent him a telegram:

> *I'VE ALWAYS ADMIRED AND RESPECTED YOUR WONDERFUL TALENTS AND ABILITY.*
>
> *THE KNOWLEDGE THAT WE WILL BE TEAMMATES IS AN INDESCRIBABLE PLEASURE.*
>
> *I AM LOOKING FORWARD TO SOME MEMORABLE DAYS FOLLOWING YOUR GUIDANCE.*
>
> *I HOPE TO REACH SOME OF THE HEIGHTS THAT MAKE YOUR RECORD STAND OUT LIKE A PINNACLE.*

IT'S ONE OF MY GREATEST THRILLS AND HAPPIEST MOMENTS TO BE ABLE TO SAY "WELCOME JACKIE TO THE GIANTS." WILLIE MAYS

Three weeks later, as the New Year introduced 1957, Robinson had an announcement of his own: he was quitting the game. On January 22, 1957, baseball approved his voluntary retirement.

II

OVER HIS FINAL TWO YEARS, Robinson was uncharacteristically muted on social issues, confirming his vulnerability. His salary dropped from $39,500 in 1954 to $31,500 in 1956, and he needed to earn a living in his second act.

He hoped to enter the mass media, but NBC was not interested and he had no future in Hollywood. That left baseball, where many people in the game, tired of his activism, could not wait for him to be gone.

Robinson had done everything in the game, except one essential thing: bank a reserve of goodwill for the time—and the time *would* come as it did for all athletes—when performance could no longer save them. Robinson always maintained he did not care if he was well-liked as long as he was respected, but likability was a quality Robinson desperately needed.

It was unclear who, if anyone specifically, had silenced him. The newspapers said it was O'Malley, who had tired of Robinson's daily controversies. Whether arguing with umpires or scolding the nation over its ambivalence toward civil rights, Jackie Robinson was always fighting and, for it, was deeply disliked in certain quarters of baseball. The vultures were descending. Jimmy Cannon, columnist for the *New York Daily News*, intimated that Robinson's rages had gone so far that he was simply mad at the world.

Because they were contemporaries and opposite personalities, Roy Campanella and Robinson were often compared. Once, when Dick

Young of the *New York Daily News* was researching a book on Campanella, Mel Jones, the farm director for Montreal when Robinson arrived in 1946, distinguished the two for Young. "Robinson, as I see him, is a formally educated, proud Negro. Campanella has had comparatively little formal education, but he is smart in another way. He's baseball smart, but I'm not referring to that.

"I mean he came up by way of hard knocks, and became just as smart, in some ways even smarter than Jackie. Like getting along with people. He has learned to maintain his poise in any company without feeling inferior. It is hard for a Negro to accomplish this in an entire lifetime."

Few newspaper articles hesitated to call Robinson exhausting. With a month remaining in the regular season, the September 1955 issue of *Sport* magazine focused on Robinson with a profile titled "The Ten Years of Jackie Robinson," which depicted a man who had lost control of himself as a professional and, in the process, the goodwill he accrued in 1947, when he was forbidden to respond to attacks against him. Within baseball, Robinson had become as famous for his temper as his baserunning.

MUCH PRAISED, MUCH DAMNED ROBINSON

As Jackie Robinson approaches the end of this tenth and possibly final season in organized baseball, he is known in many ways by many people. Because, in the beginning, Robinson endured outrage and vituperation with an almost magical mixture of humility and pride, there are those that know him as a saint.

Because today, Robinson fights mudslinging with mudslinging, and sometimes even slings mud first, there are those that know him as a troublemaker.

SPORT magazine sum paradox Robinson up this way: He had the playing ability to become a star, plus the intelligence to understand his role. He had the fighting temperament to wring the most from his ability, and the self-control to keep his temper in check. Why has he let himself go?

> One excuse might be that he's been called a nigger a thousand times in ten baseball seasons. Another is that he was scarred in his crusade.

Faced with survival, Robinson attempted restraint. First Rickey muzzled him. Two years later, Rickey gave him a friendly warning his tempestuousness was aiding his enemies. Muted for too long, Robinson did not listen. Now, in desperation, he muzzled himself. He wasn't ejected from a game during the entire 1955 season. That hadn't happened since his handcuffed rookie season, but his reputation did not soften. He attempted to conform, for landing a managing job would solve a financial issue and break another impossible racial barrier about which Robinson had been extremely (and to the white men who ran and wrote about the game, annoyingly) vocal. From Durocher to Bobby Bragan, Robinson had the requisite pugnacious qualities and baseball acumen that translated well to the bench, but it was much less likely the sport would put a Black man in charge of white players in the 1950s than it was to have a Black teammate in the 1940s.

If the exact impetus was unknown, it was clear that Jackie Robinson did not comment on the first two momentous events of the modern Civil Rights movement as they occurred—Emmett Till's murder and Rosa Parks's defiance. Till was murdered on August 28, 1955. Robinson played baseball that day, going 2-for-4, was picked off first, and caught stealing home in a 6–1 win over the Cardinals at Ebbets Field. For the rest of the season and World Series, he gave no extended comment on Till.

A week after the Series, during a massive rally held by the CIO's District 65 Retail Workers Union, which blocked traffic on 38th Street and 7th Avenue, Robinson quietly lent his name to the Till protests. Lester Rodney of the *Daily Worker* wrote up a brief in the October 16 edition. "Jackie Robinson, the popular Dodger baseball star, sent a message of greetings to the garment district rally associating himself with the nation-wide movement to avenge the murder of Emmett Till and gain freedom for Negroes everywhere." In December, Montgomery had become international news. Till was still front-page news. Cleveland star Larry Doby—the first Black player in the American League—called for the federal government to intervene. Robinson said nothing.

Survival was the likeliest explanation. The combination of Robinson hearing different voices—the threat from O'Malley, the measured common sense of Rachel, the shrewd, conservative counsel of Branch Rickey—led him to the same conclusion: commenting seriously risked what slim hopes he had for a future in baseball. Rumors swirled in 1955 that two teams—Rickey's Pirates and the Montreal Royals, the Dodger farm team where Robinson debuted—were looking at Robinson to manage. No matter how cantankerous Robinson might be, he was universally admired as a competitor. In his *Sporting News* column, following the Series, Dick Young gave Robinson a backhanded compliment typical of his standing in the game. "My own private World Series hero is Jackie Robinson. I realize this isn't a popular choice, but I'm convinced that if Robby didn't pick them up in the third game, the Brooks probably would have lost in four or five . . . and I'm further convinced he'll be gone from Brooklyn by the start of next season." Later in the column, Young wrote that Pittsburgh's financial troubles could be helped by hiring Robinson as manager to "revitalize" the franchise. ("Free suggestion . . . he'd be a box-office bonanza, and with Rickey riding reins on him, Robby just might make a fine pilot.")

Robinson was silent on civil rights, yet he still had no trouble reprising his role as Rickey's Cold Warrior. Three days after the start of the Montgomery bus boycott, Robinson traveled to Calgary to be honored by the western branch of the Canadian Council of Christians and Jews. During a two-hour Q and A session, he touched on a host of topics. Neither Till nor Montgomery were part of his remarks, but Paul Robeson was. "Unfortunate is the way he describes Paul Robeson," Robinson was summarized in the press. "He explains that had Robeson not aligned himself with the Communists, he could have been a tremendous force for the Negro. Yet Robinson feels in some way that, Robeson possibly sacrificed himself to help others of race."

Robinson also made mention of the upcoming Sugar Bowl between Georgia Tech and Pittsburgh, where the segregationist Georgia Governor Marvin Griffin pressured the schools to cancel the game because the Panthers had a Black player on the roster, fullback Bobby Grier. Robinson called the move led by the Georgia governor "ignorant."

Two weeks after the game, Rickey attended a banquet in Philadelphia and, in his remarks, mentioned Griffin, who even after the game (and Georgia Tech's 7–0 victory) said Georgia universities should never play games against teams with Black players. Rickey expressed his disappointment, but not for Grier or with an eye on the growing movement. His comments centered around Paul Robeson—how Americans were going to be perceived around the world. Rickey referred to the controversy as "an international embarrassment he caused the State Department." It was a telling reveal. While the State Department and USIA spent so much time and energy attempting to discredit Robeson, Georgia, Alabama, and the Deep South continued to prove Robeson's dissent. Branch Rickey decided to see the violence against Black citizens through lens of American Cold War propaganda, clinging to the fiction that American racism was merely communist exaggeration.

Robinson begrudgingly distanced himself from the first major steps of a movement that vindicated all he had endured since 1945, but the strategy backfired. The rumors of him as a managerial candidate never materialized. Robinson never received an interview, or even a conversation, from either Pittsburgh or Montreal. Robinson had stayed quiet and got nothing for it. The Pirates were making a different decision. After five years, they fired Branch Rickey.

III

DURING THE FIRST WEEK OF January 1957, Robinson confirmed he had retired. Photographers snapped photos of him in a suit wearing a Dodgers cap and holding his jersey one last time. A few final fights remained. The writers, most notably Red Smith, considered his act of selling his retirement to *Look* magazine (for an estimated $30,000–$50,000, nearly a year's salary) beneath him and a betrayal of the reporters who had covered him for the past dozen years. Upset because the Dodgers would have to return the player they received from the Giants (and the $30,000 in cash they'd received), Bavasi called Robinson "bush" and accused him of retiring as a leverage ploy to convince the Giants to pony up more money. Feeling Bavasi had impugned his integrity, Robinson vowed never to again wear a baseball uniform.

A few writers told elegiac tales of the great Robinson journey. Most begrudgingly acknowledged he had been one of the greatest to play the game. Others remained embittered. One writer attempted to sympathize with Robinson for surviving Rickey's early rules by noting Robinson had to rein in a "violent temper."

Robinson exited the game weary and unapologetic. He weighed 228 pounds and told reporters that trying to lose 20 pounds to get into shape for spring training felt like "torture." Attempting to compliment the spirit that made him a champion, a reporter responded that the old Robinson would have taken getting in shape as a challenge.

"I'm sick and tired of accepting challenges," he said. "That's all my life has been—a series of challenges."

In an interview with Joe Reichler of the Associated Press, Robinson held firm. He wanted the baseball world to know he and the sport were even. "I don't want anybody to imply that I am not grateful to baseball. I wouldn't be here if it weren't for baseball. But I don't believe I owe baseball a thing."

Robinson now threw himself headlong into a simmering civil rights movement. Freshly out of the baseball fight, Robinson's patience grew thin, having to live within the deferential parameters of how an athlete was expected to speak. Reichler threw Robinson a softball about the great Willie Mays losing a chance to play along the great Robinson—Mays had already sent the telegram, excited about the season. It was just sportswriter candy, a bon mot for fans to wonder tantalizingly what might have been to see Mays and Robinson wearing the same uniform. "It's about time I start thinking about Jackie Robinson," Robinson told Reichler. "Not somebody else."

When Robinson entered the league, he agreed to be sacrificed so Black players could play for every major league team. Rickey said merit would be the judge. So did *The Sporting News*. So did the writers. Robinson produced six World Series appearances and one championship. Robinson's Dodgers had finished first or second in nine of his ten seasons. Red Smith said the reaction to Robinson had always been more attributable to his personality than his race, a response typical for his ten years in the game and beyond; there was always a reason other than race.

He fulfilled the promise, blazed the trail others followed, and allowed himself to be harmed as a cost for their entry. Yet, Jackie Robinson was now retired, and, over the course of his career, three teams—the Tigers, the Phillies, and the Red Sox—had still never fielded a Black player. A year earlier in Calgary, Robinson reflected on the price of admission demanded by Rickey and America and reached a conclusion: "I lived a lie for two years."

Through all the years and the innings, pre- and-postgame press scrums, and the hundreds of personality profiles and notes about his temper and attitude, Jackie Robinson had never been interviewed by a Black sports columnist working for a mainstream newspaper because the country had never seen one. When the liberal *New York Post* hired him to a thrice-weekly column during the 1960 Presidential campaign, he became the first.

Robinson was politically conservative, which carried a different connotation than in present times. Black voters in 1960 had been surging toward the Democratic Party, but as early as 1928, Black Americans identified equally with both parties. His first decision was not choosing Richard Nixon, but rejecting Massachusetts Senator John F. Kennedy. Offended by the aloofness the senator showed toward civil rights,

Robinson said he could never vote for anyone who seemed to know so little about Black people.

In 1949, Robinson had been the anticommunist chess piece to neutralize Paul Robeson. With his *Post* column reaching a million New Yorkers and beyond, plus the cachet of being the great Jackie Robinson, the Kennedy campaign decided it was Robinson who needed to be parried. The Democrats decided to use the playbook the USIA used against Robeson: find Black athletes to offset Robinson. They chose Henry Aaron. Neither knew they were being used as Black men to diminish their idol, but Aaron and Milwaukee centerfielder Billy Bruton agreed to campaign for Kennedy. The 1960 campaign began Henry Aaron's lifelong association with the Democratic Party.

Outside of the baseball world, Robinson suffered from the lack of diplomacy that hurt him as a player. Quick to criticize, unaware—or maybe all too aware—of the impact of his words, Robinson found himself, as he did during his baseball career, in a state of constant confrontation. Politics required compromise, flexibility, and a keen awareness of when to speak and, more importantly, when not to. Robinson's willingness to always speak his mind was both a tremendous quality and liability. His confrontations were myriad and bipartisan. He collided with the NAACP, with whom his relationship was tenuous because the organization both did not like competing public voices in the fight for civil rights and because Robinson believed the group to be too passive. He collided with the growing Black power movements—the Nation of Islam and the student-led campus movements—because he steadfastly supported interracial coalitions when the movement for Black-led, Black-only organizations was percolating. He collided with both of his employers, Chock full o'Nuts, where he held the title of vice president since retiring from baseball, and the *Post,* because even the name Jackie Robinson could not alone substitute for his oft-combative political style. Robinson was discovering there was no true independence in the romantic sense when both relying on others for a paycheck and aligning with political parties, and on numerous occasions, he would clash in the outside world as surely as he did with the commissioner's office.

An even greater disappointment quickly revealed itself: civil rights was his priority, but in the mainstream white world, race was but a topic—not always urgent, always to be balanced against other priorities—as Paul Robeson discovered in 1946 when Truman told him the time wasn't right to address lynching. Between his frantic, unsuccessful appeals to Eisenhower during the Little Rock High integration in 1957 (and the president's decision to enforce the *Brown* decision, but his refusal to reveal if he supported it), his unheeded advice to Nixon that an opportunity existed to cultivate Black voters, and his feeling that civil rights was more an annoyance than a priority to Eisenhower and Nixon, Robinson was forced into a truth from which he could no longer look away: maybe for all these years, he had been signed up with the wrong team, or worse, given what little regard he held for Kennedy, there was no right team.

How did Jackie Robinson end up on the team? Robinson often referred to Branch Rickey as the father he never had (a feeling accelerated by the 1948 death of Karl Downs, Robinson's college mentor) and allowed Rickey to shape his politics. A decade after the hearings, the paths of Jackie Robinson and Paul Robeson would continue to cross, and the reason was not Alvin Stokes, John S. Wood, Lester Granger, Robinson's patriotism, or Robeson's perceived lack of it. The reason was Branch Rickey. As much as Rickey saw Robinson as the appropriate player to integrate the majors, he had also groomed Robinson to be his anti-Robeson.

IV

RICKEY SUFFERED A HEART ATTACK in February 1958. During months of convalescence, he had struck up some correspondence with Carl Rowan. Just four months earlier, Rowan had written a scathing October 1957 *Ebony* profile on Robeson titled "Has Paul Robeson Betrayed the Negro?" and had been sent to Bandung under the guise of independent journalism. Rickey was well aware of Rowan's connections with the State Department and intelligence community. Given the conservative, anticommunist politics of the two men, Rowan and Rickey quickly engaged in warm communication.

In a letter dated April 10, Rickey told Rowan he needed a favor: he had been musing about writing a magazine article on a subject he referred to as "the red threat of inferiority." The American public, Rickey wrote to Rowan, "has a sort of secret feeling that the Negro is really inferior, and I mean inferior by nature. The long years of menial service caused this sort of subconscious belief. I think the stark fact of it ought to be brought to the public's attention in every way we know how." Rickey asked Rowan to compile a master list of "prominent Negro-American intellectuals."

The result of Rickey's correspondence with Rowan appeared in the May 27, 1958, edition of *Look* magazine. With the State Department keeping Robeson under house arrest—he had now entered the ninth year of his travel ban—Rickey decided to begin his article by focusing on Paul Robeson.

HOW IT LOOKS FROM WHERE I SIT

> The intelligent victim of intolerance suffers worse than the old-fashioned whipping post could ever provide. Think that statement through. Millions of intelligent Negroes in this country know it to be true, whether white people know it or not. This was the kind of punishment that caused Negro singer Paul Robeson to become a Communist sympathizer. He just couldn't take it. He was impatient with the slow processes of democracy. Whatever love of country was obscured . . . He can say anything he pleases in this country about his government or anybody or anything and still be asked to play Othello on the New York stage. In Russia, he could not say a word against totalitarian controls without getting a free ticket to Siberia. But Robeson didn't think of this. He was hurting too badly.

Rickey's words mirrored Robinson's syndicated column from 1949—and offered insight on the degree to which Robinson had been influenced by Rickey—when Robinson asked in his *Brooklyn Eagle* column if it was possible in Russia to call the head man a louse. Not, Robinson said, unless you wanted to play centerfield in the Siberian League. Rickey, like Robinson before him, conveniently omitted a statistic the State Department did not want advertised around the world: Mississippi was the densest state of people, but the Black vote in the state was virtually nonexistent.

Rickey's disingenuousness could be seen through Robeson's current existence: In America, where Rickey wrote he could say anything he pleased, Paul Robeson lost everything. He was not asked to play Othello. No record company would sign him. He could not find work. He was not asked to sing, and in Peekskill, a violent mob tried to kill him not once, but twice. The government was currently preventing him from leaving the country. He was not free.

The fast friendship with Branch Rickey would come with a payoff for Carl Rowan: a book deal with Robinson. The collaboration made sense. They were two men of similar political sensibility: conservative-leaning and generally well-regarded in both Black and white communities. Both were of the same generation (Robinson was six and a half years older). Rickey was the connective bond, but so was being Black and navigating the mainstream, "respectable" lanes as both Rowan and Robinson worked for major newspapers. Both were connected to the NAACP, and both were Black veterans who presented themselves as firmly, if not fervently, anticommunist.

When the book, *Wait Till Next Year*, was released in 1960, the battleground for civil rights was not primarily the courtroom, as it had been for *Brown*, but in school, at lunch counters, and in the streets. Robinson revisited his HUAC testimony in a chapter titled, "A Patriot's Purgatory." Five years earlier, when he was honored in Calgary, Robinson left clues that his attitudes toward Robeson had evolved, and for ten pages of his book, he displayed a previously unseen respect for Robeson as an artist, the closest he would come to admitting testifying was a mistake and Rickey put him up to appearing. The Robinson of *Wait Till Next Year* is introspective toward Robeson. "I knew that many Negroes welcomed Robeson's remarks, not because of disloyalty, or of any other tender feelings toward the Soviet Union, but because they feared white America would never grant the Negro a position of equality simply out of a sense of justice and decency."

Robinson attempted a half-hearted lunge at debate, but their Blackness bound the two men together far more solidly than politics could divide them. "Against the facts, Robeson's Paris remarks seemed silly to me. . . . But what about Robeson? With what was I to take issue specifically? Had Robeson betrayed me? The *Negro*? The *Nation*? *The cause of freedom*? How much justification was there in the things that Robeson had said in Paris and elsewhere?"

Robinson wrote that "Negroes warned that I should beware of letting myself be used in 'that old white man's plot to divide and conquer' the colored peoples of the world."

> No one had to tell me that I did not know all I needed to know about political alignments in the United States, or about our country's position in the Cold War, or the overall state of race relations, to say what I really wanted to say about communism. I had not yet enough experience handling delicate problems of Negro progress to articulate for the nation the Negro's aspirations, especially when they had to be outlined against a background of political fear.
>
> Yet, I knew that Mr. Rickey wanted me to go to Washington. He figured that an appearance before that committee, in which I would speak boldly but wisely, would be the final stroke necessary to establish forever the Negro's place in baseball—and possibly in America.

Perhaps Robinson's conciliatory tone represented his true sentiments on the entire testimony: he had been told to perform a service by his employer and had no leverage to do anything but comply. Or perhaps Robinson was reflecting growth, fresh thoughts with eleven years of perspective and freedom from repercussion.

The most plausible answer is that the times had shifted. The domestic Cold War fever had broken. Rowan and Robinson engaged in some revisionist history, image burnishing, knowing that Robinson's testimony was no longer to Black America, if it ever was, his finest hour. Robinson also received some coaching from Rowan, and Rowan took extensive liberties with Robinson's voice. In one section, Robinson retells anecdotes about Robeson's difficult upbringing in racist Princeton, New Jersey, as famous pieces of folklore universally known by Black America. The anecdotes, however, appear in the same paragraph in Rowan's October 1957 *Ebony* profile.

Robeson was unsurprised by the change in Robinson's tone in print compared to his feisty testimony. In the same *Ebony* article, after upbraiding the Black establishment for conspiring with the federal government to attack ("If Negroes had simply remained neutral, the State Department could not have imprisoned me. In fact, they did what they did only with the active cooperation of some top Negro leadership."), Robeson saved a word for Robinson. "And Jackie," Robeson said to Rowan, "well, he was just spitting out words Lester Granger put in his mouth."

V

WITHOUT THE ENORMOUS DEBT ROBINSON felt he owed Rickey, it was unlikely he would have ever found himself placed in such opposition to Robeson, for despite his conservatism, there was no other area where Robinson politically placed being an American ahead of being a Black American. Through that lens, Robinson and Robeson had virtually no need for such a public and damaging interaction. It was Rickey and Alvin Stokes who first placed Robinson in opposition to Robeson, and the legacy of that decision placed 1960s Jackie Robinson in another conflict: a man committed to his people now at odds with the increasingly militant Black sensibility. Robinson supported Richard Nixon while the Democratic Party was rapidly becoming the political party of Black America. Following his assassination, photos of

JFK hung in Black households around the country—a show of respect for the 1960 phone call Kennedy made to a pregnant Coretta Scott King while Martin Luther King Jr. sat in a Georgia jail—a call Robinson urged Nixon to make that Nixon refused. Enraged, Robinson nevertheless remained in Nixon's camp, further highlighting his growing political distance from the Black mood of the country, distancing him from the present moment.

His allies had been aloof to civil rights, and that wounded him. Before the 1963 March on Washington, Robinson reached out to an old Dodger teammate, Clem Labine. The two had fought many a baseball battle together. Labine, Robinson thought, was one of the players who brought the Dodgers together. Labine declined. "I went to my elders and said, 'Well, what do you think? You think I should do it?'" Labine recalled. "'Jackie's a friend of mine. Should I be down in Washington?' I say now, unfortunately, I followed the advice that said, 'No, don't go down. It might not be good for your career.' . . . So, I didn't go. I'm sorry I didn't go."

Robinson took heavy criticism for leaning right, but believed Black people deserved a legitimate two-party choice. The Republican party drifted farther to the right, and his voice grew louder, but its impact weakened.

A new wave of powerful Black dissenters saw Robinson as horribly out of touch, desperate for white approval when an entire Black diaspora political consciousness rose—the Du Bois-Robeson Pan-Africanism that terrified the State Department as communist and vexed the NAACP. Four months after the March on Washington, Malcolm X went after Robinson. Malcolm once referred to Robinson as a "handkerchief-headed Uncle Tom," and the two would wage a public war of words. Part of the reason for his stinging attacks was his belief that the great Jackie Robinson had lost his way. A year earlier, it was Malcolm who interceded to settle a war of words between Robinson and Black nationalist Lewis Michaux, owner of a Harlem bookstore. To further prove his point that Robinson was allowing himself to be used, Malcolm brought up the name that now haunted Robinson—

Paul Robeson. In a letter to the *Amsterdam News* dated November 30, 1963, Malcolm wrote,

> *Shortly after the White Man lifted you from poverty and obscurity to the Major Leagues, Paul Robeson was condemning America for her injustices against American Negroes. Mr. Robeson questioned the intelligence of Negroes fighting to defend a country that treated them with such open contempt and bestial brutality.*
>
> *Robeson's brilliant stand on behalf of our people left the guilty American whites speechless: they had no defense.*
>
> *They sought desperately to find another Negro who would be dumb enough to champion their bankrupt "white" cause against Paul Robeson.*
>
> *It was you who let yourself be used by the whites even in those days against your own kind.*
>
> *You let them sic you on Paul Robeson. You let them use you to destroy Paul Robeson.*
>
> *You let your White Boss send you before a congressional hearing in Washington, D.C., (the capital of Segregationville) to dispute and condemn Paul Robeson, because he had these guilty American whites frightened silly.*

During the 1964 election cycle, Robinson and Rickey were both dismayed by what they saw as the future of the Republican Party—anti–civil rights, whiter, more conservative, and less open to remedy social maladies. Yet, neither seemed ready to flee the party. Robinson decided to lean on the personal integrity of Nelson Rockefeller, the New York governor and whom Robinson believed was the party's only hope. Outside of Rockefeller, Robinson was wholly pessimistic. A month before the bomb blast that killed four Black girls at the 16th Street Baptist Church in Birmingham, Alabama, on September 15, 1963, Robinson penned a piece for *The Saturday Evening Post* that would prove prescient titled "The G.O.P.: For White Men Only?" The magazine teed up Robinson's essay with the subtitle, "A world-famous Negro who served Nixon in 1960 blasts a right-wing tendency to turn against the Negro in 1964."

Rickey remained partisan, believing Barry Goldwater, the extreme Republican nominee, would grow into the job if he won the presidency. Rickey intensely disliked Johnson for personal reasons. Three weeks after Johnson passed the monumental Civil Rights Act of 1964, with which the federal government outlawed segregation for the first time in the 20th century, Rickey was going to back Goldwater. Writing to the influential Black Chicago pastor Archibald Carey, Rickey attempted to talk himself into comfort against his own powers of logic:

> *My chief objection to Goldwater is his civil rights stand. He is forthright but deluded. I don't think we can now tell the future of the Republican Party. . . . If Goldwater beats Johnson, I believe that the civil rights law will be enforced. I think the Arizonian has personal integrity, plenty of it—enough to conform with his oath of office.*
>
> *In the meantime, you must not acclaim or desert. For the future of the party and the future of the country . . . I am sick about everything that happened and I am apprehensive about the future conduct of the Republican National Committee. It is a machine controlled by Goldwater lieutenants.*

VI

IN 1969, JACKIE ROBINSON TURNED 50. His view of America had dimmed into darkness. It was nighttime now. He was a Hall of Famer but estranged from baseball. He feuded with the game for its lack of progress. He sparred with Hall of Famer Bob Feller during the 1969 season, who concluded Robinson just wanted a handout, a cushy front office job, just because he was Black. "There hasn't been a lick of discrimination in baseball since Jackie entered the game," Feller told reporters.

Robinson had been one of the Republican Party's most tireless defenders, but his criticisms were now taken poorly by the party. William F. Buckley, celebrated as the party's intellectual voice who had been enthusiastically conflating civil rights with domestic subversion since the 1950s, criticized Robinson with a string of condescending public attacks—claiming that Robinson was the true racist—that confirmed what Robinson believed about the conservatives was no more.

J. ROBINSON: POMPOUS MORALIZER

> It is surely time to put an end to the mischievous national habit of taking seriously this pompous moralizer who whines his way through life as though all America were at Ebbets Field cheering him on against the big bad racist Yankees. The gentleman is a philosophical moron, whose most distinctive public service would consist in going back to elementary school.

Robinson and Rickey were the most famous pioneering duo of the American 20th century, but Branch Rickey had been dead nearly four years. Two weeks before Christmas 1965, Rickey suffered a fatal heart attack at age 83, and for the first time, Robinson navigated his politics on his own. Without Rickey, Robinson's politics became less complicated. The Cold War disappeared almost entirely from his positions, a byproduct perhaps of Rickey's influence and the insistence of segregationists that only communists supported integration. Robinson focused on the issues germane to Black advancement that had always been authentically his: juvenile delinquency, education and opportunity for the young, civil rights, and job creation.

The costs had become insurmountable. Emmett Till. Birmingham. Medgar Evers. King. Malcolm X. In his sport, the next stage of integration—front office and managerial opportunities for Black candidates—seemed as unthinkable as his own signing two and a half decades earlier. With a decade of white resistance culminating in the King assassination, the violent, persistent backlash to equal rights often made him question whatever he had inspired in 1947. America was showing its true face, and it stared in hostile opposition to his.

• • •

He had finally arrived at recognition. The politically conservative white men whom he had trusted to be of different background, but similar values had disappointed him for the last time. In 1968, in full opposition to Vietnam, the war he had once supported, the war King and Muhammad Ali loudly rejected, the war that Paul Robeson had predicted two decades earlier while the country called him a traitor, Robinson broke with Richard Nixon and the Republican Party. The personal toll of his son Jackie Jr.'s drug addiction—which originated in Vietnam—and the increasing evidence the country was involved in a quagmire confirmed for him the war had been a terrible miscalculation.

He attempted to remain optimistic, but it was a struggle. The significant portion of white Americans who had once called him a hero but now seemed even more rigid in their opposition to integration hurt him deeply. Being called a communist was the most unpatriotic attack, and conservatives now called integration a communist plot. Most resounding was the number of his fellow Americans who let their feelings be known at the ballot box. Robinson was on speaking terms with, but wary of, Nixon, but it was the far-right American Independent Party, which nominated the ticket of segregationist Alabama Governor George Wallace and the General Curtis LeMay, that completed the end of his faith in his country.

"Segregation today! Segregation tomorrow! Segregation forever!" was Wallace's campaign slogan, and LeMay advocated using nuclear weapons on China, Vietnam, and the Soviet Union at various points. The duo carried five states, including Georgia, where Robinson was born—just as Strom Thurmond's segregationist Dixiecrats had won four states in 1948, repudiating Robeson and Henry Wallace. His country had spoken, and, with profound unforgiveness, he would finally listen.

Summer approached. *The New York Times* reported that American flags were selling at a record rate across the country. But in an America divided by war, the flag took on different meanings. Some interpreted the flag as a symbol of national pride. Others saw it as a conservative weapon against integration, antiwar protesters, and civil rights, a message to whom the country belonged—and to whom it did not.

Robinson had been positioned since 1947 as a symbol of the American Dream whose integration of the national pastime symbolized the inherent goodness and limitless potential of his country. So the *Times* reporter, Jon Nordheimer, called Robinson for an interview. When his story appeared on July 4, 1969, under the headline "Flag on July 4: Thrill to Some, Threat to Others," Nordheimer chose Robinson to bat leadoff for his story. "I wouldn't fly the flag on the Fourth of July or any other day," said Jackie Robinson, the former baseball star. "When I see a car with a flag pasted on it, I figure the guy behind the wheel isn't my friend."

Aftermath

Kings

I

THE PARALLEL ARCS OF PAUL Robeson and Jackie Robinson that began with belief in the American promise before descending into profound disillusionment placed the two men on a continuum with a 19th-century predecessor: Moses Fleetwood Walker. Walker was the Oberlin- and University of Michigan–educated catcher who would become the first Black player to play in the professional circuit eventually known as Major League Baseball. Fourteen years before Robeson's birth and 63 years before Robinson's historic debut, Walker played in the primitive days of baseball, when eight balls constituted a walk and the pitching mound was no mound at all, but flat ground level to home plate.

Walker played for the Toledo Blue Stockings of the American Association, the startup professional league that folded after a decade, but not before four teams—the Cardinals, Dodgers, Reds, and Pirates—joined the rival National League. Like Robeson decades later and Jackie Robinson in high school, Walker was a catcher, receiving in a bloody, bruising game that had not yet introduced chest protectors, shin guards, or even catcher's mitts. Catching fastballs with his bare hands,

Walker became an original member of the heritage of Black Americans who were optimistic that sports could be an effective proving ground for gaining social equality in the United States.

Integration in baseball lasted one year. The history books apocryphally attributed the ouster of Black players from the major leagues solely to Adrian "Cap" Anson, the determined segregationist manager of the National League Chicago White Stockings (the precursor to the Chicago Cubs), but Anson was merely a prominent voice within a larger moment of a national backlash against Black citizens. It was true that Anson used his influence to remove Black players as a condition to continuing exhibitions against Toledo (a demand joined by some of Walker's own teammates), but the real force behind their expulsion from baseball was the federal judiciary. In 1883, the year before Walker's debut and end, the Supreme Court overturned the Civil Rights Bill of 1875, laying the legal foundation for a 20th century of segregation.

Then known as "the Civil Rights Cases," the Court consolidated five cases into one sweeping judgment, ruling that the 13th and 14th Amendments that outlawed slavery and ensured equal protection under the law, respectively, did not apply to private business or individuals. The Civil Rights Bill of 1875 was ruled unconstitutional by a vote of 8 to 1, the lone dissenter being Justice John Marshall Harlan, a slave-owner until he was 32 years old. In his dissent, Harlan said the repeal stripped the 14th Amendment of its meaning.

America reinstituted segregation. Baseball followed, and the American Association expelled Walker. For a few years, Black players would survive tenuously in the minor leagues, but by 1888, professional baseball teams were completely segregated and would be for the next 58 years. The Court's repeal would be unsuccessfully challenged for the next decade, until the Supreme Court codified legal segregation in the 1896 *Plessy v. Ferguson* case. Harlan again would be the lone dissenter in *Plessy*. In its majority opinion on *Plessy*, the court agreed that in imposing a separate-but-equal doctrine, Black Americans would be subject to second-class citizenship, but only if they lacked positive thinking.

A "badge of inferiority," the court concluded, only applied if "the colored race chooses to put that construction on it."

Toledo folded after the 1884 season. That winter, a one-sentence news brief appeared in the December 13, 1884, *Xenia Daily Gazette* under the header, "Items Regarding Colored People Here and Elsewhere: M. Fleetwood Walker, the well-known colored base ball player, formerly catcher in the Toledo Club, is now in the U.S. postal service."

Banned from baseball and deprived of equal citizenship, Walker decided America was untenable. Decades later, as Robeson and Robinson would take divergent political paths to the same question, Walker believed the solution for what was called the "Negro Question" was to leave America altogether—repatriation to Africa. He had become a Garveyite.

In 1908, Walker published a searing 47-page manifesto titled *Our Home Colony: A Treatise on the Past, Present and Future of the Negro Race.* "The relations of the two races, economic, social, and industrial, are being discussed from every Negro pulpit in the country. Negro teachers and politicians are disseminating their views in every community of black people. The whites do not seem so agitated."

Walker had not lost faith in America as much as he believed he had understood it. His life in Steubenville, Ohio, had always been a taut negotiation, but the combination of the Court's decisions and the violent behavior of whites was a reminder that Reconstruction was not the norm, but an aberration.

"The Negroes without the enjoyment of social equality as we have pointed out its existence among the whites of this country—must submit to Social Inequality, and that means always at the bottom," Walker wrote. "We see no possible hope that the Negro will ever secure the enjoyment of this social freedom or equality."

The book does not reference Walker's time as a baseball player, Cap Anson, or the teammates that supported his expulsion, but it was Walker's time on the Toledo roster, traveling into Southern towns—Louisville, St. Louis, and Washington, DC—that sharpened his pessimism about integration. As an example of how firmly American segregation was cemented in American life at the turn of the century, there was nothing aspirational about sports, no rhetoric of how a game based on merit could remedy social inequalities. Baseball was simply another occupation the law allowed to belong only to whites.

Walker had studied the progressive, pre-radical positions of Du Bois and the conservative, accommodationist solutions of Booker T. Washington, but it was the Garvey option that most resonated with him. In believing Black people needed to leave America, Walker was well within mainstream thought. The American government—including Abraham Lincoln—once supported emigration from the United States, to Liberia, the American-created settlement on the West African coast. Walker wrote:

> The only practical and permanent solution of the present and future race troubles in the United States is entire separation by Emigration [*sic*] of the Negro from America. Even forced Emigration would be better for all than the continued present relation of the races; but there would be no necessary force if the proper measures are taken and the Negroes are offered reasonable help to return to their native land.

Walker stayed in America, remaining in Ohio under the increasing weight of segregation before dying of a heart attack in 1924 at age 67. His body would be buried in an unmarked grave in Steubenville. His words, long forgotten by some, never known by most, represented a fierce indictment: the American caste system was permanent. Walker wrote of the dangers for the Black people who placed their faith in the American experiment, and the coming misfortunes for the whites—such as Lincoln's Republicans—who supported improving conditions for Black citizens. "No Republican President since the enactment of the XV amendment to the Constitution can claim a majority of white voters in this country," Walker wrote. "A large majority of the white voters has always been opposed to the political party to which the Negro has been identified." Both political parties would pay the price for advocating for Black rights. After Lyndon Johnson outlawed 80 years of legal segregation with the Civil Rights Bill of 1964, the Democrats would be perceived as the party of Black America, and the price, as Walker knew from his century, would be much of white America. The Democratic Party has never since carried the white vote in a presidential election, and, with the second election of Donald Trump, have retrenched into a period reminiscent of both post-Reconstruction-era attacks on the 14th Amendment and the Cold War.

One newspaper referred to Walker's book as "hatred," but his polemic would be a prescient response to the Supreme Court decree that created 20th century conditions, including the mass exodus of Black people from the South. The Court had turned Walker into a dissident, in the tradition of the Black protest writers of the mid-19th century who inspired Paul Robeson. "The Negro should be taught he is an alien and always will be regarded as such in this country, and that equal social, industrial and political rights can never be given them. It is doubtful whether or not the Negro as a race would ever turn to Emigration as his salvation . . . but the time is fast approaching when the Negroes in very large numbers must leave the Southern states . . . they will not find open arms in the North waiting for them. When they reach the Northern States in large numbers the same condition will prevail there as now exists in the South."

Upon publication, the country entered the most intense period of racial violence against African Americans, and with the Great Migration came the Northern violence Walker predicted, which fueled the activism of Du Bois and Robeson. Instead of framing his views through the hopeful, faraway promises America constantly demanded, Walker saw only bleakness. Robeson and Robinson would soon join Walker on this continuum, and more prominently, but *Our Home Colony* remains the most ferocious critique of this country ever produced by a Black American professional athlete. Moses Fleetwood Walker looked into the soul of his country and concluded his best chance of surviving America was to leave it.

II

THE TWO MEN AMERICA PITTED against each other spent their final years failed by their bodies and underappreciated as elders. Paul Robeson would never be pulled from the depression exacerbated by his passport fight and largely disappeared from public life. Jackie Robinson did not, but his appearance was shocking to those who had not seen him recently. His journey had aged him well beyond that of a man barely out of his forties. His hair was completely white. He had suffered a heart attack and a stroke. Advanced diabetes left him blind in his right eye, preventing him from driving a car or playing golf. The racetrack, he would say, was his last remaining pleasure. His worsening conditions led doctors to tell him, Jackie Robinson, whose speed and daring sparked the imaginations of a generation, that the amputation of his legs was an inevitability.

Robinson and Robeson traveled the middle portion of the American century together, but in parallel, astonishingly having never physically met. Paul Robeson Jr. once explained it not as an inexplicable oddity but strategic. Robeson Jr. recalled once asking his father for Robinson's autograph and being refused. Robeson told his son the movement could not afford the two men to be seen publicly, for Robeson's toxicity would make Robinson's journey even more difficult. The mission of integrating the major leagues was simply too important to jeopardize.

Where they would meet was fictionally, on stage, through Edward T. Schmidt's 1990 play *Mr. Rickey Calls a Meeting*, where Schmidt imagines a 1947 conclave between Branch Rickey, the dancer Bill "Bojangles" Robinson, the boxer Joe Louis, Robeson and Robinson on the eve of Robinson's 1947 debut. Rickey controls the marionette, which is Robinson, with Robeson the skeptical, unpredictable antagonist Rickey and Robinson must overcome for Rickey's plan to succeed.

In reality, their final overlap would occur in 1972, when Robinson's final book, *I Never Had it Made*, was published. Future scholars may yet discover new material, but what appears in the book serves as his final statement on Robeson and HUAC.

In the chapter titled "My Own Man," Robinson called Robeson an "embattled and bitter man" and told Duckett, "I wasn't about to knock him for being a Communist or Communist sympathizer. That was his right. But I was afraid that Robeson's statement might discredit Blacks in the eyes of whites."

As his viewpoints darkened, Robinson mirrored Robeson. Robeson was in his late fifties during his ferocious battle with HUAC in 1956, asserting his right to his America. Robinson, writing his memoir in his early fifties, recalls his decision to testify within a familiar Double V construction, finding a lane to knit together Du Bois's conflict of two-ness. "I felt that there were two wars raging at once—one against foreign enemies and one against domestic foes—and the Black man was forced to fight both." Robinson would say he could no longer stand for the flag nor sing the national anthem. In retrospect, he said, he would have refused the HUAC invitation.

Lester Granger contended that Robinson's appearance had been a unanimous triumph when the opposite was true. Jackie Robinson was not defined by that one morning in Washington, but as the years placed his testimony in a far less heroic light, the more Robinson required confrontation on the matter—with himself.

> That statement was made over twenty years ago and I have never regretted it. But I have grown wiser and closer to painful truths about America's destructiveness. And I do have an increased respect for Paul Robeson, who over the span of that twenty years, sacrificed himself, his career, and the wealth and comfort he once enjoyed because, I believe, he was sincerely trying to help his people.

Future retellings of this period have concluded Robinson regretted appearing, but his own words suggest only partial recrimination—perhaps a final flash of his famous competitiveness, the old athlete refusing to succumb to any opponent. Nevertheless, he would sound as reflective on the McCarthy period and as rueful for his role in Robeson's destruction in the pages of *I Never Had It Made* as he had ever been.

• • •

Death was near, but too many accounts remained unsettled. By his own admission, Jackie Robinson had boycotted baseball. The game had fallen behind society. It hired very few Black coaches, and none of the 24 teams had ever hired a Black manager—nor seemed particularly eager to do so. Even into the 1960s, Black players still fought segregated housing in the South. "I don't think we'll see a black manager in my lifetime," Robinson told reporters in February 1972. Just as Black journalists and the left-wing political movements had once lobbied for him, the mainstream press now elevated Frank Robinson and Maury Wills as the leading candidates to integrate the managerial ranks. Front office jobs for Black people felt so remote, even the Black press rarely mentioned it as an aspiration.

Robinson responded with dissidence. He had sparred with Bob Feller. He called Boston's Tom Yawkey the most bigoted man in baseball. In 1969, Robinson appeared on the *Today* show, admitting he routinely declined the Dodgers' invitations to the annual Old-Timers games as a protest. He'd said no to the Mets so many times, they stopped asking. "I don't feel baseball owes me a thing, and I don't owe baseball a thing. I am glad I haven't had to go to baseball on my knees."

Nearly sixteen years after he retired and a decade after his Hall of Fame induction, the Dodgers announced the team would be retiring his iconic number 42, but Robinson had not committed to attend. The ceremony, which would also include the retiring of numbers 39 and 32, for Roy Campanella and Sandy Koufax, respectively, was scheduled for Dodgers Old-Timers Day, Sunday, June 4, 1972. Two days earlier, Robinson met with Peter O'Malley, Walter O'Malley's son, who was now the president of the club. The two men spoke within a hopeful air of reconciliation, at O'Malley's Dodger Stadium office, about the irreconcilable breach between Robinson and his father. The breach, Robinson told reporters, was created by him being collateral caught in the Rickey-O'Malley crossfire, but Robinson was never neutral. He was a Rickey man. Months earlier, Robinson gave an interview on the topic of hiring in baseball and said—knowing full well the O'Malleys were still a powerful influence in the sport—"Baseball needs its next Mr. Rickey."

When Robinson decided to attend his own number retirement ceremony, he said it was his fondness for his old Dodger teammate Don Newcombe that made the difference—and the positive energy from his meeting with Peter O'Malley. O'Malley spoke earnestly and optimistically of post-career opportunities for Black players. Robinson enjoyed a similar conversation earlier in the year with Mike Burke, the Yankees president. A new generation of baseball executives seemed more receptive to enacting the kinds of changes that would bring him back to the game. "We need younger men in the front office," Robinson said. "The old men are bigots and bigotry cannot be changed." Another encouraging sign came when new Mets owner Joan Payson announced that upon retirement, Willie Mays would be hired as a team ambassador.

Late the next night following his meeting with Peter O'Malley, on the eve of the ceremony, a tired Robinson lay in his hotel bed, conducting an interview with Ron Rapoport, a talented young reporter from the *Los Angeles Times*. In his piece, Rapoport portrayed a man who had washed his hands of the game, not out of bitterness, but out of acknowledgment. "As you probably know, baseball and Jackie Robinson haven't had much to say to each other," Robinson told Rapoport. "It's hard to look at a sport which black athletes have virtually saved and when a managerial job opens they give it to a guy who's failed in other areas just because he's white."

Despite his reservations, Robinson's nature wasn't to reject an overture he believed to be sincere, and he took Peter O'Malley at his word: optimism and intention from a person in power was where change could begin. "I guess I would say that the major weakness—and also one of his great strengths—was his tendency to trust people because he felt he was trustworthy," Rachel Robinson would say of her husband. "In other words, to think that people's values and codes were like his own. . . . So, he made some mistakes and trusted the wrong people.

Frankly, I'd rather be on that side than someone who is not trusting and who can't really relate to people because of that."

Robinson left the O'Malley meeting encouraged. Two days later, he arrived at Old-Timers Day and seemed genuinely moved by the immortalizing of his number. The Associated Press said the Dodgers billed the event their "Salute to Casey Stengel"—who appeared at Dodger Stadium in Yankee pinstripes. This was the same Stengel who defeated the Dodgers so many times, the Stengel who was one of the great nemeses of Jackie Robinson. It was the same Stengel to whom multiple versions of an anecdote about the Yankees' call-up of Elston Howard in 1955 as their first Black player were attributed: "When we finally get a nigger, we get one who can't run." Reynolds, Joe DiMaggio, and Mickey Mantle were all in attendance. In reporting the event, the wire services wrote about the Dodgers honoring Stengel, noting the number retirements of Robinson, Campanella, and Koufax as an afterthought.

Peter O'Malley would own the Dodgers until 1998. Over the 26 years since that buoying Friday afternoon conversation with Jackie Robinson, O'Malley would not hire a Black manager—from 1954 to 1996, the Dodgers would only have two managers, Robinson antagonist Walter Alston and Tommy Lasorda. As a franchise, the Dodgers would not hire a Black manager until 2016, nearly two decades after O'Malley sold the team. The New York Yankees, established in 1901, through the 2025 season have never hired a Black manager.

Four and a half months after his number retirement, virtually 27 years to the day Rickey announced his signing, Jackie Robinson was dead. His last public appearance, before Game Two of the 1972 World Series in Cincinnati, provided an appropriate backdrop for a prolific and taxing quarter century. On the Riverfront Stadium artificial turf—a surface that did not exist during his playing days—Robinson was honored pregame. The American League president, Joe Cronin—the Joe Cronin who was the manager of the Red Sox during Robinson's performative, humiliating April 1945 tryout in Boston—refused to join him on the field.

With Cronin underneath the stands eating a hot dog—a living embodiment of the crude attitudes toward Robinson and integration in baseball—Robinson famously made the same plea publicly that he had made privately to Peter O'Malley: to one day see a Black face managing a major league team. Earlier in the year, he predicted he would not live to see a Black manager—and he did not.

III

FOR A TIME, JACKIE ROBINSON lived on awkwardly in death: deeply mourned and respected but not universally celebrated and years away from the universal reverence of today. If segregation and racism robbed baseball fans of seeing a young and unburdened Robinson play in the major leagues for a full career, the world was robbed of what Jackie Robinson would have become as an older man. It was undeniable that by the end of his life, Robinson had concluded the established systems he had once supported needed dismantling, or at least reform. He supported elements of the Black Panther Party. When the baseball establishment ostracized Curt Flood and notable top stars such as Willie Mays and Carl Yastrzemski did not support him, Robinson—whose mentor Branch Rickey once accused supporters of free agency of being communists—testified on Flood's behalf that players should have the right to self-determination once their contracts expire. When the athletes famously mobilized political action around the 1968 Olympics in a break from the State Department–sponsored propaganda trips of USIA, it was Robinson who supported the revolutionary spirit of Dr. Harry Edwards, Tommie Smith, and John Carlos.

He was unwaveringly dedicated to the Black community, but his 1949 testimony left the belief he had been a pawn for white political and social interests. His conservative politics only heightened the suspicions.

Death prompted a kinder appraisal. In a reflection published two weeks after Robinson passed, the official newspaper of an old, sometimes adversary, the Black Panther Party, erased some of the ambiguity.

WE REMEMBER JACKIE ROBINSON

Jackie Robinson was a man who refused to see Black people denied or exploited in the field of sports. A man who loved baseball and found great dignity in winning, for his people; he fought hard to have Black men included in major league teams.

On October 24, 1972, Jackie Robinson died of a heart attack in Stamford, Connecticut. He had been almost forgotten by his contemporaries and was relegated to legendry by young people. He died no longer a star, a great Black man. To many he was a "Tom," to some, a lost man.

The Black Panther Party believes that he was a great Black man; that his contributions were great, his courage undeniable . . . we extend our deepest sympathies to the family of Jackie Robinson, who had endured great suffering (their son was killed last summer in an automobile accident). We would like to say only that the contributions to the total liberation of Black and all oppressed people have been many, from all segments of the Black community, in the past and in our present . . . we remember Jackie Robinson.

ALL POWER TO THE PEOPLE

For being the sport most steeped in history, baseball was never particularly adept at praising its players, and over the years, Robinson drifted into an unclaimed void, adjacent to the celebrated history of the sport but too significant to be reduced to its dustbin. He was the mirror that reflected all the game had been—and all it had not.

He was the game's forever conscience, but Jackie Robinson ceased belonging to any one obvious place. He was the Brooklyn Dodger whose team played in Los Angeles; the Southern Californian who never played for the Los Angeles Dodgers; the fixture of New York's history, but an adversary of both the Yankees and the Giants; and the former Queens resident, whose new team, the Mets, did not exist when he lived there.

He was what made the sport special, sociological, and political. *Important.* "The problem of the 20th century is the problem of the color line," Du Bois wrote in 1903. It was on a dramatic, national scale that baseball would confront race for the country. In the 1970s, however, a weary America did not want to talk about race anymore, except within a conservative movement committed to dismantling civil rights gains by taking a page from the 1883 Supreme Court: race was an impediment, not systemically or legislatively, but only if Black people allowed it to be.

With no anchor tethering Robinson, at risk of a certain cultural ambivalence, it was Rachel who rehabilitated him. Robinson symbolized a moment baseball seemingly wanted to forget—and, as he knew in life, the public preferred to address race out of benevolence, not responsibility.

During his Hall of Fame induction in 1962, Robinson had written a conciliatory letter to Walter O'Malley, hoping, unsuccessfully, to make the peace, but Rachel leveraged her respect and elegance to rebuild the relationships Robinson had frayed, first with Peter O'Malley and the Dodgers, and later within the larger baseball community, the commissioner's office, in particular. Since he was a New Yorker during his playing days, the Mets adopted Robinson as one of their own. Jackie may not have attended Mets functions, but Rachel did, and her diplomacy and presence created a posthumous lane for Robinson that previously did not exist. By the end of the 20th century, Robinson would be etched in the national conscience as an undisputed American legend. On April 15, 1997, at the suggestion of Len Coleman, who succeeded Bill White as president of the National League, baseball would retire his number 42 across the entire league in perpetuity. No player who wasn't currently wearing the number could request it. Upon his retirement in 2013, the last grandfathered number 42, New York Yankees pitcher Mariano Rivera, would be the last player to wear Robinson's number.

It would take years for Rachel's persistence to be rewarded. "She has also tried to perpetuate her husband's memory, as a man as well as a great ballplayer," a reporter wrote of her in 1976. "She believes he's been neglected."

On April 6, 1987, when baseball celebrated the 40th anniversary of Robinson's major-league debut, Roger Kahn and Al Campanis, Robinson's old teammate from the 1946 Montreal Royals, joined the journalist Ted Koppel on the ABC program *Nightline* to discuss Robinson and the issue Robinson stressed was the essential next stage of integration in the sport: seeing Black men in the manager position and within the front office.

The bookend to baseball's infamous 1946 Commissioner's Report that revealed the depths to which the game believed the inclusion of Black people would financially kill baseball was not completely apparent until 41 years later, when Koppel's exchange with Campanis exposed the sport and its internal attitudes.

ROGER KAHN: Although we can all rejoice in the progress that baseball has made on integration, I think if Jack were alive today, Jack would say, "How come there are no Blacks running ball clubs?"

TED KOPPEL: Mr. Campanis, it's a legitimate question. You're an old friend of Jackie Robinson's. It's a tough question for you. You're still in baseball. Why . . . why is it there are no Black managers, no Black general managers, no Black owners?

AL CAMPANIS: Well Mr. Koppel there have been some Black managers, but I can't really answer that question directly. The only thing I can say is, you have to pay your dues when you become a manager. Generally, you have to go to the minor leagues. There's not very much pay involved, and some of the better-known Black players have been able to get into other fields and make a pretty good living in that way.

TED KOPPEL: Yeah but you know in your heart of hearts, and we have to take a break for a commercial, you know that's a lot of baloney. *(Campanis laughing)* There are a lot of Black players, a lot of great Black baseball men who would dearly love to be in managerial positions. And I guess what I'm really asking you, is, you know, peel it away a little bit. Just tell me: why do you think it is? Is there still that much prejudice in baseball today?

AL CAMPANIS: No, I don't believe it's prejudice. I-I truly believe that they may not have some of the, the uh, necessities to be a field manager or perhaps a general manager.

TED KOPPEL: You really believe that?

AL CAMPANIS: Well, I don't say all of them, but they certainly are short. How many quarterbacks do you have? How many pitchers do you have that are Black? It's . . .

TED KOPPEL: I gotta tell you that sounds like the same kind of garbage we were hearing 40 years ago about players, you know, "Not really cut out . . ." Hey, you remember the days of, "Hit a Black player in the knees and . . ." That really sounds like garbage if you forgive me saying so.

AL CAMPANIS: It's not garbage, Mr. Koppel. I played on a college team and the centerfielder was Black, and in the backfield at NYU and the fullback was Black. Never knew the difference whether he was Black or white. We were teammates. It just might be . . . why are Black men, or Black people not good swimmers? Because they don't have the buoyancy.

(Laughter)

TED KOPPEL: Or maybe they don't have the access to all the country clubs and the pools. But let's take a break and we'll continue our discussion in a moment.

Over four decades, between the day Robinson joined the majors and the night his old Montreal teammate Al Campanis exposed the racism that lived within the bloodstream of the game on national television, only Frank Robinson had ever managed a team from the start of spring training through the end of the season. Three years after Jackie Robinson's death, Cleveland hired Frank Robinson as baseball's first Black manager for the 1975 season. Seven years later, the Giants made Robinson the first Black manager in the National League. By that time, Jackie Robinson had been dead nearly 10 years. As an interim manager, Larry Doby helmed the White Sox for the second half of the 1978 season. Maury Wills took over in mid-1980 for the Seattle Mariners, started the 1981 season, but lasted only 24 games.

In the five seasons following the Campanis debacle, Frank Robinson, Hal McRae, Cito Gaston, Don Baylor, and Dusty Baker all received managerial jobs. Bill White, for whom Jackie Robinson was a hero during his playing days and an inspiration for White's activism to fight segregated housing in spring training, was named president of the National League in 1989. Len Coleman would succeed him. In 1993, Houston named Bob Watson general manager. In 1992 and 1993, Gaston would win the World Series in consecutive years with Toronto. Baker would manage 26 years, be named Manager of the Year three times, win the 2022 World Series, and retired with 2,183 managerial wins, at the time the seventh-highest total in baseball history.

At the time of the *Nightline* segment, the NFL had employed one Black head coach in its 67-year history: Paul Robeson's old friend Fritz Pollard (in 1921). Over the next half decade, NFL teams hired more Black coaches in five years than it had in its previous 70.

Even 15 years after his death, during a seminal, infamous moment in American television, it was the posthumous aura of Jackie Robinson that forced changes to problems his contemporaries said were of his imagination, changes he himself never lived to see.

The players would be another matter. Major League Baseball and the Dodgers would benefit for decades from a reputation neither would maintain through their actions. Baseball would lose its connection to African American players by diverting its development resources to Latin America—as Rickey had originally planned before signing Robinson. The Dodgers' heyday for developing Black players ended in the early 1970s, and the annual league-wide celebration of Robinson is more a commemoration of a past triumph than a current success. There were more Black players in the league when Robinson died than there are playing in the majors today.

IV

PAUL ROBESON DIED ON JANUARY 23, 1976, in West Philadelphia. There would be no neat reconciliation between himself and his country. Neither through banquet nor plaque nor testimonial would he be made whole. Robeson would spend his last years in seclusion—protected from hostility by family, burdened by chronic pain and physical and mental decline, and, after six decades in the American cauldron, reclaiming the agency of his privacy. There would be celebratory moments (a 1973 tribute to him at Carnegie Hall, for example), but over the last dozen years of his life, Robeson would grant virtually no interviews. His last recorded public speech occurred in 1964. "He was a public person for many years," his son told a reporter in 1975, months before his father's death. "Now he has chosen to be a private person." Even those words were met with heavy skepticism, for it was unclear if Robeson's isolation was from a personal choice, his family shielding him, or his body making its own decision as his diminished faculties ended the public-facing portion of his life.

While in Europe, Robeson had suffered a nervous breakdown in early 1961—including a suicide attempt. Speculation raged publicly and privately, the FBI noted dutifully. It had been said that he had acknowledged the USSR's atrocities committed against minority groups and its duplicity, and that his "misplaced faith" in communism had broken him. For once, the FBI and Essie agreed: both believed his radical politics to be firmly intact. One newspaper noted that proof of the depths of Robeson's repudiation for his old positions could be found not in what he had said, but what he left unsaid. One outlet concluded the roots of his distress could be confirmed through Essie's refusal to allow anyone access to him. "It is indeed possible that, after more than a decade, he saw through the communist fraud . . . Until he speaks for himself, we shall not know the truth."

Robeson retreated into the 1960s. The communist movement aged; its giants faded. In January 1965, Robeson's protégé Lorraine Hansberry died of pancreatic cancer. Robeson gave one of the eulogies. Eleven months later, Eslanda Robeson lost her yearslong battle with cancer. Robeson's great friend Benjamin Davis died of cancer in 1964. In late August 1963, on the eve of the March on Washington for Jobs and Freedom, which catapulted Martin Luther King Jr. into international renown, the great lion W.E.B. Du Bois died quietly in Ghana. Born three years after the Civil War, Du Bois advocated for Black people over the course of nearly a century as no other. A week after his death, one newspaper noted Du Bois went "unmourned in this nation," while another framed Du Bois with echoes of Moses Fleetwood Walker, and a foreshadowing of Jackie Robinson. Du Bois, the newspaper wrote, had grown disillusioned with the Negro's progress. He had broken with the NAACP in 1948 for its lack of militancy, and in 1961, he joined the Communist Party. In 1962, he settled in Ghana and became a citizen. Before leaving for Ghana, he would concede the twoness of America could not be conquered, writing, "I was not an American. I was not a man. I was, by long education and daily reminder, a colored man in a white world."

By the end of the 1960s, Robeson had not been seen publicly in nearly five years. His last great public moment occurred April 22, 1965 at the Americana Hotel in New York. His "Welcome Home" birthday party in 1965 was supported by dozens of Black luminaries from James Baldwin to John Coltrane. He had made no statement regarding the March on Washington. The American government committed to break his spirits, and, to some degree, it succeeded. During a month of surveillance in the fall of 1966, the New York FBI office concluded not to interview Robeson because "subject has been described as mentally ill and is also in poor health. It is felt no useful purpose would be served by interviewing him at the risk of great embarrassment to the Bureau is considerable."

Yet the FBI continued to hound him. A year earlier, Robeson moved to Philadelphia to live in the comfort of his sister Marian's home at 4951 Walnut Street, several blocks from the University of Pennsylvania campus. The Philadelphia Bureau was watching him, assigned him a local number (100–38128), and, after six weeks of surveillance (from January to March 1971), the Bureau reported it was "reevaluating" the necessity of Robeson's active security file on the grounds that Robeson, who had never committed a crime in his life, "is now nearly 73 years old and evidently not personally dangerous." In 1974, after 32 years of harassment, eight years of barring him from traveling abroad, and nearly a dozen years of hostile treatment at home, the FBI ceased its surveillance of him.

In absentia, his supporters looked for him and tried to restore him as the mood of the country briefly demanded an apology from its institutions—from the people responsible for the carnage inflicted on his life. There would be a late, triumphant re-release of *Here I Stand* by progressive Boston publisher Beacon Press in 1971, but there would be no second memoir. On August 6, 1972, the front of *The New York Times*' Arts section asked the question, "Time to Break the Silence on Paul Robeson?" Yet, no lengthy interview would follow; no final statement would come from the great bass baritone himself for history to interpret and reinterpret.

At Rutgers—where Robeson had been its greatest student and football player, only to be disowned by his alma mater during the second Red Scare—a joint student and alumni movement sought to make things right. It was 1970, and Robeson had been out of the public eye for a half dozen years. The College Football Hall of Fame was located on the Rutgers campus, but Big Paul had never been inducted. A newspaper noted that *Who's Who in America*, the famous reference book, contained Robeson's name in every foreign edition, but he was not listed in the American edition. Nor had Robeson yet been restored to the Walter Camp All-Americans for 1917 and 1918. No player who had ever made the All-America list twice had been excluded from the Hall of Fame, except Paul Robeson.

Three days before Robeson's 72nd birthday, the school honored him. Mason Gross, the university president, took to the lectern and told the audience, "Paul Robeson suffers from being ahead of his time. He started out 50 years ago on a fight we are still trying to carry out now."

Citing illness, Robeson did not attend. Paul Jr. was there, accepting the honors for his father and reciting his defiant responses to

HUAC during his 1956 appearance. Three months later, Rutgers held another event, announcing the renaming of its student center after Robeson.

Like Jackie Robinson, there would be the requisite gestures over the years. In 1995, the College Football Hall of Fame finally inducted Paul Robeson. His induction biography would make no mention of his politics—or an explanation for his exclusion. The postal service would issue a Paul Robeson stamp in 2004. In addition to Rutgers, Penn State and even Princeton would adorn buildings with his name, but the 21st century would be the century of billionaires.

The 2011 Occupy Wall Street movement used the wealth inequality metaphors—the 1 percent versus the 99 percent—that Robeson used in the 1940s. The late-2010s "Oscars So White" protest against the lack of opportunity and recognition for African American artists in Hollywood echoed Robeson's words from 1939, when he quit the field: "The industry was not prepared to permit me to portray the life or express the living interests, hopes and aspirations of the struggling people from whom I come," he said. "You bet they will never let me play a part in a film in which a Negro is on top."

His name would still survive the way important names do—faintly, regally, hovering mysteriously with importance—but would be devoid of the most critical, unrecoverable element: knowledge of who he was, what he had been and stood for, and how his country had treated him. Robeson's name would loom vaguely, guiltily in death, over America and a Black America, in particular, that should have known him but did not. Like Robinson, he would stand as an eternal conscience for Black America.

The street where Paul Robeson lived his final days is not a high foot-traffic area and not a convenient destination for tourists. It is Black, working-class, and unpretentious. Paying tribute to him requires a pilgrimage to an unassuming West Philadelphia block in the Cedar

Park neighborhood, to where the people live. In 1991, the Pennsylvania Historical and Museum Commission marked Marian Forsythe's house at 4951 Walnut Street with a plaque.

PAUL ROBESON

(1898–1976)

A RUTGERS ATHLETE AND COLUMBIA LAW GRADUATE, ROBESON WON RENOWN AS A SINGER AND ACTOR. HE WAS A NOTED INTERPRETER OF NEGRO SPIRITUALS. HIS CAREER SUFFERED BECAUSE OF HIS POLITICAL ACTIVISM AND HE LIVED HIS LAST YEARS HERE IN RETIREMENT.

At 45th and Chestnut Streets—blocks from where he took in his last breaths—rising up across the street from Paul Robeson High School stands a four-story-high mural of Robeson. It was completed by artist Peter Pagast. In 1999, it would be retouched by Ernel Martinez. In the mural, Robeson wears a three-piece suit, stands against a golden backdrop, and looks out at the vast universe of man. Just above his head is a title: 1898—PAUL ROBESON—1976. Underneath his feet reads a caption: "Citizen of the world."

Four days after Robeson died, a column on the front page of the *Philadelphia Inquirer*'s Metro section told a story of Phil Coren, a West Philadelphia podiatrist who recalled receiving a phone call some time in 1974 from Marian Forsythe, who asked Coren to see her brother. "I recognized his face," the doctor said. "You don't forget a face like his. He was still very handsome. He still had that great dignity, that magnificent demeanor."

Coren would visit Paul Robeson for the final two years of his life. He stood in proximity of the great man, full of curiosity, but did his job. He did not pry. If Robeson felt Coren's nervous, quavering interest in him, he did not encourage dialogue. Robeson, Coren recalled, "seldom spoke."

For the final chapter of Paul Robeson's life, a life which had spanned from the 19th century to the American bicentennial, Coren would engage in a self-test of willpower, holder of one of the rare remaining keys capable of unlocking a singular wisdom, never able to use it. "There was so much I wanted to ask him about his life, about his troubles, but he was always so quiet. He always seemed so occupied with his own thoughts. He always demanded privacy.

"Perhaps Paul Robeson was bitter," Coren recalled. "Perhaps, he was old and sick and tired. But I'll never know.

"He didn't say. And, of course, I never asked."

V

REMNANTS OF THE COLD WAR lingered in various forms well into the 21st century, and while the domestic period where average Americans persecuted one another at the government's urging finally faded, de-escalation came at an enormous cost. What would remain of far-left, liberal politics would be unwillingly absorbed into the Democratic Party: cautious defenses of civil and women's rights; Lyndon Johnson's ambitious vision of a "Great Society" followed by an unconvincing, tepid defense of it; meek ownership of the New Deal principles; and timid advocacy of American labor overwhelmed by a conservative revolution.

Supreme Court victories returned openly communist and socialist candidates to political ballots, but the United States would demonstrate preferences—just as it did in the 1930s to enable the coalition of Hitler, Mussolini, and Franco—that favored authoritarianism over the socialist principles of government regulation, wealth equality, and antifascism. The positions that were once the baseline of the radical politics of Robeson and Du Bois, and their accompanying pre-McCarthy labor movements, were swept to the fringes of American politics as protest votes often without substantial influence.

Despite a dynamic upheaval of colonialism and the establishment of independent African nations, Black American mainstream political thought would emerge from the McCarthy period as an almost exclusively domestic exercise—but Black athletes remain valuable propaganda tools. A 2018 photo op posed basketball star Draymond Green as a sniper as a guest of the Israeli government, yet attempts to couple Black American politics with the world were often met with disinterest within the Black community and, most prominently in the case of the Black Panthers, FBI aggression. The assassinated Lumumba in the Congo and deposed Nkrumah in Ghana were high-profile examples of CIA-backed violence. Nelson Mandela's release and rise to the South African presidency came to be seen in America as a humanitarian cause more than a political one.

Accompanying Robeson's silence has been the greatest casualty of the radical left's demise: a virtually nonexistent critique of capitalism and colonialism. The country would react to correct some of the sins of the period—HUAC was dissolved in 1975; Pat McCarran's name was formally removed from Las Vegas airport in 2021, which was renamed after Democratic Nevada Senator Harry Reid. Save for the brief Occupy protests, however, anticapitalism has virtually disappeared from our discourse, even as the 21st century has become the age billionaire. Black Americans trumpet the success of individual celebrities—the dynamic against which Robeson had warned since the 1930s—as the wealth gap between Blacks and whites, rich and poor, inexorably widens. As the 1960s gave way to a conservative political revolution symbolized by Ronald Reagan—the Hollywood anticommunist who first ran for President the year of Robeson's death—the prevailing political view of America would belong to Branch Rickey, whose anti–New Deal, unregulated vision of Christian capitalism and American democracy as one would outlive him.

Rockwell Kent, whose passport case, talented life as an iconoclastic renaissance man, and socialistic politics mirrored that of Paul Robeson, died in 1971. In placement similar to the front-page, below-the-fold obituary Robeson would receive five years later, Kent received a lengthy profile in addition to his obit in *The New York Times*, which eulogized the artist and also the bygone American generation of political progressives who saw the radical labor movements of Eugene Debs and the moral crises of the Spanish Civil War as central to a just political worldview and insisted that wealth inequality was disconnected to—in fact, anathema to—a healthy democracy.

"When I was a young fellow, I was very much disturbed by there being some people with lots of money and lots of people with no money. I thought a lot about it and I read a lot about it, so that when I voted for the first time, I voted Socialist," Kent was quoted as saying. "I'm still disturbed by the fact that there are some people with a lot of money and a lot of people with no money and a few million with no jobs, and that the world is rich in resources and that, people are starving to death, and that all the people in the world want to live and yet a good part of the time they're busy killing each other."

Victor Grossman, who left his Army post in 1952 and swam across the Danube into communist Austria for fear of being jailed for being a communist, would live in East Germany for the remainder of its existence and stay in Germany after the country reunified in 1990. The U.S. government would monitor him, the Army for his desertion and the FBI for his establishment of the Paul Robeson Archives in the mid-1960s. The Army would drop his desertion charge in 1994. He then received a U.S. passport for the first time in nearly a half century. Well into his nineties, his defense of socialism remained total. "In 38 years, I never saw one person sleeping on the street, and I never saw one beggar. This is the kind of thing that impressed me," he said in 2019. "There were terrible problems, and one of them was people always looked to the West, which was beaming in on TV all the time the propaganda of how wonderfully they lived, not only in West Germany, but in the U.S. as well. The TV show *Dallas* you may remember. This wonderful life on oil farms. People in East Germany believed that's how people lived in the West. Wouldn't it be nice to live that way? It was very clever propaganda, a combination of Goebbels and Madison Avenue."

VI

THOSE WHO STOOD BY PAUL Robeson saw no need for reappraisal because their belief in him had never waned. The Tallest Tree in the Forest. The Great Forerunner. Citizen of the World. He had provided the shade for those with his commitment and values, and in return, he received their protection, gratitude, and veneration. Along with many others in remembrance of Robeson, one letter to the editor, in particular, appeared as an indictment of society and the individuals who only now, too late, understood the true scope of Robeson, and, as Jackie Robinson would describe it when recalling his own part in Robeson's downfall, "America's destructiveness." As one letter would say of Robeson, "He wasn't mentioned in history books, like Nathan Hale. He wasn't mentioned on football game broadcasts, like Red Grange. He wasn't mentioned in dramatic reviews, like Barrymore. He wasn't mentioned by opera critics, like Caruso. The man who was never mentioned despite the fact that he truly excelled not in one of the above fields, but in all of them.

"Now that the fires that raged in him cool and he is put lifeless into the ground, we mention and accept the fact that he lived. Now, safely silenced, he is suddenly mentioned as a 'great American' and newspapers write editorials about him and soon halls of fame and history books will doubtless find a place for him and we can pat ourselves on our bicentennial backs for living in a country where even the dissident can be a hero, once he is dead."

Ten months after Robeson's death, on October 16, 1976, Al Cohn of *Newsday* published a Q and A interview with Rachel Robinson under the headline, "Mrs. Jackie Robinson: I See Jack as a Civil Rights Leader." In it, Rachel eloquently placed Robinson in a historical context ("I think his memory can only be perpetuated through the efforts of those who saw him as a great man.") and confronted the roots of his greatest conflicts with the Black community.

Q: I'd like you to talk some more about mistakes.

MRS. ROBINSON: There were two major mistakes that Jack made . . . he regretted them very much . . . He didn't think he did wrong things when he was doing them. But his judgment about these people changed as time went on. One mistake was Nixon. The other was his statement against Paul Robeson and his appearance before the House Un-American Activities Committee. I think we got some bad advice, and we didn't really fully understand the committee, which was then fairly new. I think, for me, it's the difference between living on the West Coast and living in the East. In the West you just don't get the political sophistication that you get in the East . . . When Jack was asked to testify, he conferred with Mr. Rickey and with black leaders who were heads of organizations. Jack was at that time very patriotic—his-country-right-or-wrong. But we were still uncertain enough about it to check it out with a lot of different people. You must also remember that we came out of conservative families that were afraid of communism. He had various people help write [his testimony]. . . . Most writers praised him because they wanted to see one black condemn another. He got misused in that respect. But it was a regret, and something I regret. Perhaps if I had had a different perspective on it, I could have influenced him. But I didn't.

By October 1976, it did not require a great reserve of courage to criticize Richard Nixon, history's disgraced president. Rachel would call Nixon "the albatross," referring to the constant criticism Robinson received for supporting him, criticism Jackie Robinson's name has carried for more than 60 years. Neither would survive the disapproving glare of history. Both Nixon and HUAC were discredited symbols of paranoia and shame that Americans wanted to forget, a period when America ruined so many of its own people—a period whose return new generations now dread. The shock of the Trump administration's assault on the arts and universities, its immigration and visa restrictions, and domestic attacks on citizenship may feel unprecedented because many of today's generation have no firsthand memory of the first half of Cold War and cannot envision Americans comfortable with the police-state tactics, but what is past is prologue: Trump is merely reinstituting the playbook of the McCarthy 1950s, the time of Robeson and Robinson, American versions of authoritarianism.

Rachel Robinson's words would be the last on the subject from its only surviving primary figure, and what did require courage was to indirectly place a level of responsibility at the feet of Branch Rickey, the man whose advice Robinson took in appearing before the committee, whose role and wisdom had never been questioned. Perhaps her words carried less meaning because they had arrived so late, from the safest ground, and nothing could ever undo what the morning of July 18, 1949, had done, but the *Newsday* interview did its part to place her and, posthumously, her husband, on the right side for posterity. If not always in life, Jackie Robinson and Paul Robeson were in death no longer adversaries. The account between the two men, for history, had been squared.

Acknowledgments

I am in the unpayable debt of too many people to count, for every piece of advice, resource, and conversation that contributed positively to this book. This one would not have been possible without the tireless research and watchful eye of Brooks Melchior. With precious few possible exceptions, I cannot think of a person in the country who has devoted more personal time to the story of Jackie Robinson, especially his early, pre–major league years. For the past three years, Brooks has worked on making sure this project was afforded the benefit of every magazine article, newspaper story, video clip, cartoon, and photograph of Jackie Robinson and Paul Robeson. Every author should have such an ally and friend.

For the terrific historian Paul Dickson, the Robeson-Robinson intersection had been something of a white whale. Upon hearing I was undertaking the story of that fateful day before HUAC, Paul graciously sent a legal box of meticulously sorted (by year and subject) materials on Robeson and Robinson. His previous work and research on Robinson and Robeson were of extreme help when writing this book.

The folks at the National Baseball Writers Hall of Fame and Museum were, as always, gracious with their time, resources, and friendship. Chief amongst them are Bill Francis, Cassidy Lent, Tom Shieber, and Jon Shestakofsky, all mainstays at the old institution. Bill has been a friend to me and virtually all of my projects for what has now been a quarter century. Cassidy, as always, was patient and professional, fielding incessant questions about the collections and citations and providing a proper road map through the voluminous letters, telegrams, and correspondence leading up to the day in 1943 when Paul Robeson addressed the game's owners.

Thank you also to Ryan Reft and Adrienne Cannon at the Library of Congress, to Della Britton of the Jackie Robinson Foundation, Jenn Jensen, formerly of the Foundation, and Musa Jatta at the Schomburg Center for providing resources, insights, and road maps to finding specific materials related to Robinson's HUAC testimony and Robeson's reactions. The following staffs were extremely helpful in navigating their archives: the Tamiment Library at New York University, the W.E.B. Du Bois Library at the University of Massachusetts, the Society for American Baseball Research, and the New Haven Railroad Historical and Technical Association.

Philip Foner's *Paul Robeson Speaks: Writings, Speeches, Interviews, 1918-1974*; Martin Duberman's *Paul Robeson: A Biography*, which remains the standard work on Robeson; Paul Robeson Jr.'s two-volume *The Undiscovered Paul Robeson*; David Levering Lewis's two-volume biography on Du Bois and accompanying Du Bois reader; Victor Navasky's *Naming Names*; and James Yates's memoir, *Mississippi to Madrid*; and Janus Films and the Criterion Collection's restoration of Robeson's films were of immense value. YouTube, in all of its mysteries, also proved essential, as did Ancestry.com, Newspapers.com, and the FBI Vault.

Thank you also to the constant guidance of the great Dr. Harry Edwards, the always generous David Maraniss, Susan Robeson, and to Spike Lee. Thank you to Tisa Bryant, Lisa Davis, Chris Sauceda, Joanna Cornish, Andreen Soley, Laura Harrington, William Astore, Erin McDermott, Todd Schmidt, and Deirdre Mullane. Thank you to the legend, Brad Mangin, for tracking down the images for the photo insert, and to Toni Smith for use of her invaluable family collection of books on Paul Robeson and making important introductions.

And, lastly, thank you to the most supportive editor in the business, Rakia Clark at Mariner Books.

Bibliography

Branch, Taylor. *Parting the Waters: America in the King Years, 1954–1963*. New York: Simon and Schuster, 1988.

Buhle, Paul, and Dave Wagner. *Hide in Plain Sight: The Hollywood Blacklistees in Film and Television, 1950–2002*. New York: Palgrave, Macmillan, 2003.

Carew, Joy Gleason. *Blacks, Reds and Russians: Sojourners in Search of the Soviet Promise*. New Brunswick, NJ, and London: Rutgers University Press, 2010.

Carroll, Fred. *Race News: Black Journalists and the Fight for Racial Justice in the Twentieth Century*. Champaign, IL: University of Illinois Press, 2017.

Dickson, Paul. *Bill Veeck: Baseball's Greatest Maverick*. New York: Walker and Company, 2012.

———. *Leo Durocher: Baseball's Prodigal Son*. New York: Bloomsbury, 2017.

Duberman, Martin. *Paul Robeson: A Biography*. New York: The New Press, 1989.

Du Bois, W.E.B. *Black Reconstruction in America, 1860–1880*. New York: Free Press, 1998.

Early, Gerald L. *A Level Playing Field: African American Athletes and the Republic of Sports*. Cambridge, MA: Harvard University Press, 2011.

Editors of Freedomways. *Paul Robeson: The Great Forerunner*. New York: International Publishers, 1998.

Falkner, David. *Great Time Coming: The Life of Jackie Robinson from Baseball to Birmingham*. New York: Simon and Schuster, 1995.

Foner, Philip S. *Paul Robeson Speaks: Writings, Speeches, Interviews, 1918–1974*. New York: Bruner/Mazel Inc., 1978.

Fussman, Cal. *After Jackie: Pride, Prejudice, and Baseball's Forgotten Heroes: An Oral History*. New York: ESPN Books, 2007.

Goodman, Jordan. *Paul Robeson, A Watched Man*. London and New York: Verso Books, 2013.

Grossman, Victor [Stephen Wechsler]. *Crossing the River: A Memoir of the American Left, the Cold War, and Life in East Germany.* Amherst and Boston, MA: University of Massachusetts Press, 2003.

Halberstam, David. *The Coldest Winter: America and the Korean War*. New York: Hyperion, 2007.

Heideman, Paul. *Class Struggle and the Color Line: American Socialism and the Race Question 1900–1930*. Chicago: Haymarket Books, 2018.

Hervieux, Linda. *Forgotten: The Untold Story of D-Day's Black Heroes, at Home and at War*. New York: HarperCollins, 2015.

Hochschild, Adam. *American Midnight: The Great War, A Violent Peace, and Democracy's Forgotten Crisis*. New York: Mariner Books, 2022.

———. *King Leopold's Ghost: A Story of Greed, Terror, and Heroism in Colonial Africa*. New York: Mariner Books, 2020.

Isserman, Maurice. *Reds: The Tragedy of American Communism*. New York: Basic Books, 2024.

Kahn, Roger. *The Era: When the Yankees, the Giants and the Dodgers Ruled the World*. New York: Ticknor and Fields, 1993.

Kelley, Robin D.G. *Hammer and Hoe: Alabama Communists During the Great Depression*. Chapel Hill, NC: The University of North Carolina Press, 1990.

Lanctot, Neil. *Campy: The Two Lives of Roy Campanella*. New York: Simon and Schuster, 2011.

Levering Lewis, David. *W.E.B. DuBois: The Fight for Equality and The American Century, 1919–1963*. New York: Henry Holt, 2000.

———. *W.E.B. DuBois: A Reader*. New York: Henry Holt, 1995.

Lowenfish, Lee. *Branch Rickey: Baseball's Ferocious Gentleman*. Lincoln, NE, and London: University of Nebraska Press, 2007.

Lumpkin, Beatrice. *"Always Bring a Crowd!": The Story of Frank Lumpkin, Steelworker*. New York: International Publishers, 1999.

———. *Joy in the Struggle: My Life and Love*. New York: International Publishers, 2013.

Marable, Manning. *Race, Reform, and Rebellion: The Second Reconstruction in Black America, 1945–1990*. Jackson, MS: University of Mississippi Press, 1991.

Maraniss, David. *A Good American Family: The Red Scare and My Father*. New York: Simon and Schuster, 2019.

Maxwell, William J. *New Negro, Old Left. African-American Writing and Communism Between the Wars*. New York: Columbia University Press, 1999.

McCullough, David. *Truman*. New York: Simon and Schuster, 1992.

Michaeli, Ethan. *The Defender: How the Legendary Black Newspaper Changed America*. Boston and New York: Mariner Books/Houghton Mifflin Harcourt, 2016.

Moffi, Larry, and Jonathan Kronstadt. *Crossing the Line: Black Major Leaguers, 1947–1959*. Iowa City: University of Iowa Press, 1994.

Navasky, Victor S. *Naming Names*. New York: Viking, 1980.

Peary, Danny. *Jackie Robinson in Quotes: The Remarkable Life of Baseball's Most Significant Player*. Salem, MA: Page Street Publishing, 2016.

Pittman, Margrit. *Chapters from My Life*. Self-published memoir.

Rampersad, Arnold. *Jackie Robinson: A Biography*. New York: Alfred A. Knopf, 1997.

Ransby, Barbara. *Eslanda: The Large and Unconventional Life of Mrs. Paul Robeson*. Chicago: Haymarket Books, 2022.

Redmond, Shana L. *Everything Man: The Form and Function of Paul Robeson*. Durham, NC, and London: Duke University Press, 2020.

Robeson, Paul. *Here I Stand*. Boston: Beacon Press, 1958.

Robeson, Paul Jr. *The Undiscovered Paul Robeson: An Artist's Journey, 1898–1939*. New York: John Wiley and Sons, 2001.

———. *The Undiscovered Paul Robeson: Quest for Freedom, 1939–1976*. New York: John Wiley and Sons, 2010.

Robeson, Susan. *The Whole World in His Hands: A Pictorial Biography of Paul Robeson*. Secaucus, NJ: Citadel Press, 1981.

Robinson, Jackie. *Baseball Has Done It*. Brooklyn, NY: IG Publishing, 2005.

———. *I Never Had it Made: The Autobiography of Jackie Robinson*. Hopewell, NJ: Ecco Press, 1995.

Robinson, Robert, and Jonathan Slevin. *Black on Red: My 44 Years Inside the Soviet Union*. Washington, DC: Acropolis Books, 1988.

Rowan, Carl T., and Jackie Robinson. *Wait Till Next Year: The Story of Jackie Robinson*. New York: Random House, 1960.

Silber, Irwin. *Press Box Red: The Story of Lester Rodney, the Communist Who Helped Break the Color Line in American Sports*. Philadelphia: Temple University Press, 2003.

Solomon, Mark. *The Cry Was Unity: Communists and African Americans, 1917–1936*. Jackson, MS: University Press of Mississippi, 1998.

Stone, I.F. *The Truman Era, 1945: A Nonconformist History of Our Times*. Boston and Toronto: Little Brown and Company, 1953.

Tye, Larry. *Satchel: The Life and Times of an American Legend*. New York: Random House, 2009.

Tygiel, Jules. *Baseball's Great Experiment: Jackie Robinson and His Legacy*. New York and Oxford: Oxford University Press, 1983.

———. *The Jackie Robinson Reader: Perspectives on an American Hero*. New York: Dutton, 1997.

Von Eschen, Penny M. *Race Against Empire: Black Americans and Anticolonialism, 1937–1957*. Ithaca, NY: Cornell University Press, 1997.

Washburn, Patrick S. *A Question of Sedition: The Federal Government's Investigation of the Black Press During World War II*. New York and Oxford: Oxford University Press, 1986.

Yates, James. *Mississippi to Madrid: Memoir of a Black American in the Abraham Lincoln Brigade*. Seattle: Open Hand Publishing, 1989.

Notes

Preface: Twoness

4 *"This waste of double aims"*: "Strivings of the Negro People," *The Atlantic Monthly*, August 1897.

8 *"One feels his two-ness"*: "Strivings of the Negro," *The Atlantic Monthly*, August 1897.

Chapter One

14 The Boston Globe*:* "Dutch Catholic Jews Deported in Reprisal for Church Protest," *The Boston Globe*, August 15, 1942.

16 *"I feel that in London"*: "A Black Man as Othello," *New York Daily News*, October 24, 1943.

17 Time *magazine reported:* "Another Othello," *Time* October 7, 1935.

17 *Six days before opening*: "Margaret Webster feels sure 'Othello' was Negro," *The Boston Globe*, August 4, 1942.

18 *The Associated Press asserted:* "Paul Robeson's Othello Wins Critics' Praise," *The Morning Union*, August 11, 1942.

19 *"In these war days"*: "Paul Robeson Creates an Immortal Othello Up in Cambridge," *Daily Worker*, August 16, 1942.

19 *Low, the sports editor:* "Pirates to Try Out Negroes," *The Sporting News*, July 27, 1942.

20 *"Has the war"*: "Hope for the Negro," *Minneapolis Spokesman*, August 21, 1942.

21 Baltimore Sun *critic:* "Straw-Hat Theatre's 'Othello' Is a Hit," *The Baltimore Sun*, August 30, 1942.

21 *"Rich Princeton was white"*: Paul Robeson, *Here I Stand* (Boston: Beacon Press, 1958), 10.

21 *"Just as in youth"*: Ibid., 11.

22 *"Paul Robeson has majesty"*: "Majesty and Dignity Illuminate Negro Paul Robeson's 'Othello,'" *New York Daily News*, October 20, 1943.

22 *"At least once"*: "Straw-Hat Theatre's 'Othello' Is a Hit," *The Baltimore Sun*, August 30, 1942.

22 *"There can be no question"*: Philip S. Foner, *Paul Robeson Speaks: Writings, Speeches, and Interviews, 1918–1974* (New York: Brunner/Mazel, 1998), 144.
22 *"Nothing the future brings"*: Ibid.,143.
23 *"hated her own"*: Federal Bureau of Investigation. *File 100–353031: Lena Horne*, Part 1 of 1, J. Edgar Hoover Building, Washington, DC.
23 *"The cheers were long"*: "Paul Robeson Plays 'Othello' to the Loudest Cheers in Years," *Brooklyn Eagle*, October 20, 1943.
23 *"What other worlds"*: "Saga of a Nonpareil," *New York Daily News*, October 31, 1943.
24 *"arrogant minorities who"*: "Would Have Negro Vote Abolished," *The Black Dispatch*, August 15, 1942.
26 *"I have no doubt"*: W.C. Tuttle to Judge W.G. Bramham, October 15, 1943, Letter, Race Relations Folder, National Baseball Hall of Fame and Museum, Cooperstown, NY.
26 *Tuttle told the two Black newspapers:* Letter from W.C. Tuttle to W.G. Branham, October 15, 1943, Integration Folder, National Baseball Hall of Fame and Museum, Cooperstown, NY.
27 *A Landis loyalist:* W.G. Bramham to Kenesaw Mountain Landis, October 20, 1943, Race Relations Folder, National Baseball Hall of Fame and Museum, Cooperstown, NY.

Chapter Two

30 *On November 24:* NAACP to K.M. Landis, November 24, 1943, Letter, Integration files, Box 1, Folder 8, National Baseball Hall of Fame and Museum, Cooperstown, NY.
30 *Barnett remarked that:* Claude A. Barnett to K.M. Landis, November 26, 1943, Letter, Integration files, Box 1, Folder 8, National Baseball Hall of Fame and Museum, Cooperstown, NY.
30 *On congressional stationery:* Rep. William L. Dawson to K.M. Landis, November 23, 1943, Letter, Integration files, Box 1, Folder 8, National Baseball Hall of Fame and Museum, Cooperstown, NY.
30 *Or had it?:* "My Brother Jackie," *Ebony*, July 1957.
45 *Quinn had answered:* JML MTG, December 3, 1943, National Baseball Hall of Fame and Museum, Owners Meeting files, Box 1.

Chapter Three

46 *It was said:* "Foxy Griff Feathers Nest at Pow-Wows," *Brooklyn Eagle*, December 4, 1943.
46 *The* San Francisco Examiner: "The Low Down," *San Francisco Examiner*, December 8, 1943.
47 *"Because baseball is"*: Philip S. Foner, *Paul Robeson Speaks: Writings, Speeches, and Interviews, 1918–1974* (New York: Brunner/Mazel, 1998), 127.
47 *"clean-cut, tactical"*: "Inside Story on Onslaught Against Organized Baseball Told by New York Writer," *St. Paul Recorder*, December 10, 1943.
47 *The Black press:* Ibid.
48 *In a companion column:* "Frick Says Owners Were Impressed by Publishers," *Pittsburgh Courier*, December 11, 1943.
49 *"When they go"*: "Demi-God in Action," *St. Paul Recorder*, December 10, 1943.

49 *Two headlines in:* "Clark Griffith Won't Budge on Use of Colored Players," *The Washington Afro-American*, December 11, 1943.
49 *"I have no objection"*: "Yankee Boss Oks Colored Players," *The Washington Afro-American*, December 11, 1943.
49 *"Can We Beat the Japs?"*: "Can We Beat the Japs?" *The Washington Afro-American*, December 11, 1943.
50 *"paid-for propaganda"*: Clark Griffith to Kenesaw Mountain Landis, Letter, Integration Folder, Box 1, Folder 9, National Baseball Hall of Fame and Museum, Cooperstown, NY.
50 *"Dear Mr. Griffith"*: Kenesaw Mountain Landis to Clark Griffith, Letter, Integration Folder, Box 1, Folder 9, National Baseball Hall of Fame and Museum, Cooperstown, NY.
51 *"The solution, logically"*: "Baseball Manpower Shortage Solved," *The Boston Record*, January 26, 1943.
51 *The same day:* Eddie Collins to William Harridge, January 26, 1943, Letter, Integration Folder, Box 1, Folder 9, National Baseball Hall of Fame and Museum, Cooperstown, NY.
51 *"Dear Judge:"* Alvin Gardner to Judge Landis, Letter, Integration Folder, Box 1, Folder 9, National Baseball Hall of Fame and Museum, Cooperstown, NY.
52 *Despite Wendell Smith's:* "Frick Says Owners Were Impressed by Publishers," *Pittsburgh Courier*, December 11, 1943.
54 *The right-wing:* "City of Cool Relations," *Wisconsin State Journal*, July 26, 1948.
55 *"Now, gentlemen"*: Report of Joint Meeting of American and National Baseball Clubs: Official Minutes. National Baseball Hall of Fame and Museum, Cooperstown, NY.
57 *"Singer Paul Robeson"*: "Singer Paul Robeson Lauds Robinson Deal," *Montreal Gazette*, October 24, 1945.
58 *"More power to Robinson"*: "Good and Bad: Various Comments of O.B. Writers on Negro's Case," *The Sporting News*, November 1, 1945.
58 *MacPhail's fellow owners:* William Benswanger to Larry MacPhail, Letter, Integration Folder, Box 1, Folder 9, National Baseball Hall of Fame and Museum, Cooperstown, NY.
58 *From the White Sox:* Harry Grabiner to Larry MacPhail, Letter, Integration Folder, Box 1, Folder 9, National Baseball Hall of Fame and Museum, Cooperstown, NY.
59 *The most telling:* Connie Mack to Larry MacPhail, Letter, Integration Folder, Box 1, Folder 9, National Baseball Hall of Fame and Museum, Cooperstown, NY.
59 *"I used to have"*: Jules Tygiel, *Baseball's Great Experiment: Jackie Robinson and His Legacy* (New York: Oxford University Press, 2008), 109.

Chapter Four

63 *The war was over:* Research Starters: World War II Deaths, The World War II Museum, https://www.nationalww2museum.org/students-teachers/student-resources/research-starters/research-starters-worldwide-deaths-world-war.
64 *"It is quite conceivable"*: "Negro Player Issue Heads for Showdown," *The Sporting News*, November 1, 1945.
65 *as "a symbol of emancipation"*: "Player Prize Added to Robinson's Honor List," *The Sporting News*, November 23, 1949.

65 *Over the following*: "Branch Rickey Tells Courier," *Pittsburgh Courier*, November 3, 1945.
65 *"Whether Jackie Robinson"*: "Democracy on the Diamond," *St. Louis Post-Dispatch*, December 12, 1945.
66 *"When we saw"*: "Jack Robinson's Courage Admired by Ex-Colonels," *The Sporting News*, April 9, 1947.
67 *"Rickey has turned"*: "Dodgers Rate Van Cuyk no. 1 in Rookie Crop," *The Sporting News*, January 8, 1947.
68 *"The $64 Question Mark"*: "He's the $64 Question Mark," *The Sporting News*, January 8, 1947.
68 *"the Negro player"*: "Bramham Scores 'Raid' Against Negro Loop," *The Sporting News*, November 1, 1945.
68 *"Members of these"*: Report of Major League Steering Committee for Submission to the American and National Leagues, August 27, 1946, National Baseball Hall of Fame and Museum, Integration Folder. Original is located in the A.B. Chandler Papers, University of Kentucky, Box 162.
70 *"The individual action"*: Report of Major League Steering Committee for Submission to the American and National Leagues, August 27, 1946, National Baseball Hall of Fame and Museum, Integration Folder. Original is located in the A.B. Chandler Papers, University of Kentucky, Box 162.
70 *"Father Divine"*: "Bramham Scores 'Raid' Against Negro Loop," *The Sporting News*, November 1, 1945.
71 *"Robinson's sensational playing"*: "Jackie on First for Brooklyn," *Pittsburgh Courier*, March 29, 1947.
72 *"As long as he's not"*: "Difference of Opinions Rife on Dodgers on Signing of Negro by Branch Rickey," *Windsor Star*, October 25, 1945.
72 *On the third:* "Dodgers Split on How They Feel About Jackie Robinson as Potential Teammate," *The Post-Standard*, March 4, 1947.
73 *"It was not so much"*: Ibid.
74 *"Robeson, the colored lad"*: "Rutgers Machine Sweeps Newport to Defeat," *Brooklyn Eagle*, November 25, 1917.
75 *"You just can't"*: Roger Kahn. *The Era: When the Yankees, the Giants and the Dodgers Ruled the World* (New York: Ticknor and Fields, 1993).
76 *"the Negro people"*: Arnold Rampersad, *Jackie Robinson: A Biography* (New York: Alfred A. Knopf, 1997), 160.
77 *"especially in the South"*: "A Negro in the Major Leagues," *The Sporting News*, April 23, 1947.

Chapter Five

79 *"Not charity but a chance"*: "Headline Action," *The Call and Post*, March 15, 1947.
81 *Rickey's trusted assistant:* Arthur Mann, *The Jackie Robinson Story* (New York: F.J. Low, 1950), 117.
82 *"The next two years"*: "We Salute Robeson," *Chicago Star*, April 26, 1947.
83 *"ATTEMPT ON LIFE"*: "Attempt on Life of Paul Robeson After Crusade," *St. Louis Argus*, January 31, 1947.
84 *"Rumor has it"*: "Forgotten GA Murder Under Scrutiny," *The Omaha Guide*, August 24, 1946.

84 *"The British Empire"*: Philip S. Foner, *Paul Robeson Speaks: Writings, Speeches, and Interviews, 1918–1974* (New York: Brunner/Mazel, 1998), 173.

85 *"Millions of Negro"*: "Singer Denies He's Communist," *Reno Gazette-Journal*, October 8, 1946.

85 *"a speaker or artist"*: "Peoria Bans Robeson: He Vows to Sing," *Chicago Tribune*, April 18, 1947.

86 *He held to his:* Paul Robeson, *Here I Stand* (Boston: Beacon Press, 1958), 39.

86 *"To be a poor man"*: *The Atlantic Monthly*, August 1897.

86 *"Under the caste system"*: Paul Robeson, *Here I Stand* (Boston: Beacon Press, 1958), 10.

86 *"Vanished also is"*: Adam Hochschild. *Spain in Our Hearts: Americans and the Spanish Civil War, 1936–1939* (Boston and New York: Mariner Books, 2016), xix.

87 *"Negroes are lynched"*: *The Messenger*, November 1917.

88 *"It means little"*: Philip S. Foner, *Paul Robeson Speaks: Writings, Speeches, and Interviews, 1918–1974* (New York: Brunner/Mazel, 1998), 142.

89 *"The blacks who chose"*: Joy Gleason Carew, *Blacks, Reds and Russians: Sojourners in Search of the Soviet Promise* (New Brunswick: Rutgers University Press, 2010), 5.

91 *"Harlem Negroes have"*: "Italian Paper Raps America for Lynchings," *The Afro-American*, August 10, 1935.

91 *"A warmth stirred"*: James Yates, *Mississippi to Madrid: Memoir of a Black American in the Abraham Lincoln Brigade* (Seattle: Open Hand, 1988), 132.

93 *"You became the tool"*: Philip S. Foner, *Paul Robeson Speaks: Writings, Speeches, and Interviews, 1918–1974* (New York: Brunner/Mazel, 1998), 107.

93 *"What I won't do"*: Ibid., 126.

94 *"The Bureau desires"*: Federal Bureau of Investigation, *File 100–12304: Paul Robeson, Sr.*, Part 3 of 31, J. Edgar Hoover Building, Washington, DC.

Chapter Six

97 *"No statement by"*: "Truman Talk Forecasts War, Bankruptcy, Wallace States," *San Francisco Examiner*, January 21, 1949.

97 *"A sequel may"*: "Parties Differ on Speech Aims," *San Francisco Examiner*, January 21, 1949.

97 *"sick at heart"*: I.F. Stone, *The Truman Era, 1945–1952: A Nonconformist History of Our Times* (Little Brown & Co, 1972), 58.

98 *"Guilt by association"*: "Clark's Letter Listing Subversive Groups," *Buffalo News*, December 5, 1947.

99 *"I think one man"*: Farrell Evans, "Why Harry Truman Ended Segregation in the U.S. Military in 1948," History, https://www.history.com/news/harry-truman-executive-order-9981-desegration-military-1948.

100 *"jolly drawling Negroes"*: "Tris Coffin's Washington Daybook," *The Herald-Sun*, July 27, 1948.

102 *According to Truman:* David McCullough, *Truman* (New York: Simon and Schuster, 1992), 739.

102 *"I talked to my manager"*: Philip S. Foner, *Paul Robeson Speaks: Writings, Speeches, and Interviews, 1918–1974* (New York: Brunner/Mazel, 1998), 187.

Chapter Seven

103 *"Who does he think he's fooling?"*: "Dickey Front," *The Daily Tribune* (Wisconsin Rapids, WI), April 28, 1949.

105 *In an obvious:* Federal Bureau of Investigation, *File 100–12304: Paul Robeson, Sr.*, Part 3 of 31, 30, J. Edgar Hoover Building, Washington, DC.

105 *Three weeks later:* Ibid., 32.

105 *The next day:* Ibid., 37.

105 *Hoover did not:* Adam Hochschild, *Spain in Our Hearts: Americans and the Spanish Civil War, 1936–1939* (Boston and New York: Mariner Books, 2016), 166.

105 *"in jail"*: "Edward Barsky, Surgeon, Dies; Joined Spanish Republican Side," *The New York Times*, February 13, 1975.

105 *Du Bois described Robeson:* David Levering Lewis, *W.E.B. Du Bois: A Reader* (New York: Holt Paperbacks, 1995), 799.

106 *He would also call:* Ibid.

106 *In Oslo:* Philip S. Foner, *Paul Robeson Speaks: Writings, Speeches, and Interviews, 1918–1974* (New York: Brunner/Mazel, 1998), 197.

108 *"His writings indicate"*: Federal Bureau of Investigation, *File. No. 100–99729: William (EB) Du Bois*, part 1, 3, J. Edgar Hoover Building, Washington, DC.

109 *Robeson reasoned Africa's:* Adam Hochschild, *King Leopold's Ghost: A Story of Greed, Terror, and Heroism in Colonial Africa* (New York: Mariner Books, 2020), x.

109 *repay American corporations:* Philip S. Foner, *Paul Robeson Speaks: Writings, Speeches, and Interviews, 1918–1974* (New York: Brunner/Mazel, 1998), 207.

109 *"We were enriched"*: Adam Hochschild, *King Leopold's Ghost: A Story of Greed, Terror, and Heroism in Colonial Africa* (New York: Mariner Books, 2020), x.

109 *"taken so soon"*: David Levering Lewis, *W.E.B. Du Bois: A Reader* (New York: Holt Paperbacks, 1995), 1.

112 *"A white man"*: "Paul Robeson Awarded 30th Spingarn Medal for His Leadership," *Minneapolis Recorder*, October 26, 1945.

113 *Nine days later:* "Robeson Lauds Russia at Spingarn Banquet," *Pittsburgh Courier*, October 27, 1945.

113 *"National Association"*: "A Meeting in Atlanta," *The New Yorker*, March 9, 1956.

113 *"Upstanding Harlemites are"*: "The Broadwayite," *Michigan Chronicle*, November 3, 1945.

115 *"The general theory"*: Martin Duberman, *Paul Robeson: A Biography* (New York: The New Press, 1989), 344.

116 *"Since Mr. Robeson"*: "Paul Robeson Speaks for Paul Robeson." *The Crisis*, May 1949.

116 *"One of the most"*: Martin Duberman, *Paul Robeson: A Biography* (New York: The New Press, 1995), 348.

117 *"Then what about"*: "Mrs. Paul Robeson Defends Husband's Stand at Boston Meet," *The New England Bulletin*, May 14, 1949.

117 *"We Negroes are Americans"*: Ibid.

118 *"Are we to be thus"*: Richard Newman, Patrick Rael, and Philip Lapsansky, eds., *Pamphlets of Protest: An Anthology of Early African American Protest Literature, 1790–1860* (New York: Routledge, 2001), 140.

118 *"During the Wallace campaign"*: Philip S. Foner, *Paul Robeson Speaks: Writings, Speeches, and Interviews, 1918–1974* (New York: Brunner/Mazel, 1998), 202.

119 *"And I say"*: Ibid.

120 *"The old Paul Robeson"*: "Paul Robeson: Tragic Dupe," *Lincoln Evening Journal*, April 25, 1949.

120 *The speech made:* "Paul Robeson, Oppressed," *Salem News*, April 23, 1949.

121 *"The House Un-American Activities"*: "Ballplayer to Refute Slur on Race," Associated Press, July 8, 1949.

Chapter Eight

127 *A* Miami Herald*:* "Loyalty to Friends," *Miami Herald*, February 1, 1949.

129 *"As you know"*: Leslie Perry to Jackie Robinson, July 11, 1949, Telegram, Arthur Mann Papers, Manuscript Division, Box 1, Folder 3, Library of Congress, Washington, DC.

130 *To get him in shape:* Ibid., Box 5, Folder 6.

131 *"It would be"*: Dan W. Dodson to George Weiss, Mayor's Committee on Unity, [Date missing], Letter, Integration Folder, National Baseball Hall of Fame and Museum, Cooperstown, NY.

131 *"He is colored"*: C.T. McManus to George Weiss, Letter, Integration Folder, National Baseball Hall of Fame and Museum, Cooperstown, NY.

131 *According to Dodger:* David Falkner, *Great Time Coming: The Life of Jackie Robinson from Baseball to Birmingham* (New York: Simon and Schuster, 1995), 214.

132 *Rickey would tell:* "Jackie Lauds Rickey as His Guiding Star," *The Sporting News*, February 1, 1950.

132 *An editorial in:* "The Jackie Robinson Situation," *The Sporting News*, March 23, 1949.

133 *"Jackie, man!"*: Roger Kahn. *The Era: When the Yankees, the Giants and the Dodgers Ruled the World* (New York: Ticknor and Fields, 1993), 96.

133 *"We are stunned"*: Mr. and Mrs. John Hester to Jackie Robinson, July 11, 1949, Telegram, Arthur Mann Papers, Manuscript Division, Box 1, Folder 3, Library of Congress, Washington, DC.

135 *"leads me to believe"*: U.S. House of Representatives. Committee on Un-American Activities. *Hearings on Communist Infiltration of Minority Groups*, Eighty-First Congress, First Session, July 13, 14, and 18, 1949, 425–426.

135 *"special attention to"*: Ibid.

140 *"How small can"*: Lester Granger to Branch Rickey, Letter, Arthur Mann Papers, Manuscript Division, Box 1, Folder 3, Library of Congress, Washington, DC.

140 *"the smear technique"*: "Rabbi Benjamin Schultz, Crusader Against Communist Infiltration," *The New York Times*, April 25, 1978.

140 *"One enemy is"*: U.S. House of Representatives, Committee on Un-American Activities, *Hearings on Communist Infiltration of Minority Groups*, 462.

141 *"And so it isn't"*: Ibid., 480.

142 *Robinson finally addressed:* Ibid., 482.

143 *"We can win"*: Ibid.

Chapter Nine

145 *"his achievements in"*: "The Two Worlds of Robeson and Robinson," *The Paducah Sun-Democrat*, July 20, 1949.

145 *Granger wrote:* Lester Granger to Jackie Robinson, July 19, 1949, Letter, Arthur Mann Papers, Manuscript Division, Box 1, Folder 3, Library of Congress, Washington, DC.

146 *"circulated for five hours"*: Ibid.

146 *In a simplistic attempt:* "Jackie Robinson Speaks," *Minneapolis Star-Tribune*, July 20, 1949.
147 *"must have asked":* "Toombs Countians Not Talking on the Subject of Robert Mallard," *The Columbus Ledger*, December 5, 1948.
148 *"All I want to do":* Philip S. Foner, *Paul Robeson Speaks: Writings, Speeches, and Interviews, 1918–1974* (New York: Brunner/Mazel, 1998), 220.
149 *"Jackie Robinson says":* "Drop That Gun, Jackie," *Baltimore Afro-American*, July 16, 1949.
150 *Branch Rickey was actively:* "Jackie Out, Sam In for Brooks?," *New York Age*, August 27, 1949.
152 *As Helen Rosen:* Helen Rosen, "Paul Robeson: Here I Stand," American Masters Digital Archive (WNET), April 7, 1998, https://www.pbs.org/wnet/americanmasters/archive/interview/helen-rosen
152 *"Chapter by chapter":* "Soviet Atomic Bomb Has Upset Europe's Power Relationship," *Buffalo News*, October 1, 1949.
153 *"I hardly knew":* Helen Rosen, "Paul Robeson: Here I Stand," American Masters Digital Archive (WNET), April 7, 1998, https://www.pbs.org/wnet/americanmasters/archive/interview/helen-rosen.
153 *No one was arrested:* "3-Hour Riot at Paul Robeson Concert," *The Virginian-Pilot*, August 28, 1949.
154 *"Our objective was":* "Reports Differ on Cause of Riots," *The Reporter-Dispatch*, August 29, 1949.
155 *"The contention here":* "Now, an Oppenheimer," *Sioux City Journal*, June 16, 1949.
155 *"I'm in the headlines":* Philip S. Foner, *Paul Robeson Speaks: Writings, Speeches, and Interviews, 1918–1974* (New York: Brunner/Mazel, 1998), 224.
157 *"I think those rioters":* "Jackie Blasts Mob Attack," *Daily Worker*, August 4, 1949.
157 *"Lynch the big":* "The Sidewalk," *The California Eagle*, September 8, 1949.
157 *The next day:* "Robeson Riot Hurts 60," *Detroit Free-Press*, September 5, 1949.
158 *Helen Rosen would:* Helen Rosen, "Paul Robeson: Here I Stand," American Masters Digital Archive (WNET), April 7, 1998, https://www.pbs.org/wnet/americanmasters/archive/interview/helen-rosen.
158 *"I really had":* Ibid.
160 *"You no longer":* "Letter to the Editor," *The Central Jersey Home News Tribune*, September 4, 1949.
160 *Three days after:* "D.A. Clears N.Y. Cops in Concert Violence," *York Daily Record*, September 7, 1949.
161 *"Any person of his stature":* "Buzzin' with Cuzzin," *The Future Outlook*, September 10, 1949.
161 *"His presence here":* Editors of Freedomways, "The Robeson Phenomenon," *The Black Dispatch*, September 10, 1949.
161 *"When my wife":* *Paul Robeson: The Great Forerunner* (New York: International Publishers, 1998), 312.
162 *"Robeson being the only Negro":* "The Sidewalk," *The California Eagle*, September 8, 1949.

Chapter Ten

163 *Robeson was ineligible:* "Bill Cunningham Pays Tribute to Football Stars," *Buffalo News*, November 16, 1954.
164 *"In his books":* Arnold Rampersad, *The Life of Langston Hughes*, vol. 2: (Oxford University Press, 2002), 230.
164 *"Instead of helping":* "Robeson vs. Ryan," *New York Daily News*, January 6, 1948.

164 *"In 1954"*: Editors of Freedomways, *Paul Robeson: The Great Forerunner* (New York: International Publishers, 1998), 312.
165 *"If you want"*: Federal Bureau of Investigation, *File 100–12304: Paul Robeson, Sr.*, part 3 of 31, 98, J. Edgar Hoover Building, Washington, DC.
166 *at an April luncheon:* "Rickey Claims Commies Seek Baseball Ruin," *The Dayton Journal*, April 14, 1949.
166 *"If You Oppose"*: *The Mexico (MO) Ledger*, April 14, 1949.
167 *"Fire all the Reds"*: "The Institute of Pacific Relations and the Betrayal of China: The Senate Testimony of Alfred Kohlberg," https://www.dcdave.com/article5/120207.htm.
167 *The June 1948:* "Letter 54," *Counterattack*, June 4, 1948.
171 *"softhearted and hardboiled"*: "Soft-Hearted Ruth Shipley Hard Boiled Passport Chief," *Montreal Star*, August 12, 1941.
171 *When Shipley retired:* Jeffrey Kahn, "The Extraordinary Mrs. Shipley: How the United States Controlled International Travel Before the Age of Terrorism," *The Connecticut Law Review*, vol. 43, no. 3, February 2011.
171 *Bea Lumpkin:* Interview with Bea Lumpkin.
172 *"intended to make"*: "Making America a Police State," *I.F. Stone's Weekly*, May 2, 1953.
175 *During a string*: Federal Bureau of Investigation. *File 100–353031: Lena Horne*, part 1 of 1, 51–52, J. Edgar Hoover Building, Washington, DC.
175 *"The first time"*: "Paul Robeson: Scandalize My Name," https://www.zinnedproject.org/materials/scandalize-my-name.
176 *"I am not a Communist"*: "Actor Canada Lee Denies He is a Red," *Winston-Salem Journal*, July 7, 1949.
176 *"As everyone must know"*: "Canada Lee Corrects Walter Winchell," *The Gulf Informer*, November 5, 1949.
176 *José Ferrer, Robeson's:* "Ferrer on Robeson," *The Sandusky Register*, January 21, 1953.
178 *"the racial dimensions"*: David Caute, *Red List: MI5 and British Intellectuals in the Twentieth Century* (London: Verso, 2022), ch. 9.
178 *"his frequent criticism"*: Martin Duberman, *Paul Robeson: A Biography* (New York: The New Press, 1989), 389.
180 *"The teams were selected"*: "McLin's Sports Parade," *Tampa Bay Times*, July 19, 1952.
180 *On the story:* "Robinson, Back from Europe, Raps Phony Stories by Reds," *The Fresno Bee*, January 3, 1951.
181 *"There have been"*: "The Strange Case of Paul Robeson," *Ebony*, February 1952.
181 *"Paul Robeson—The Lost Shepherd"*: "Paul Robeson—The Lost Shepherd," *The Crisis*, November 1951.
182 *"With Robeson and Du Bois"*: "Paul Robeson Revisited," *The New York Times*, October 16, 1973.
184 *in the inaugural issue:* "Candidates Speak for Peace and Civil Rights," *Freedom*, November 1950.
184 *"We won, 6–1"*: "Here's My Story," *Freedom*, November 1951.
185 *"At that instant"*: "Note on Newcombe," *The Tablet*, February 2, 1952.
185 *"It is astounding"*: "Blast at Big Don," *Baltimore Afro-American*, February 23, 1952.

Chapter Eleven

189 *"It was really"*: John Bricker to Branch Rickey, Branch Rickey Papers, Manuscript Division, Library of Congress, Washington, DC.

190 *"I can show them to you"*: "Jackie Robinson Says: Robeson Has Wrong Outlook," *The Washington Post*, August 30, 1949.
191 *The day of the second:* "Negro Killed by Gun Blast," *Omaha World-Herald*, September 4, 1949.
192 *"no other man"*: "Jackie Lauds Rickey as His Guiding Star," *The Sporting News*, February 1, 1950.
194 *It is there: The Jackie Robinson Story*, directed by Alfred E. Green (Los Angeles: Eagle-Lion Productions, 1950).
194 *"But I'm certain"*: Ralph Carhart, ed., *Not an Easy Tale to Tell: Jackie Robinson on the Page, Stage, and Screen* (The Society for American Baseball Research, 2022).
197 *"I have heard it said"*: Federal Bureau of Investigation. *File 100–353031: Lena Horne*, part 1 of 1, J. Edgar Hoover Building, Washington, DC.
197 *A final scene:* "The Way I See It," *Minneapolis Spokesman*, May 26, 1950.
198 *"Whether Robinson"*: "Commie Views of Jackie," *The Sporting News*, March 1, 1950.
200 The Sporting News*:* "Few, If Any, Colored Stars Ready to Join Majors, Says Negro Scribe," *The Sporting News*, January 12, 1949.
200 New York Daily News*:* David Falkner, *Great Time Coming: The Life of Jackie Robinson from Baseball to Birmingham* (New York: Simon and Schuster, 1995).
201 *In a stunning interview:* Branch Rickey Papers, Interview with Davis J. Walsh, Box 58, Folder 8, Library of Congress, Washington, DC.
201 *"I think it's telling"*: Ralph Kiner, *Baseball Forever* (Chicago: Triumph Books, 2004), 78–79.
201 *Both Rickey and history:* Dan W. Dodson to Charles E. Hughes, July 27, 1945, Memo, National Baseball Hall of Fame and Museum, Cooperstown, NY.
201 *"The one I dreaded the most"*: Branch Rickey Papers, Interview with Davis J. Walsh. Library of Congress. Box 58, Folder 8, Library of Congress, Washington, DC.
202 *"Jackie straights out"*: "Will the Yankees Hire a Negro Player?," *Our Sports*, July 1953.
202 *"We have no intention"*: Ibid.
203 *"I don't care what"*: Ibid.

Chapter Twelve

206 *James Baldwin:* James Baldwin, *The Harlem Ghetto* (Boston, Beacon Press, 1956).
206 The Daily Telegraph *of London:* "Un-American Bar," *The Daily Telegraph*, June 14, 1956.
207 *The USIA responded:* "'Diplomats in Short Pants,'" *Corpus Christi Caller-Times*, December 18, 1955.
209 *over the 60-minute hearing:* Philip S. Foner, *Paul Robeson Speaks: Writings, Speeches, and Interviews, 1918–1974* (New York: Brunner/Mazel, 1998), 413.
215 *Three handwritten responses:* "Race and Ethnicity," The American Soldier in World War II, https://americansoldierww2.org/surveys/a/S144.Q85.F.15922524.
217 *"Believe me"*: "Robeson Has Wrong Outlook," *The Washington Post*, August 30, 1949.
218 *A published letter:* "Americans for Robeson," *The Washington Afro-American*, June 23, 1956.
218 *"Imagine anywhere else"*: "Others' Views—About Paul Robeson," *Santa Barbara News-Press*, July 2, 1956.
220 *Du Bois would not:* David Levering Lewis, *W.E.B. Du Bois: A Reader* (New York: Holt Paperbacks, 1995), 556.

220 *Nor would Robeson:* Philip S. Foner, *Paul Robeson Speaks: Writings, Speeches, and Interviews, 1918–1974* (New York: Brunner/Mazel, 1998), 429.

221 *Privately, like most radicals:* Ibid., 430.

221 *Two years later:* "Court Bars Red Oath Rule for Passports," *New York Daily News*, June 17, 1958.

222 *a great painter:* Martin Duberman, *Paul Robeson: A Biography* (New York: The New Press, 1989), 406.

222 *He would often:* "A Man of Multiple Skills," *The New York Times*, March 14, 1971.

223 *"I am forced to the conclusion":* Ken Germander, "Rockwell Kent's Historic Passport Case," http://www.kenmcculloughpoet.com.

224 *Nearly a year later:* "Robeson Will Make London Headquarters," Associated Negro Press, May 21, 1959.

Chapter Thirteen

227 *"depend on the deal":* "Whether Jackie Will Quit If Trade," *The Sporting News*, January 18, 1956.

228 *Alston told reporters:* "Robinson Plans to Play Next Year," *The Courier-Journal*, October 30, 1956.

228 *He was stunned:* "Willie Is Proud to Have Jackie as a Teammate," *Pittsburgh Courier*, December 22, 1956.

229 *Because they were contemporaries:* "He Knows How to Get Along with People," *The Sporting News*, October 19, 1955.

230 *"As Jackie Robinson":* "The Ten Years of Jackie Robinson," *Sport Magazine*, September 1955.

231 *"Jackie Robinson, the popular":* "Urges Civil Rights March as Racist Strives for Whitewash," *Daily Worker*, October 16, 1955.

232 *"My own private World Series hero":* "Clubhouse Confidential," *The Sporting News*, October 19, 1955.

232 *Robinson was silent:* "The Way I See It," *The Calgary Herald*, December 8, 1955.

233 *Robinson also made mention:* Ibid.

233 *Two weeks after:* "Rickey Raps Georgia Governor," *The Sporting News*, January 25, 1956.

234 *A few writers:* "In the Wake of the News," *The Chicago Tribune*, January 7, 1957.

234 *Robinson exited the game:* "Robinson Explains Decision," *The Times* (Muenster, IN), January 8, 1957.

238 *The American public:* The Papers of Branch Rickey, Manuscript Division, Box 26, Folder 3, Library of Congress, Washington, DC.

238 *The result of Rickey's:* "How It Looks from Where I Sit," *Look*, May 27, 1958.

239 *When the book:* Carl Rowan and Jackie Robinson, *Wait Till Next Year* (New York: Random House, 1960), 202.

240 *Robinson wrote that:* Ibid., 205–206.

242 *"I went to my elders":* Jackie Robinson, WGBH-TV, Boston, https://www.youtube.com/watch?v=iNCYFTVSjwA.

242 *To further prove:* "Open Letter from Malcolm X," *The Amsterdam News*, November 30, 1963.

243 *A month before:* "The GOP: For White Men Only?," *The Saturday Evening Post*, August 10, 1963.

244 *In 1969:* "Feller Says Jackie Robinson Has Always Been 'Bush,'" *Winston-Salem Journal*, July 25, 1969.

244 *William F. Buckley:* "J. Robinson: Pompous Moralizer," *Greensboro Daily News*, August 14, 1968.

246 *Summer approached:* "Flag on July 4: Thrill to Some, Threat to Others," *The New York Times*, July 4, 1969.

Aftermath: Kings

249 *In its majority:* University of Louisville Brandeis School of Law, Harlan's Great Dissent, *Plessy v. Ferguson*, https://louisville.edu/law/library/special-collections/the-john-marshall-harlan-collection/harlans-great-dissent.

250 *"Toledo folded after":* "Items Regarding Colored People Here and Elsewhere," *Xenia Gazette*, December 13, 1884.

250 *In 1908:* Moses Fleetwood Walker, *Our Home Colony* (Pranava Books, 2022), 1.

250 *"The Negroes without":* Ibid., 19.

251 *The American government:* Ibid., 31.

251 *"A large majority":* Ibid., 16.

252 *"The Negro should be taught":* Ibid., 31.

254 *In the chapter:* Jackie Robinson, *I Never Had it Made: The Autobiography of Jackie Robinson* (Hopewell, NJ: Ecco Press, 1995), 84.

254 *"I felt that there":* Ibid., 84.

254 *Lester Granger contended:* Ibid., 86.

255 *"I don't feel baseball":* "Jackie Robinson Seeks and Finds Sensitivity," *Los Angeles Times*, June 5, 1972.

256 *A new generation:* "Jackie Robinson Still Seeks Equality," *The Waterloo Region Record*, June 15, 1972.

256 *In his piece:* "Jackie Robinson Seeks and Finds Sensitivity," *Los Angeles Times*, June 5, 1972.

256 *"I guess I would say":* "Mrs. Jackie Robinson: I See Jack as a Civil Rights Leader," *Newsday*, October 16, 1976.

258 *In a reflection:* "We Remember Jackie Robinson," *The Black Panther*, November 4, 1972.

264 *His last recorded:* "Robeson, 77, Quietly Guards His Privacy," *Asbury Park Press*, September 28, 1975.

264 *"It is indeed possible":* "Iron Curtain Crashes. Paul Robeson Silent," *Marshfield News-Herald*, November 23, 1963.

264 In late August 1963: "William Du Bois and the Long Trail," *The Charlotte News*, September 2, 1963.

265 *"I was not an American":* "Du Bois: A Far-Reaching Shadow," *The Charlotte Observer*, September 6, 1963.

265 *During a month:* Federal Bureau of Investigation, *File 100–12304: Paul Robeson, Sr.*, part 30 of 31, J. Edgar Hoover Building, Washington, DC, https://vault.fbi.gov.

265 *Yet the FBI:* Ibid., 29.

266 *Three days before:* "Rutgers Hails Robeson," *Central New Jersey Home News*, April 6, 1970.

267 *The 2011 Occupy:* "Time to Break the Silence on Paul Robeson?," *The New York Times*, August 6, 1972.

269 *For the final chapter:* "The Last Lonely Days," *Philadelphia Inquirer*, January 27, 1976.

271 *"When I was a young"*: "Man of Multiple Skills," *The New York Times*, March 14, 1971.

271 *The U.S. government:* "Victor Grossman. A Socialist Defector," Community Church of Boston, May 26, 2019, https://youtu.be/v8CP6fomR8w.

272 *"Now that the fires"*: "Letters to the Editor," *Los Angeles Times*, February 1, 1976.

272 *Ten months after:* "Mrs. Jackie Robinson: I See Jack as a Civil Rights Leader," *Newsday*, October 16, 1976.

Index

ABOUT MARINER BOOKS

MARINER BOOKS traces its beginnings to 1832 when William Ticknor cofounded the Old Corner Bookstore in Boston, from which he would run the legendary firm Ticknor and Fields, publisher of Ralph Waldo Emerson, Harriet Beecher Stowe, Nathaniel Hawthorne, and Henry David Thoreau. Following Ticknor's death, Henry Oscar Houghton acquired Ticknor and Fields and, in 1880, formed Houghton Mifflin, which later merged with venerable Harcourt Publishing to form Houghton Mifflin Harcourt. HarperCollins purchased HMH's trade publishing business in 2021 and reestablished their storied lists and editorial team under the name Mariner Books.

Uniting the legacies of Houghton Mifflin, Harcourt Brace, and Ticknor and Fields, Mariner Books continues one of the great traditions in American bookselling. Our imprints have introduced an incomparable roster of enduring classics, including Hawthorne's *The Scarlet Letter*, Thoreau's *Walden*, Willa Cather's *O Pioneers!*, Virginia Woolf's *To the Lighthouse*, W.E.B. Du Bois's *Black Reconstruction*, J.R.R. Tolkien's *The Lord of the Rings*, Carson McCullers's *The Heart Is a Lonely Hunter*, Ann Petry's *The Narrows*, George Orwell's *Animal Farm* and *Nineteen Eighty-Four*, Rachel Carson's *Silent Spring*, Margaret Walker's *Jubilee*, Italo Calvino's *Invisible Cities*, Alice Walker's *The Color Purple*, Margaret Atwood's *The Handmaid's Tale*, Tim O'Brien's *The Things They Carried*, Philip Roth's *The Plot Against America*, Jhumpa Lahiri's *Interpreter of Maladies*, and many others. Today Mariner Books remains proudly committed to the craft of fine publishing established nearly two centuries ago at the Old Corner Bookstore.